Understanding Terrorism in the Age of Global Media

Understanding Terrorism in the Age of Global Media

A Communication Approach

Cristina Archetti
University of Salford, UK

palgrave
macmillan

First published 2013 by
PALGRAVE MACMILLAN

Palgrave Macmillan in the UK is an imprint of Macmillan Publishers Limited,
registered in England, company number 785998, of Houndmills, Basingstoke,
Hampshire RG21 6XS.

Palgrave Macmillan in the US is a division of St Martin's Press LLC,
175 Fifth Avenue, New York, NY 10010.

Palgrave Macmillan is the global academic imprint of the above companies
and has companies and representatives throughout the world.

Palgrave® and Macmillan® are registered trademarks in the United States,
the United Kingdom, Europe and other countries.

ISBN: 978–0–230–36049–5

This book is printed on paper suitable for recycling and made from fully
managed and sustained forest sources. Logging, pulping and manufacturing
processes are expected to conform to the environmental regulations of the
country of origin.

A catalogue record for this book is available from the British Library.

Library of Congress Cataloging-in-Publication Data

Archetti, Cristina.
    Understanding terrorism in the age of global media : a communication
approach / Cristina Archetti.
        p. cm.
    Includes bibliographical references.
    ISBN 978–0–230–36049–5
    1. Terrorism and mass media. 2. Terrorism in mass media. 3. Terrorism –
Press coverage. I. Title.

P96.T47A83 2013
363.325—dc23   2012033367

10 9 8 7 6 5 4 3 2 1
22 21 20 19 18 17 16 15 14 13

Printed and bound in the United States of America

To my mum and dad on the occasion of their 40th wedding anniversary. Because they really did a great job in raising four kids.

Contents

List of Figures		viii
Acknowledgements		ix
Introduction: A Different Perspective on Terrorism		1
1	The Problems with Terrorism Research	12
2	Terrorism, Communication, and the Media	32
3	A Communication Approach	60
4	Explaining Radicalisation	101
5	The Role of Narratives	125
6	The Al Qaeda Narrative as a Brand	144
7	The Way Forward	169
Notes		180
Bibliography		185
Index		209

Figures

1.1	Three hypothetical sets of causal connections among variables	21
3.1	The social construction of the individual narrative	82
3.2	Evolution of the individual narrative over time	85
3.3	Compatibility between individual narratives and collective narrative within a group	86
3.4	Changing membership of a group over time: compatibility/dissonance of individual narratives with a collective narrative	87
4.1	"Radicalisation process" (New York Police Department)	105
4.2	"Radicalisation and mobilisation dynamics framework" (US National Counterterrorism Centre)	105
5.1	The global communication environment as a hall of mirrors: the simultaneous coexistence of multiple individual narratives.	135
5.2	Old models of communication: the linear transmission of a message	137
6.1	Kapferer's identity prism	152
6.2	Application of the identity prism to mapping the Al Qaeda narrative	156
6.3	Application of the identity prism to mapping the UK government narrative	156
6.4	The brand platform as a definition of "success" in terrorism and counterterrorism	166

Acknowledgements

Although this book was completed during my sabbatical (between September 2011 and January 2012), the research that supports its arguments started much earlier. All those who accompanied me along that journey, present and past colleagues at Leeds University and Salford University, are forever in my heart.

I am indebted to Robin Brown for reading a draft of the manuscript and providing his usual frank and invaluable feedback.

My greatest gratitude, as always, is for my husband, Robin. His love and generosity have no boundaries: he tolerated having a less-than-well-tempered creature living in the study next door; he was always willing to discuss her ideas; effectively, he endured talking over dinner about the same topic for four months.

Having moved into a new house has also made a difference. I have enjoyed glancing beyond my computer screen to the Yorkshire countryside while writing. In my thoughts, I chased the people and stories travelling on the planes coming and going from Leeds Bradford airport in the distance.

With its ups and downs, teamwork in the household has worked to perfection once again. I look forward to the next project.

Introduction: A Different Perspective on Terrorism

This book is about explaining terrorism in an age of interconnectedness and globalisation. It argues that we cannot truly understand terrorism in the twenty-first century – let alone counter it effectively – unless we also understand the processes of communication that underpin it. In doing so the book challenges the very notion of violent extremism and the state of terrorism research.

Talking about communication – the sharing and transmitting of information – also means engaging with the role of the media. Over the past decade much has been said about the role of technologies like the Internet and global communication networks in sustaining transnational terrorism, the spread of its ideology, and its recruiting activities. Also, many have been the claims about the implications of live instantaneous reporting of terrorist attacks and negative coverage of conflicts in foreign lands in serving terrorists' objectives. There is a widespread realisation that communication is crucial, not least in the acknowledgement that the international fight against terrorism is, ultimately, beyond its military dimension, a confrontation of ideas – a struggle for the moral high ground and for the "hearts and minds" of global audiences. So much so that "strategic communication" is the buzzword in official circles, think tanks, and academia alike. The notions of "narrative" or "brand" have often been drawn into the analysis of the roots of terrorism or advocated as an essential part of a counterterrorism response: the idea, for instance, that we should rewrite the "narrative" of grievance promoted by terrorists to radicalise new followers.

Despite its centrality, however, there has been very little effort to establish an analytical framework that rigorously and comprehensively explains the role of communication in the development of violent extremism. This is a problem whose scope cannot be overstated.

1

Twenty-first century politics takes place in a fast-paced, media-saturated, and increasingly interconnected world. Yet, our foreign policy and security are being read through analytical lenses that were developed, at best, during the Cold War. Effectively, without an understanding of communication in the digital age, the way research is being conducted in these domains can be compared to exploring the frontiers of space with Galileo's telescope.

In this perspective the book demonstrates that current assessments about the role of communication in terrorism research are shaped by outdated theories. Core terrorism research, more specifically, appears to be conceptually stuck in the early twentieth century. This is the same research that attracts huge amounts of public funding and that, by informing counterterrorism policies, has a far reaching impact on our everyday life – think about restrictions of civil liberties, surveillance, even just the screening of hand luggage at airports. This is by no means to say that good research does not exist. Rigorous research on the role of communication, though, is at the margins of the field. When policymakers require advice, they tend to seek the contributions of core terrorism scholars, even if reality has evolved more quickly than the traditions of these researchers' respective disciplines. The result is that "our" security (and foreign policy) is being influenced by scholars who know very little about how to make sense of global mediated politics. This book aims to bring communication right at the centre of our approach to contemporary terrorism.

The purpose of this book is not to draw attention to the communicative aspects of terrorism – its aim being playing to an audience, or the fact that, as former British prime minister Margaret Thatcher put it, publicity is the "oxygen" of terrorism; that information is a "weapon"; or that the use of email can be helpful in the organisation of a terrorist plot, for that matter. These are all hardly new points. We know, as a range of scholars has eloquently argued over the years (Schmid and de Graaf 1982; Crelinsten 1987; Nacos 1994, 2002a, for instance), that terrorism *is* communication and, as such, it is really aimed at the people watching. And this is no exclusive characteristic of the contemporary era either. Alex Schmid (1989: 541) famously associated the rise of modern non-state terrorism to the invention of the rotary press and of dynamite. Terrorism, however, existed before the advent of the mass media. It simply relied on alternative forms of communication like rumours and gossip (Rapoport 1984). We know that new communication technologies, by enabling individuals to transmit information instantaneously across distances and to communicate with global publics at almost no cost, do make a difference. In contrast to the previously mentioned gossip, where information spread relatively slowly and within the immediate circle of personal acquaintances, "Cheap and easy-to-use video cameras, digitalisation, CD-burners, plus the demands of 24-hour rolling news, means that anyone now has access to the airwaves. Home videos end up being broadcast to hundreds of millions" (Burke 2004).

Indeed, effective communication constitutes a powerful weapon, but military strategists have been well aware of this since the time of Sun Tzu (2009 [sixth century BC]). In counterinsurgency operations in Afghanistan or Iraq, for example, coalition opponents do not possess substantial military, financial, or material resources. Yet, through the persuasive power of ideas, such as extremist ideologies, they can mobilise audiences across national borders to affect events in the theatre of operations and persuade new recruits to join their fight. We know that the communication aspect of terrorism and counterterrorism are so important that Ayman Al-Zawahiri, leader of Al Qaeda following Osama bin Laden's death, has himself famously acknowledged that "More than half" of what the United States calls the global fight against terrorism "is taking place on the battlefield of the media, [for] we are in a media battle in a race for the hearts and minds [of Muslims]" (in Rumsfeld 2006). His words might reflect his own biased perception of a political conflict in which he is too directly involved to have any genuine sense of perspective. Alternatively, he might be strategically motivated by the attempt to raise Al Qaeda's status: in the media domain even a small group of poorly armed individuals can pick a fight with a global superpower. Yet the statement appears to potently capture the notion that ideas and values matter – a notion shared by his opponents, too. In fact, although this point applies more broadly than to the Al Qaeda case, the 9/11 Commission concluded in its final report that eliminating the threat of extremism ultimately requires not only dismantling its network, but also "prevailing in the longer term over the ideology that gives rise to Islamist terrorism" (National Commission on Terrorist Attacks upon the United States 2004: 363).

This book, instead, develops a more radical argument. It suggests that, if we want to understand the role of communication in the construction of the terrorism phenomenon, we must first develop a reading of society as *relational*. Communication, in fact, is the very fabric of social life. *Before* tackling the terrorism problem, we must realise that communication is essential to the very way in which ordinary citizens interact with one another, exchange information and ideas, form groups (or networks) and mobilise for political purposes. The fact that some individuals embrace extremist ideas and participate in terrorist organisations, within this perspective, should not be regarded as an inexplicable abomination, but as claim-making beyond the limits of mainstream political discourse. In this sense the book provides a new way to think about contemporary events in a world constantly constructed and reconstructed by an incessant production, exchange, processing of information and by the stories, or "narratives," as it is now fashionable to say (that is, interpretations), that social actors construct about it. In this view terrorist networks are not clearly distinguishable groups of people who are somehow isolated from the rest of society. Although they do develop a distinctive outlook on their surrounding reality, they still belong to networks within an overlapping, broader set of relationships. This matters, as it will be explained, when it comes to explaining how the position of an individual within a constellation of social ties affects that actor's identity and, in turn, actions. In this perspective terrorist groups are, effectively, social movements. They act within structures of opportunities that constantly evolve as a result of their actions and those of their political antagonists. These structures are not only defined by material resources, but also by perceptions. What could be dismissed as "immaterial" and irrelevant, especially when it comes to explaining physical harm and destruction of property, is actually very important. In fact, mobilisation of a movement's members requires a constant process of meaning construction in which stories serve to define who the members are, where they are coming from, what they are trying to achieve, and why they act. All these communication processes – in terms of the content of the exchanges, the number of interlocutors, the way in which the conversations take place, and the effects they will have on connected actors – are highly contingent. Not only are they context-bound but also time-specific. In this respect, the book combines the approaches of relational sociology (White 2008), social movements' theory (Tarrow 1998; Tilly 2002), and actor network theory (Latour 2005) to make sense of social interactions, mobilisation in an increasingly mediated society, and the role of both communication technologies and media organisations in the mobilisation of extremist groups. In doing so, the book provides both conceptual tools and suggestions on how to *apply* them to assess practical situations and, ultimately, thinking along alternative (perhaps more innovative?) lines of enquiry.

There is an ongoing debate about the boundaries of terrorism scholarship, and this book is not the most appropriate place to get into the details of the controversy. Although the precise borders of the terrorism field of study are contested, not least by the recent addition of Critical Terrorism Studies,[1] there is nonetheless an identifiable body of work that deals with the issue of terrorism, which I will here refer to in its entirety, as do others (such as Reid 1993, 1997; Gordon 2001, 2004, 2005, 2007; Silke 2004a, c, d; Reid and Chen 2007; Ranstorp 2007a), as the field of Terrorism Studies. The book is a response to a series of interconnected shortcomings within this broad body of literature.

To start with, while the frequent references to the "media" signal an increasing recognition of the fact that communication is an important component of the terrorism phenomenon, media's role is not at all problematised. In fact, beyond a few good texts, the literature on the relationship between terrorism and the media is not immune from flaws associated to terrorism studies in general: reliance on secondary and recycled data, scarce engagement with conceptual issues, and scholarship largely produced by "one timers" (Gunning 2007: 365–369). While the mobility of researchers who contribute one article to the field and then move on to a different subject encourages the study of terrorism from the perspectives of different disciplines (see also Reid and Chen 2007), it also constitutes an obstacle to scientific accumulation. Indeed, one can say from a theoretical point of view that there are no genuine explanatory frameworks as to why individuals become engaged in terrorism beyond largely descriptive studies about the organisation, background, and activities of specific groups or individuals.

Media – whether approached as communication technologies or organisations – are often mentioned, but it is clear that their role is taken as obvious, even self-explanatory, to the point that, as we will see, even in academic texts by highly esteemed terrorism scholars, claims about the media's function and effects are often made in a surprisingly casual way. Statements that would appear highly questionable, if not extreme, to a media researcher – "the proliferation of jihadist entities is strongly fuelled by the [I]nternet" (Hegghammer 2008: 15) to give just one example – are made without a solid base of empirical evidence. The sentence just given as an illustration is a telling example of how even authoritative researchers often come to rely on small blocks of taken-for-granted knowledge, especially when those blocks fall outside the core domain of the researchers' respective expertise. At closer examination, what appears like an uncontested "fact," turns out to be constructed out of often-repeated anecdotes. The same sentence, in fact, would spark a whole set of questions for a imaginary scholar of the media: Of what does the "fuelling" role of the Internet consist? Could one say that the Internet is the *cause* of the proliferation of jihadi groups?

Would they exist without the Internet? Is the technology "only" helping them to have a public presence? What difference does that make? How does the Internet combine with other technologies, including advances in transportation and in the manufacturing of explosives, for instance? And the questions could go on to include issues of media effects on audiences. As will be discussed in detail in the following chapters, this kind of systematic distortion in (mis)interpreting the role of the media is related to the lack, in Terrorism Studies, of a theoretical framework for conceptualising that role.

Clearly, this book cannot hope to single-handedly solve the problems of an entire field of study. In fact, the experience of writing this book can be compared to working on an archaeological site: the very first idea was to write a text to explain the relationship between terrorism and the media. Metaphorically, I saw debris emerging from the ground and started digging. That was the realisation that terrorism studies did not really understand the role of communication and the media. The more I dug, however, the more artefacts and skeletons emerged from beneath the ground. I realised that the role of communication and the media could not be tackled without developing a broader framework to explain how the communicative aspects of social interaction lead to violent action. Within its self-contained scope, this book has therefore turned into a first step towards producing an explanatory framework for the way in which terrorism is socially constructed through communication, with a particular focus on the twenty-first century context. While it is only scratching the surface of the deepest problems within Terrorism Studies, it nonetheless aims to make four interconnected contributions.

First, it provides an explanatory framework of the way communication – more or less mediated by technologies – plays a key role in the mobilisation of terrorist groups within and across geographical borders, online and offline. More specifically, it maps, defines, and more solidly grounds, in a broader sociological horizon, a range of concepts that are already widely used. The notions of "radicalisation," "network," "narrative," and "brand," for instance, are already part of current explanations of terrorist activities and the spread of extremism. Some terms, like "narrative," have become popular among counterterrorism practitioners: "narrative" (or "counter-narrative") figures 25 times in the latest UK government's *Prevent* counterterrorism strategy document (Home Office 2011). These terms, however, are used inconsistently and inaccurately. Beyond not being clearly defined, they are used to refer to different phenomena. For example, "narrative" is used in some cases to refer to a more or less sophisticated "story" (Casebeer and Russell 2005; Quiggin 2009), in other cases to denote a more complex interpretation. In this latter respect, *Prevent* (Home Office 2011: 108) defines "narrative" as "the particular interpretation of religion, history and politics that is associated with Al Qa'ida and like minded groups. The narrative connects 'grievances' at a local and/or global level, reinforces the portrayal of Muslims as victims of Western injustice and thereby purports to legitimise terrorism. It combines fact, fiction, emotion and religion and manipulates discontent about local and international issues" (see also Corman 2011).

In addition, various researchers apply these terms in separate contexts. For example, researchers who write about "networks," tend to be different individuals from those who talk about "narratives." In an interesting and early demonstration of the role of communication networks in affecting an individual's understanding of the world, those who apply the concept of "network" tend to have been trained in quantitative methods (Sageman 2004, 2008, for instance), while those who apply the notion of "narrative," instead, lean towards an academic training rooted more in the humanities (the ethnographic approach of Belaala [2008], for instance). This book aims to overcome this compartmentalisation of the conceptual landscape and to show that these different terms describe, in reality, the same connected social world. As will be shown, networks and narratives, to continue with the example just provided, are tightly related. In fact, no significant social tie within a network would exist if there was not a "story" attached to it.

The second contribution of this book is that it approaches the relationship between terrorism and communication in a multidisciplinary perspective that combines communication and media studies with a range of other disciplines – apart from Terrorism Studies, Sociology, International Communications, Political Communication – in a way that illuminates the partiality of each. By explaining how communication technologies, both old and new, fit with other forms of communication including face-to-face interaction, this book challenges the homogenising and generalised claims about the role of the media that are currently made in terrorism literature. These are the questions the book engages with: Are the advances in communication technology, as embodied by the Internet for instance, the key to the spread of Al Qaeda's ideology? Are they also responsible for the "radicalisation" phenomenon? Why do apparently ordinary citizens embrace Al Qaeda's message? Can Al Qaeda's recruitment be explained in terms of brand appeal? Is the global fight against terrorism a "clash of narratives"?

How can our societies counter the terrorist groups' narrative/s? How can we measure "our" governments' progress in countering extremism? Osama bin Laden's death in May 2011 has brought Al Qaeda back into both the media spotlight and the international political agenda. While some argue that the loss of this charismatic and unifying figure has made a dent in the organisation's brand (Braiker 2011; Fink 2011; Muir 2011), others have pointed out that the disappearance of even the most widely known figure is not expected to have a significant operational impact on the group's activities, which were largely decentralised anyway (Musharbash 2011; *The Economist* 2011; Temple-Raston 2011). Al Qaeda, this last argument goes, is "more than just bin Laden." It is an ideology and a social movement with a global reach. In this respect, the book will contribute to the debate by enabling a deeper understanding of the exact nature of extremist organisations and the process through which the mobilisation of supporters is carried out.

The yearning for democracy and civil freedoms that has driven protesters during the "Arab Spring" of 2011 and the developments following the fall of the Quaddafi regime in Libya might suggest that large parts of the Arab world and its neighbouring countries are not supporting the Al Qaeda ideology. In this respect, the book suggests ways to actually measure the extent to which the Al Qaeda narrative is being embraced (or not) at a local level.

The third contribution is that the analysis seamlessly integrates perceptions and stories into explanations of the way social actors mobilise and take action in the real world. In so doing it fully embraces Charles Tilly's (2002: 13) invitation to explore the link between stories, identities and political change. More specifically, it takes the author's analysis further by applying it to the mobilisation of violent extremist groups and more explicitly tackling the role of communication and the media in contemporary politics.

It should be borne in mind, however, that this link among stories, identities, and political action is a highly dynamic one. Not only because we live in a world which changes at a very fast pace (and not just because communication technologies change quickly and terrorists evolve in their tactics), but because the configuration of opportunities that might lead to terrorism is actually different in every specific social domain – read: temporal, relational, spatial-infrastructural, technological. Media have different roles in different societies and contexts. For example, the Internet might play a significant role in the process of radicalisation (the embracing of extremist ideologies) in a country like the United States or the United Kingdom, where access to this technology is widely available. It is plausible that in our media-saturated societies, the Internet figures among the platforms used by terrorists to distribute extremist material and engage in conversations with potential recruits. The same thinking could not be applied to remote areas of Afghanistan where not only is the Internet not available, but literacy rates are extremely low. There, extremism could be most effectively encouraged through shabnamah, night letters affixed by Taliban supporters on the walls of government buildings or mosques during the night and read by literate villagers to their neighbours (Johnson 2007).

What the following pages are not going to offer is some kind of "silver bullet" to the problem of terrorism. The conceptual tools and arguments presented in this book cannot tell, for example, which kind of message sent through which kind of media is able to trigger that spark that will lead an apparently ordinary citizen – the London bombers were described as fathers, friends, colleagues, one of them a teaching assistant (*BBC* News 2005b) – to engage in acts of extreme violence. The purpose of the discussion, instead, is to make visible the processes to learn this within a specific political and social context at a given time. In fact, understanding extremism requires the ability to be critical and to raise questions. Ultimately, this book is going to be useful in the hands of those who are prepared to apply the conceptual tools to find the answers that are relevant to their contingent setting.

As the fourth contribution: understanding the way in which social networks affect our thinking, expectations and interpretation of the world, beyond supporting a better understanding of the processes that underpin terrorism, can also support a critical reflection by researchers about their own positions in the academic field. To what extent is this position – our allegiance to specific paradigms, theories, and methodological traditions – affecting the way we think? To what extent are our expectations already establishing limits to what we can find? The book, in this respect, also suggests ways in which researchers can become more aware of the (somehow inevitable) group-think of closed academic circles and communities of enquiry.

While this book mainly focuses on Al Qaeda, its arguments can be broadly applied to the terrorist activities of other organisations and more general forms of political extremism. In fact, this is really a study of the way extremist ideologies are collectively constructed, shared, and remoulded over time. The applicability of the book's arguments, as I will illustrate through a range of examples, extends well beyond the Al Qaeda case. The examples span the right-wing-inspired killings that took place on the Norwegian island of Utøya and in Oslo in July 2011,[2] the Red Brigades in Italy (1970s and 1980s), the Red Army Faction in Germany (1970–90s), Armenian terrorism (1970–80s), and contemporary radicalisation across Denmark, France, Spain, and the United Kingdom.

The arguments that will be presented take a moderate pro-government normative standpoint. This is intended, aimed at producing analysis that can inform the activities of practitioners involved in counterterrorism. It does not at all equate with an endorsement of government policy against terrorism. The use of expressions like "ours" and "theirs," as well as "struggle for hearts and minds" and "war of ideas," within this perspective, should not be read as a reproduction of governmental sound bites. Indeed, as a political communication scholar herself, the author is well aware of the mechanisms of strategic communication and how rhetorical choices do reflect specific political agendas. The adoption of this language is, in this context, a deliberate way to more closely connect with existing debates. For better or worse, they are de facto shaped by both governmental rhetoric and journalistic accounts whose jargon is routinely derived from intelligence and security sources. Starting from what is widely available and read about in the public domain is a way to carve an entry point for then questioning, challenging, and problematising existing understanding of the role of communication as well as the very notion of terrorism in an age of global media. Lastly, the adoption of this language is also a way of signalling the author's inevitably biased standpoint as a law-abiding member of a Western society.

Ultimately, this book offers a very different take on the nature of terrorism and the role within it of communication and the media, especially in the contemporary context. The following pages draw concepts, theories, and insights, from a range of disciplines. The approach might cause some frustration to the scholars of each of them. In fact, the journey outlined by the chapters' progression might feel like a rollercoaster ride: the angles and perspectives of analysis are going to change quickly; they are going to take deep dives and sharp turns across Terrorism Studies, Sociology (Relational Sociology, social movements' theory, Actor Network Theory, Symbolic Interactionism), Communication, Media Studies, Marketing (branding), International Communication, Political Communication, and Journalism Studies. The purpose is precisely to shake the reader's view of the subject, turn it upside down, and to lead to the consideration – even if just for the sake of disagreement – of new possibilities and avenues for future research.

Writing this book has been fun after all. Hopefully, the reader will enjoy the ride, too.

Chapter 1 sets the stage for the arguments to be developed by outlining the state of research in Terrorism Studies, particularly the lack of engagement with theory. Chapter 2 further highlights the deep misunderstandings about the relationship between terrorism and the media. Chapter 3 suggests a new communication model to explain the development of violent extremism in an interconnected world. This model is then going to be applied to explaining radicalisation, in Chapter 4, and the role of narratives in both the development of violent extremism and counterterrorism, in Chapter 5. Chapter 6 shows that the multidisciplinary approach adopted in the book can inform innovative empirical research. It demonstrates the applicability of the concept of branding to measuring progress in counterterrorism. The conclusions identify the implications, for the future of terrorism studies and the practice of counterterrorism, of a communication approach to understanding violent extremism.

1
The Problems with Terrorism Research

To understand terrorism in an age of interconnectedness and globalisation we need to engage with the question of the role of communication and the media in the phenomenon of political extremism. Communication and the media cannot, however, be approached in isolation. To comprehend the difference media can possibly make in the exchange of information, its processing, and its effects, they need to be "fitted" into the broader picture of how social interactions occur, identities are constructed, and groups mobilise for political purposes. The aim of this chapter is to show that this framework, within the broadly conceived field of terrorism studies, does not currently exist.

The chapter starts from a critique of the very definition of terrorism and explains the way in which the term will be used in the rest of the book. It then proceeds to pointing out that, despite the volume of research, the field does not overall offer a satisfactory explanation for the terrorism phenomenon in terms of *causal processes*. We may know a great deal about the chronology and planning of single attacks, about the tactics of specific groups, the contents of organisation's manifestos and extremist ideologies, the background and life stories of individual terrorists. Indeed, we even know what kind of perfume one of the hijackers wore before he embarked on his last mission in the early hours of 11 September 2001.[1] We can easily download Al Qaeda training manuals (US Department of Justice n.d.); get a good idea of the contents of the group's latest magazine in English, *Inspire* (Ambinder 2010; Joscelyn 2011a,b) read about the way an ordinary Muslim became a radical in Ed Husain's *The Islamist*, to name just one memoir. But beyond this ocean of minutiae, why does terrorism exists? How does it arise? How does it develop? Why does it end? This claim might sound odd considering that there are a number of well-known works precisely addressing these questions.

One can think, for instance, about Martha Crenshaw's widely quoted articles, "The Causes of Terrorism" (1981) and "How Terrorism Declines" (1991),[2] or the book *The Root Causes of Terrorism* (Bjørgo 2005b). By using these works as examples I will suggest that it is not that they do not contribute to further our understanding of the phenomenon. They certainly do. But only to a certain extent: against the very objectives of the respective authors, they consist of useful sets of *descriptive observations* related to specific cases and contexts – for instance selected terrorist groups or countries – rather than genuine *explanations*. Acknowledging the lack of explanatory frameworks – or theories – for the terrorism phenomenon, as well as the reasons for this gap, is the first step in understanding why there is a general inability to make sense of the role of communication and the media.

1.1 The fragmentation of terrorism research

Many have lamented the fact that the field of terrorism studies lacks an engagement with theoretical frameworks (Crenshaw 1981, 1991; Tarrow 1995: vii; Silke 2004b; Cronin 2006). Leonard Weinberg and Louise Richardson (2004: 138) openly state that "the study of political terrorism has largely been a a-theoretical undertaking." Andrew Silke (2004d: 207) further finds that in the 1990s less than two per cent of all articles published in the two main journals within the field, *Terrorism and Political Violence* and *Studies in Conflict and Terrorism*, addressed conceptual issues. And the situation does not appear to have changed to this day (Smith 2009). Most conceptual debate, in fact, seems to be absorbed by defining terrorism. Given that the discussion, whether in an article or the introduction of a book, invariably ends with an acknowledgement that "one's terrorist is another person's freedom fighter" and that any definition (including the purposive use of the label to suit a political agenda) is inevitably biased, ritually repeating the same points contributes very little to advancing our understanding. Beyond the sterile discussion about definitions, little effort has been made in developing theoretical frameworks to explain terrorism beyond the detailed descriptions of single groups' cases. After explaining the definition of terrorism that I reluctantly adopt for the purposes of this book, I will turn to examining the explanatory shortcomings of the field.

1.2 Redefining terrorism

Alex Schmid (1984), in his first edition of *Political Terrorism*, discussed more than a hundred definitions of terrorism. Proving how difficult it is to find a consensus on the matter (but also how persistent researchers have been in engaging in such a fruitless task), in the second edition of the book, over 20 years later, he and Albert Jongman write that "the search for an adequate definition of terrorism is still on" (Schmid and Jongman 2005: 1). Discussing the suggestions on how to define terrorism that were received through a survey of about 50 members of the political terrorism research community (ibid.: 2), they raise the question of whether a satisfactory way to characterise the phenomenon should include references to symbolic violence: "the intent of terrorism is psychological or symbolic, not material" (ibid.: 8); whether it should be broad or narrow: for example, is it unnecessary to include in a definition a description of the outcomes of terrorism, such as fear, or would such omission make the definition too broad to be "operationally useful?" (Ibid.: 10). Should there be distinctions among different kinds of terrorism, for instance that perpetrated by states rather than by individuals? Should terrorism be defined as a "method of combat," thereby evoking the idea of a war context, which could lead to the exclusion of insurgency and guerrilla activities? (Ibid.: 16). Could it exist without "terror?" In other words, how much fear should it cause to distinguish it from ordinary violence? (Ibid.: 20). Or should the communication function of terrorism be emphasised as the main motive behind it? (Ibid.: 21–25).

These points raise legitimate questions about the analytical merit of adopting a definition of terrorism that distinguishes it from other politically motivated activities. For the purpose of showing both the ambiguity of the term and the fact that it might in itself constitute an obstacle towards examining similarities across patterns of political action that are, instead, placed into a different category, I will briefly examine the relationship between "terrorism," "extremism," "guerrilla warfare," and "insurgency." The following examples show that the lines between the sets of activities falling under each category are extremely blurred. Indeed, it almost looks as if researchers are trying to slot reality into arbitrary conceptual boxes that hardly fit.

Extremism, according to Roger Eatwell and Matthew Goodwin (2010a: 8), "is typically related to actions and value systems that lie beyond the moral and political centre of society." Having been associated with authoritarian regimes, like Nazism, the term is not value-neutral. Such historical association, they add, supports the notion that extremism "involves either the implicit or overt acceptance of violence as legitimate" (ibid.: 9). In this perspective, it is not clear where the line between extremism and terrorism should be drawn. Some, for instance, would call the ideological extremism of the Nazi regime and the organised violence it supported against Jews "state terrorism" (Perdue

1989). Others draw a distinction on the basis of moral legitimacy: Jason Franks (2009: 154), for instance, explains how "Orthodox Terrorism Studies," as opposed to Critical Terrorism Studies, tends to construct non-state violence as terrorism, while state violence is seen as legitimate. Besides, there is also no clear dividing line between violent and non-violent extremism. In this respect *Prevent* (Home Office 2011: 19), the United Kingdom's current strategy against terrorism, states that non-violent extremism is part of the broader terrorist problem on the grounds that, in order to become engaged in acts of terrorism, individuals often pass through a phase in which they support non-violent extremist views:

> In assessing drivers of and pathways to radicalisation, the line between extremism and terrorism is often blurred. Terrorist groups of all kinds very often draw upon ideologies which have been developed, disseminated and popularised by extremist organisations that appear to be non-violent (such as groups which neither use violence nor specifically and openly endorse its use by others).

On the relationship between terrorism, guerrilla warfare and insurgency, in *Inside Terrorism*, a seminal text in terrorism literature,[3] Bruce Hoffman (2006: 35), writes that:

> terrorism is often confused or equated with, or treated as synonymous with, guerrilla warfare and insurgency. This is not entirely surprising, since guerrillas and insurgents often employ the same tactics (assassination, kidnapping, hit-and-run attack, bombings of public gathering places, hostage-taking, etc.) for the same purposes (to intimidate or to coerce, thereby affecting behaviour through the arousal of fear) as terrorists. In addition, terrorists as well as guerrillas and insurgents wear neither uniform nor identifying insignia and are often indistinguishable from non-combatants.

Why do we need to distinguish them then? Although it is acknowledged that "none of these are pure categories and considerable overlap exists" (ibid.) the explanations provided as to why they should be kept separate are not compelling, particularly because they appear to be applied inconsistently across contexts and groups involved. As Hoffman (ibid.) continues:

> "Guerrilla" ... is taken to refer to numerically larger groups [one could ask: larger than which number?] of armed individuals who operate as

a military unit, attack enemy military forces, and seize and hold territory ... while also exercising some form of sovereignty or control over a defined geographical area and its population. "Insurgents" share the same characteristics; however, their strategy and operations transcend the hit-and-run attacks to embrace what in the past has been called "revolutionary guerrilla warfare," "modern revolutionary warfare," or "people's war"[;] ... insurgencies typically involve coordinated informational (e.g., propaganda) and psychological warfare efforts designated to mobilize popular support in a struggle against an established national government, imperialist power, or foreign occupying force. (Ibid.)

Would not these aspects describe the activities of Al Qaeda-affiliated groups in Afghanistan or Iraq? Indeed, Edwin Bakker (2006: 3) sees guerrilla warfare as a feature of "jihadi terrorism":

Jihadi terrorism in Afghanistan or Iraq is of an entirely different nature than that witnessed in Indonesia, Kenya, Spain, or the United Kingdom. In Afghanistan and Iraq, the jihadi fight has the characteristics of guerrilla warfare and civil war, with tens or hundreds of victims every week. In Europe, fortunately, jihadi terrorism has been much less lethal.

The fact that what constitutes terrorism is not clearly recognisable is further demonstrated by the application of the term, over history, to designate a wide variety of activities. One understands, of course, that the application of the term has tended to reflect political agendas, particularly the power of institutions (most times governments and states) to define meaning in society: the political opponent of the day would normally be turned into the "enemy" by being called a "terrorist." This nonetheless has varied from labelling "terrorism" the abuse of office (as in the French revolutionary *régime de la terreur*), anarchism (such as the activities of the Anarchist International in the late nineteenth century), the actions of nationalist and separatist groups (like the Irish Fenians, Revolutionary Brotherhood and Clan na Gael in the second half of the nineteenth century), the mass repression of totalitarian regimes (Nazism and Fascism in the early twentieth century), anticolonial movements (like the Front de Libération du Québec or the Basque ETA (Hoffman 2006: 3–20). Indeed, as Hoffman admits, in current everyday language the term "terrorism" would be used to describe "virtually any especially abhorrent act of violence perceived as directed against society – whether it involves the activities of antigovernment dissidents or government themselves, organized crime syndicates, common criminals, rioting mobs, people engaged in militant protest, individual psychotics, or lone extortionists" (ibid.: 1).

The use of the term "terrorism" appears thus motivated more by the emotional reaction triggered by the extent and barbarity of the violence, the choice of targets, the unexpectedness of the action, the radical nature of the terrorists' message, than any clear-cut difference from other similar and politically motivated violent activities.

Despite these considerations about the dubious utility of applying the "terrorism" conceptual category at all, the term is de facto widely used and there is practically little choice but to do the same here. The criteria for selecting the cases in which to apply it will adhere to the rule of thumb often suggested to students to recognise terrorism – the presence of four key features: (a) its being an act of violence, (b) motivated by political reasons, (c) directed against innocents, (d) to frighten a broader audience (Yungher 2008: 6). I take this as a common denominator, a shared conceptual ground with the reader to allow the arguments in the following chapters to unfold. These four aspects, however, are not free from problems.

In relation to the violence aspect of terrorism, Eatwell and Goodwin (2010a: 9) point out that extremism (also defined, in their view, by violent action), that "few in the contemporary world would admit to supporting 'violence'": Palestinians would not say they are engaged in "violence" (let alone "terrorism") against Israeli soldiers, but in "acts of resistance." Thatcherism applied "force," not "violence," both to solve the Falklands' dispute and to restore social order in 1984–85, when the coal miners would not comply with authorities' requests (ibid.). Also what is "political" is not at all straightforward. The fact that what is political is a social construction and derives its meaning from a specific cultural (often national) context is underlined by these words of Ulrike Meinhof, a member of the German Red Army Faction (RAF): "[in Germany] If you throw a stone, it's a crime. If a thousand stones are thrown, that's political. If you set fire to a car, that's a crime. If a hundred cars are set on fire, that's political" (in Post 2007: 127). The idea of "innocents," too, begs the question of: innocent in whose perspective? By common social standards – including the author's own – victims do not "deserve" death, injury or trauma, but that is not always the view of the perpetrators. To follow with the RAF example, Jerrold Post (ibid.: 131) reports the reply that the leader of the Heidelberg cell of the RAF gave to a new member of the organisation, shocked at hearing that the group was planning to set off firebombs in a KADeWe store:

> "Gott in Himmel" he blurted out. "There will be all these inno-cents victims." ... "Hans," asked the leader, in an icy tone, "have you been to a KADeWe store? If you have been, you will know that these people who shop there are not innocent victims, they are capitalist consumers. They deserve to die."

As I will explain in Chapter 2, interpretations of social reality (or stories) are crucial to the establishment of a group's identity and to its mobi-lisation. Dismissing the perspective of the perpetrators only because it conflicts with "ours," means denying ourselves the opportunity to fully understand social action (Zulaika and Douglass 2008).

The purpose of influencing a wider audience is also not exclusive to terrorists. Any citizen who joins a street march wants to communicate with a wider audience. Chaining oneself to a tree to protest against the removal of a forest and the building of a retail park is an action taken to attract the attention of broader constituencies. Nor is "ter-ror" a good choice as a defining feature of terrorism. First, because it appears to depend on a presumed reaction to a "terrorist" act rather than being a characteristic of the act itself. This, in principle, could be acceptable if the "terror" reaction regularly and invariably manifested itself upon the occurrence of "terrorism." But this, at a closer look, is not at all the case. In fact, despite the spectacular nature of the attacks and the high human toll in terms of lives lost, how many people were truly "terrorised" by 9/11? By "terror" I mean an incapacitating state of psychological paralysis, different from either "anxiety" or "con-cern" for the victims. A person living in New York, on the morning of 11 September 2001, might have felt his or her life to be at risk without necessarily experiencing "terror." Somebody living in a small town in either the middle of Kansas, the Scottish Highlands, or the Chinese countryside – hardly terrorist targets – might have felt sorry for the people killed, but would have certainly not been afraid of becoming victims themselves. How many people should truly be "terrorised" in order to call the act "terrorism"? Is there any geographical proximity or time frame within which the "terror" reaction should materialise?

A better defining feature than "terror," in this book's view, is the perception that the political claim made by the extremist group is a threat to the view of the world and identity (which we might call values) of the majority it aims to address. The perception of threat, in this perspective, would come from the imagined "distance" between an extremist group's claim and the view of the world shared by the majority. In this sense a terrorist group like Al Qaeda would be positioned, by the political standards of British society, far up on a long spectrum of political claims that can range from advocating the establishment of community-led response to climate change and shrinking supplies of energy by the "Transition Network" (not really a threat, just a different lifestyle);[4] to calling for a ban on immigration (more of a threat, but still within the limits of legitimate democratic debate, as demonstrated by the fact that the British National Party is not illegal);[5] to dismantling democracy and applying Sharia law ("existential" threat posed by Al Qaeda).

Obviously without condoning it, I take distance from the idea that terrorism is some form of aberration or extraordinary occurrence. I prefer to approach it more neutrally as a form of action purposely chosen by social actors to make extreme political claims. In fact, as I will explain in Chapter 3, terrorist groups are regarded in this book as social movements. Violent extremism will be used as a synonym for terrorism.

1.3 The missing "whys" of terrorism

It has been argued that terrorism research is "haunted by bad social science" (Amm Sam 2010). This statement was made by a contributor to the *Free Radicals Blog* at the London-based International Centre for the Study of Radicalisation and Political Violence, in relation to the understanding of why people become terrorists. The observation, while it referred to the explanation of a specific phenomenon within terrorism studies, appears to apply to the wider state of the field, as several others have pointed out. Audrey Cronin (2006: 10), for example, talks about the "thinness of terrorism studies": "Terrorism studies are often event driven, spurred by attacks and the need to analyze and respond more effectively to a specific threat. As a result, the bulk of traditional research on terrorism has been descriptive analysis focused on one group, detailing its organization, structure, tactics, leadership" (Cronin 2006: 8). Silke (2004a: 1–2), in his analysis of the achievements and failures of the field writes that "while the volume of what has been written is both massive and growing, the quality of the content leaves much to be desired. So much is dross, repetitive and ill-informed." Michael Smith (2009: 320) suggests that "much of what passe[s] for terrorism research [is] susceptible to superficiality and the production of dull typologies and inconsequential historical catalogues." He is not as scathing about the quality of scholarship as is historian Michael Howard (quoted in Smith 2009: 319), who argues that terrorism studies have "been responsible for more incompetent and unnecessary books than any other outside ... of sociology[;] it attracts phoneys and amateurs as a candle attracts moths."

The reasons normally presented for the general lack of empirical enquiry are that some information, guarded under the label of "national security," is simply off-limits to researchers and that first-hand analysis can be costly and/or time-consuming (Schulze 2004). This forces most researchers, who tend to operate on their own (Silke 2004d: 191), to rely on colleagues' publications, open access government documents, and media reports (Schulze 2004: 161–164; Horgan 2007: 108). Silke (2004c: 59), more to this point, finds that the researchers he reviewed in the period 1995–1999 "were not producing substantively new data or knowledge" but were "reworking old material which already existed" – a trend that Schmid and Jongman (2005: 137) confirm for the more recent period: from their survey of terrorism researchers, it appears that only 46 per cent of the experts they approached could rely on data they had themselves generated.

I argue that the root of the poor conceptual development of the field is, however, neither the little empirical research, nor the timid explicit engagement with conceptual issues. In fact, engagement with conceptual issues is not achieved, as is often suggested, only by means of debating abstract matters or agreeing on what terrorism refers to (as Silke 2004a argues, for instance). It can be more thoroughly achieved through reflection on the very process through which observations about the world are turned into knowledge. The thorny issue, in this perspective, is the elaboration of explanations – or theories – about terrorism. I will now elaborate further on this aspect by addressing, in turn, the neglect of *explanatory* research, the lack of genuine engagement with causal mechanisms, the limited pursue of comparative research, and the lack of theory testing.

1.3.1 The neglect of explanatory research

David de Vaus (2001) establishes a distinction between descriptive research and explanatory research. Descriptive research, he explains, answers the question *"What* is going on?" Explanatory research is, instead, concerned with the: "Why is it going on?" (Ibid.: 1). Descriptive research, as he writes, "encompasses much government sponsored research including the population census, the collection of a wide range of social indicators and economic information such as household expenditure patterns, time use studies, employment and crime statistics" (ibid.). In relation to the subject of terrorism, examples of descriptive research could cover statistics about terrorist incidents available on the Global Terrorism Database,[6] a compilation of translated texts by Osama bin Laden and Ayman Al-Zawahiri (Hegghammer 2005; Mansfield 2006; Kepel and Milelli 2008), or a book on the history of the Irish Republican Army (IRA) (English 2004).

Descriptive research is not only statistics-based and can involve addressing "more abstract" questions like: "is the level of social inequality increasing or declining?" (de Vaus 2001: 2) or, again in the case of terrorism, "is terrorism on the rise?"; or "are more individuals embracing extremist views – or becoming radicalized – than five years ago?" Explanatory research, instead, develops causal explanations: it is one thing to say, for instance, that more recruits are joining Al Qaeda today than five years ago, another thing to explain *why*. A causal explanation involves establishing a link between a phenomenon, X (the embracing of extremist views – radicalisation – for example), and a factor, Y, – what Gary King, Robert Keohane, and Sidney Verba (1994) would call "variable" (terrorist extremist propaganda material, for instance). The causal relationships between variable/s and outcome can be more or less complex. They can be, as illustrated in Figure 1.1, straightforward as in case A. This can involve a chain of variables, as in B. Alternatively, this can present more complex sets of causal connections, as in C. Any link between a variable and outcome, that is, any answer to the "why question," is a *theory* (de Vaus 2001: 5).

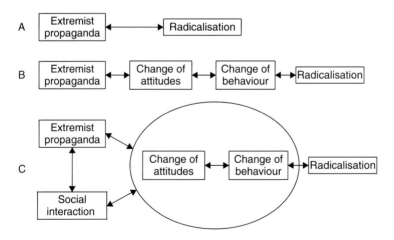

Figure 1.1   Three hypothetical sets of causal connections among variables

The fact that terrorism research is event-driven, empirical, and stimulated by the immediate needs of the security community (Cronin 2006: 8) does not necessarily have to translate into descriptive research, although this would likely be the very first outcome, especially in relation to emerging terrorist groups about which little previous research might exist. Nothing, however, in principle stops researchers from asking "why" questions about any topic any time. Besides, descriptive research is not somehow inferior to explanatory research. On the contrary, as de Vaus (2001: 1) points out, it is "fundamental to the research enterprise." Without good descriptive research it would not be possible to pursue the "why" questions. To continue with the example made earlier, we cannot ask why, for instance, more people could be becoming radicalised than five years ago if we do not detect the existence of this trend in the first place. The problem is that there is little good descriptive research going on to sustain explanatory research. While, as mentioned earlier, some data is classified, accessing former terrorists does not need to be a dangerous enterprise (Dolnik 2011a). Indeed there is an "increased availability of disengaged individuals and movements in several regions" (Horgan 2009: 17), historical and archival resources (Duyvesteyn 2007), and an unprecedented volume of terrorists' statements, videos, publications, manuals, discussions on online fora that can be accessed at the click of a button on the Internet. These mines of empirical data are either underestimated, conveniently ignored, or not considered as sources of relevant data at all.

1.3.2   The lack of comparative research

Where the focus on either single terrorist organisations or cases leads to descriptive research, this tends not to be systematically taken to the next level. This is related to the general lack of comparative approaches. As Guy Swanson (1971 in Ragin 1987: 1) put it: "Thinking without comparison is unthinkable. And, in the absence of comparison, so is all scientific thought and scientific research." The point he is making is that we cannot even begin to explain a phenomenon unless we get a sense of which aspects of the phenomenon we need to focus our attention on. And we cannot identify those but through detecting similarities and differences when we compare our phenomenon to other cases. As Charles Ragin (1987: 1) writes, "virtually all empirical social research involves comparison of some sort … . Comparison provides a basis for making statements about empirical regularities and for evaluating and interpreting cases relative to substantive and theoretical criteria."

A comparative approach can be both longitudinal (comparison of cases over time) but also cross-sectional (across countries, for example). Comparisons produce observations that, inductively, can lead to formulating an explanation of the phenomenon being studied – theory building (de Vaus 2001: 5–6). However, no matter how good the selection of cases to be compared, comparisons alone cannot guarantee the formulation of reality-proof theories. While comparisons sensitise the researcher to regularity and variation, they have only a limited role in causal inference (Hallin and Mancini 2005: 216). Alexander George (1997: 1), in this respect, describes the method of "controlled comparison" as "the method of studying two or more cases that resemble each other in every respect but one, thereby achieving or approximating the functional equivalent of an experiment which makes it possible to rely on experimental logic to draw causal inferences." The method allows the researcher to eliminate variables competing for the production of an outcome: "a condition present in both cases cannot account for the difference in case outcomes." As the author points out, however, in reality it is extremely difficult to find two cases that resemble each other in every respect but one (ibid.). Indeed he says that "practically all efforts to make use of the controlled comparison method fail to achieve its strict requirements" (ibid.: 5). For one main practical reason, the method of controlled comparison can hardly be applied to social phenomena involving a multiplicity and complexity of causes: there are too many variables and too few cases a researcher can possibly handle (ibid.: 2). The author further adds that relying on covariance alone as a basis to draw causal inferences does not tackle the problem of equifinality. Equifinality occurs when "the *same* type of outcome can emerge in different cases via a *different* set of independent variables" (George and Bennett 2005: 157, their emphasis). It is, therefore, imperative that any theory be thoroughly empirically tested (on a new set of data) before being taken as an accurate explanation of reality.[7] This is particularly important because all scientific knowledge cannot but be "provisional" (de Vaus 2001: 5), especially in the social sciences. Whichever theory – or causal relationship between one or more variables and an outcome – we formulate, it will never work with the regularity of a physical law – "whenever water is heated to 100° C it always boils."[8] Most causal explanations in the social sciences are thus *probabilistic* rather than *deterministic* (Suppes 1970 in de Vaus 2001: 5, his emphasis).

The relevance of all the points made so far to understanding terrorism can be better illustrated through an example. If, by examining the Al Qaeda case, we noticed that a substantial number of individuals convicted of terrorist activities had become radicalised after having come into contact with extremist propaganda material, such as jihadi videos, over the Internet, we might be led to formulating the causal explanation (theory) that extremist propaganda (variable), distributed over the Internet, for example, is leading to radicalisation (outcome). Believing that this is an accurate description of reality, if not an explanation for radicalisation, however, would not be legitimate. In fact, this brings up the difference between correlation and causation. As de Vaus (2001: 4) explains: "Confusing causation with correlation also confuses prediction with causation and prediction with explanation." Going back to our example, having observed a correlation between exposure to extremist propaganda and radicalisation, we might think that we can predict one from the other. This, however, is not the same as being able to explain why (indeed if!) extremist propaganda leads to radicalisation: "*Good prediction does not depend on causal relationships. Nor does the ability to predict accurately demonstrate anything about causality*" (de Vaus 2001: 4, his emphasis). In other words, it might be that all radicalised individuals we have observed have been exposed to extremist propaganda over the Internet; still, this does not tell us anything about the causal mechanism, why they have embraced the Al Qaeda cause. Is it because individuals are "infected" by the extremist message? Is it because individuals become more sensitive to an extremist interpretation of reality, which they then develop on their own? Is it because at the stage when they access the extremist material (which they might have actively searched for) the radical views they had already developed (perhaps through a circle of like-minded acquaintances) became reinforced? The possibilities are countless and they should include the hypothesis that the extremist propaganda material is not at all the point of departure within our provisional causal explanation, but one among many variables within a longer chain of connected variables. What if, for instance, the real starting point of the causal explanation was the position of the individual in a constellation of social relationships that affects the way s/he interprets reality? The access to extremist material on the Internet, in that case, could just be related to the fact that the Internet is a convenient and available tool for accessing information. In a society in which that technology was not available – in a remote area of Yemen, for instance – radicalisation might still occur, but perhaps it would not involve the Internet. This, however, would not be "visible" unless we *compared* radicalisation processes across countries with different levels of development and diffusion of communication technologies. The comparison does not help the researcher in this case to establish for certain what causes radicalisation, but sensitises the investigator to the fact that the Internet might just be another variable within the explanatory causal chain, which needs further research.

1.3.3 The lack of engagement with causal explanation

Current causal accounts of terrorism present two main problems. The first is that that they are based on a questionable categorisation of variables. As Crenshaw notes in "The Causes of Terrorism" (1981: 380): "Even the most persuasive of statements about terrorism are not cast in the form of testable propositions ... . A narrow historical or geographical focus is also common ... . In general, propositions about terrorism lack logical comparability, specification of the relationship of variables to each other, and a rank-ordering of variables in terms of explanatory power." Despite the good intentions, the same article in which the author expresses her critique of existing studies does not offer a radically different alternative. In all fairness to the author, she states that the purpose of her paper is to present "a preliminary set of ideas about the problem of causation" (ibid.), not a real explanation for terrorism. The distinctions she makes between "preconditions" – both "enabling" and "permissive" factors that "set the stage for terrorism in the long run" (ibid.: 381) – and "precipitants" – "similar to the direct causes of terrorism" (ibid.) – however, appear to be nothing more than arbitrary categories attached to specific cases. As such they are far from providing any insight into the causation of terrorism.

For example, the first condition Crenshaw identifies as "a direct cause of terrorism" is the existence of "concrete grievances among an identifiable subgroup of a larger population, such as an ethnic minority discriminated against by the majority" (ibid.: 383). What she writes, though, equally suggests that the grievances might well be held by majorities, such as colonial national movements: "A social movement develops in order to redress these grievances and to gain either equal rights or a separate state; terrorism is then the resort of an extremist faction of this broader movement. In practice, terrorism has frequently arisen in such situations: in modern states, separatist nationalism among Basques, Bretons, and Quebecois has motivated terrorism. In the colonial era, nationalist movements commonly turned to terrorism" (ibid.). Indeed, she further undermines the role of the "existence of grievance" as a "direct cause of terrorism": "This is not to say, however, that the existence of a dissatisfied minority or majority is a necessary or a sufficient cause of terrorism. Not all those who are discriminated against turn to terrorism, nor does terrorism always reflect objective social or economic deprivation. In West Germany, Japan, and Italy, for example, terrorism has been the chosen method of the privileged, not the down-trodden" (ibid.). How can a "direct cause" apply in some cases but not others? Besides, the existence of grievances in itself does not necessarily lead to terrorism. The real question a causal explanation of terrorism should address, one could argue, is: How do grievances lead to violent action?

Similar points could be made about a "second condition" she describes: "lack of opportunity for political participation" (ibid.). This identified precondition does not necessarily translate into terrorist violence. Under which further circumstances would this outcome arise?

The arbitrariness of such categories is even more obvious when one compares them to those outlined in another work that addresses the issue of what explains terrorism. Tore Bjørgo's (2005b) *The Root Causes of Terrorism* also differentiates between preconditions and precipitants on virtually identical terms. In fact, Bjørgo acknowledges he is bor-rowing their distinction from Crenshaw (1981), although he considers them as two ends of a continuum rather than two neatly distinct cat-egories (ibid.: 258). Preconditions, he adds, "are of a relatively general and structural nature, producing a wide range of social outcomes of which terrorism is only one. Preconditions alone are not sufficient to cause the outbreak of terrorism. Precipitants much more directly affect the emergence of terrorism. These are the specific events or situations that immediately precede, motivate or trigger the outbreak of terror-ism" (Bjørgo 2005a: 258). The preconditions in Bjørgo include: "lack of democracy, civil liberties and the rule of law," "failed or weak states," "rapid modernization," and "extremist ideologies." Among the precipi-tants are "the experience of social injustice," "the presence of charis-matic ideological leaders," and "the experience of discrimination on the basis of ethnic or religious origin" (ibid.: 259–260). For Bjørgo the lack of democracy is a precondition for terrorism. For Crenshaw the "lack of opportunity for political participation" – which could be alternatively called lack of democracy – is a precipitant. At the end it might just all be a matter of definitions, but one cannot escape the suspicion that what is a "precondition" and what is a "precipitant" could be relative to each individual case. This example also points to a greater conceptual contradiction. Both authors argue that terrorism is the outcome of dif-ferent factors. This means that terrorism would not exist unless those factors are combined. The bottom line is that, wherever it might fit, earlier or later, in what might look to the researcher like a prominent role – "immediately ... motivate or trigger" (ibid.: 258) – or on the side – "set the stage for terrorism in the long run," (ibid.) – either a factor is causal or it is not. The distinction between "precondition" and "precipitant" might just be related to the chronological manifestation of the factors. In fact, in Bjørgo, there seems to be an assumption that what occurs more closely in time ("immediately precede") to the outbreak of terrorism is somehow "more causal" than what happens at greater distance in the chronology of events.

The second problem with existing causal accounts of terrorism is that the identified variables might apply to a much broader set of phenomena than terrorism. As Michael Smith (2009: 328) bluntly puts it in reviewing the *Root Causes of Terrorism*: "The problem with these 'preconditions' is that they apply to *all* conflicts, not just those that may be afflicted with terroristic [*sic*] violence." Where, therefore, does their explanatory power in relation to the specific phenomenon of terrorism reside? Going back to the example given earlier, the presence of grievances could well be a cause for terrorism, but it needs to be fitted into an explanation of how they exactly generate extremist violence. Some level of grievance, in fact, is what characterises any political arena, even the most democratic, civilised and far removed from violence. Without such explanation, the presence of grievances could be seen as the cause of countless other phenomena, including peaceful strikes, road rage, perhaps even depression. In fact, Doug McAdam, Sidney Tarrow and Charles Tilly (2001: 24) define a causal explanation as "a delimited class of events that alter relations among specified sets of elements in identical or closely similar ways over a variety of situations." James Mahoney (2003: 4) phrases it more simply: "a [causal] mechanism is a cause that affects outcomes in similar ways across diverse contexts." Although law-like regularity cannot be expected in explaining the social world, the problems with current "explanations" of terrorism is that they might apply to one case and not to another one with no well-defined reason as to why the variation occurs. Cronin (2006: 17–18), in explaining why terrorism ends, for instance, identifies seven reasons:

(a)   capture or killing of the leader;
(b)   failure to transition to the next generation;
(c)   achievement of the group's aims;
(d)   transition to a legitimate process;
(e)   undermining of popular support;
(f)   repression;
(g)   transition from terrorism to other forms of violence.

Why did each of them work for some organisation and not for others? Why for instance did not the killing of Osama bin Laden lead to the demise of Al Qaeda as it happened in the case of the execution of Shoko Asahara, leader of Japan's Aum Shinrikyo (ibid.: 21)? If the presence of a "viable successor" or the "structure of the organisation" can make a difference, as the author suggests *in passim* (ibid.: 18), how do these aspects exactly fit within the causal explanation? And how do they relate with the other reasons about why terrorism ends?

1.3.4   The missing dimension of theory testing

The building of a theory is not complete without thorough testing. The testing involves deriving a set of propositions – or hypotheses – from the theory that allow either to verify the existence of the relationships among the variables or to better define the conditions under which the theory is valid. This set of propositions should be formulated "so that if the theory is true then certain things should follow in the real world" (de Vaus 2001: 6–7). This is vital to ensure that the provisional knowledge contained in the causal explanation we have formulated on the basis of our observations actually reflects reality. In other words, to ensure that the causal mechanisms we think exist, do in fact exist. The lack of a deep engagement with causal mechanisms and the absence of this process are the reasons why, ultimately, after decades of research, there is still no real comprehensive theory of terrorism. The difference between identifying isolated factors that might lead to a phenomenon and actual knowledge about it is not always appreciated, as this recent policy statement suggests: "Since the last *Prevent* strategy, academic, intelligence and other Government work has illuminated the drivers of radicalisation, the characteristics of people who have been radicalised and who have joined terrorist groups, and the specific pathways to support for, and participation in, terrorist acts" (Home Office 2011: 17). As Chapter 4 will point out, the existence of multiple and contrasting accounts of the radicalisation process shows that, in reality, neither consensus on, nor knowledge of the matter has been achieved.

1.4   Why no theories?

Theory building and theory testing – the latter as the refinement of causal explanations to identify their respective conditions of validity – are crucial to the development of science, but due to four further reasons they do not appear to be taking place in Terrorism Studies. They are related to the structure of the field.

The first is that the bulk of research is produced by first-timers. Silke writes that 83 per cent of articles published in major terrorism journals (like *Terrorism and Political Violence* and *Studies in Conflict and Terrorism*) in the 1990s were produced by one-timers (Silke 2004d: 191) with "no real interest in making a substantial contribution to the field" (Silke 2004c: 69). This finding is supported also by Avishag Gordon (2007): through an analysis of terrorism-related publication patterns over time, he confirms that, despite the growing amount of literature on the subject, the bulk of terrorism research is produced by researchers who contribute to the field with one or two articles and then move on to a different subject.

Although this trend is widely seen in negative terms, it is not necessarily for the worse. On the one hand, Cronin (2006: 9) writes that the one-timers are "scholars who are relatively new to the subject and unaware of the body of work that has gone before." This leads to their inability to understand terrorism beyond its "present political context" (ibid.). This is, in itself, an obstacle to longitudinal comparative research. On the other hand, the mobility of researchers encourages the study of terrorism from the perspectives of different disciplines (see also Reid and Chen 2007). Indeed, all the best works about the relationship between terrorism and the media come from scholars who are not "core" terrorism researchers (Paletz and Schmid 1992; Awan, Hoskins, and O'Loughlin 2011; Seib and Janbek 2011). It is nonetheless true that the transient nature of research does not help scientific accumulation. Either the descriptive research does not lead to explanatory research, as mentioned earlier, or the theories being built are never refined through the identification of their conditions of validity or systematically tested.

A second reason is the history of the way the field has developed over time and the fact that, as Cronin (2006: 9) writes: "The agenda reflects the strengths of established international security and defence community, where there is far more expertise, for example, on nuclear weapons and proliferation than on the Arab-speaking networks that might use them." Smith (2009: 321), further on this point, suggests that the low quality of scholarship is explained by the fact that:

> With few exceptions, contemporaneous international relations theorists, historians and strategic experts, who might have had something to contribute to informed discussions about violent non-state actors, absented themselves from the debate in favour of the technical-managerial obsessions of Cold War defence that usually fixated upon

arcane, banal, hairsplitting exchanges over nuclear deterrence, arms control and weapons systems.

This leads, in turn, to a third reason for theory building lagging behind in Terrorism Studies. Researchers who contribute to terrorism studies come from different research backgrounds. Disciplines have methodological traditions that tend to define the approaches scholars take in developing research both in terms of the level at which analysis is conducted and the methodology used. Approaches in terrorism studies tend to gravitate towards either the micro- or the macro-level of analysis with very little in between. This lead to producing perfectly acceptable explanations within their respective domains (see, for instance, Horgan [2009] for a micro- and meso-level analysis, Weinberg and Richardson [2004] for a macro approach). What is the link, however, between the micro and the macro? How do we explain, in other words, the connection between individual motivation and structural influences in leading to terrorism? This, as it will be explained in the next chapter, is important: to make sense of the role of the media, which can have an impact ranging from affecting individual perceptions, to contributing to the organisation of a group, to supporting mobilisation on a worldwide scale, it is necessary to fit them within a framework that spans these two dimensions. At the same time some research domains are more established and influential than others. As for the predominance of certain methodologies, Marc Sageman (2008: 173) talks about an overemphasis by governmental funders on statistical "modeling over data collection." Jonathan Githens-Mazer (2010: 47) similarly points out that literature on extremism is biased towards quantitative studies and profiling. Jeroen Gunning (2007: 371) characterises the "problem-solving approach" of Orthodox Terrorism Studies as "positivist and objectivist."

As a fourth point, despite the fact that Terrorism Studies involves a variety of disciplines, it is questionable the degree to which the field is truly *inter*disciplinary. Theories do not appear to be developed across academic departmental lines. Eatwell and Goodwin (2010a: 14), in this respect, identify the tendency to examine different kinds of extremism in isolation from each other: "Studies on the contemporary extreme right rarely engage with the literature on Islamic extremism and vice versa." The degree of compartmentalisation becomes even more evident when one compares theories in Terrorism Studies to theories from neighbouring disciplines, whose insights could be very relevant to explaining violent extremism. For instance, explaining why individuals engage in political action is important in both producing an explanation of radicalisation (why individuals resort to violent action) and social movements literature (why individual get involved in political collective action, which might well turn violent). Radicalisation literature, including official documents like *Prevent* (Home Office 2011), often mentions "grievances" as drivers towards extremism. It states that "We know that extremists can play on a sense of grievance to reinforce their messages" (ibid.: 87) and that the Al Qaeda narrative "connects 'grievances' at a local and/or global level, reinforces the portrayal of Muslims as victims of Western injustice and thereby purports to legitimise terrorism" (ibid.: 108). If we look at social movements theories, however, we discover that "grievance theory" was popular in the 1950s and 1960s (Tarrow 1998: 13–14). It was inspired by a Marxist focus on conflict between class-based interests. This has long ago been abandoned in favour of a more sophisticated explanation of social movements that does not only examine the sources of conflict (the grievances) but also look at the formation of collective identity, the circumstances within which resources can be mobilised, and action takes place. This innovation, however, is not contributing to progress in Terrorism Studies. Indeed, Silke (Silke 2004a: 9) points out that "The activities of terrorist groups, and the nature of their membership, have by and large been studiously ignored by social scientists." Tarrow (1998: 211, n. 3) reciprocally observes that scholars of social movements normally concentrate on the "'civil' movements of liberal democracies" with little regard for the "'bad' movements."

The aim of this discussion was to show not only the conceptual gaps, but also the reasons for the theoretical limitations within the field of Terrorism Studies. They help in explaining the problems in the subset of literature that deals with terrorism as a form of communication, particularly in explaining the role of the media. This is the subject we are going to turn to in the next chapter.

2
Terrorism, Communication, and the Media

This chapter examines the approaches to the study of terrorism that emphasise its communicative dimension. The field's conceptual gaps highlighted in the first chapter particularly help in placing into context the current problems in making sense of the role of the media. Indeed, Brian Simmons (1991: 36) observes that "much literature concerning the mass media's coverage of terrorism is speculative in nature": "Often, sweeping statements are made without any substantive proof." Robert Picard (1991), assessing the "contagion hypothesis" – the idea that media reporting of terrorism generates more of it – talks about "dubious science" (ibid.: 49) and a "lack of scientifically acceptable evidence" supporting the arguments (ibid.: 60). David Paletz and John Boiney (1992: 12) write that the literature which tends to see media coverage as beneficial to terrorists is marked "by a reliance on the same incidents and on anecdotal information." Jeffrey Ross (2007: 215–216), reviewing research on the relationship between media and terrorism finds that "there is a striking similarity among ... monographs; they cover many of the same topics and often reprint well-cited journal articles, therefore adding little new information."

The analysis is divided into two parts. The first will show that the role of the media is interpreted in contradictory terms. For instance, for some the media are manipulated by terrorists, for others by governments; in yet another scenario they are independent, have a will of their own, and even have the power to manufacture an alternative reality. Not only is it not always clear what "media" refers to in these accounts, but the term appears to be used indistinctively to conflate communication technologies, content carried by media platforms, and media organisations. There is also a lack of perspective in assessing the role of new communication technologies like the Internet and social media.

In addition to this, if we look at the claims made from the point of view of external disciplines, like Communication Studies or Political Communication, they would also either sound extremely questionable or reflect outdated theories.

The second part of the chapter makes the point that communication is far more relevant to the understanding of terrorism than existing literature gives it credit for. Communication is important not only because terrorism is about transmitting a message or because terrorists might be disseminating their ideology through the Internet. Communication is the very enabler of social interaction. Acknowledging the relevance of communication allows understanding how identities are formed, how people come to share a political cause and mobilise around it, as well as how political action can turn to violence. Besides, communication is not just relevant at times of terrorist attacks but at *all times*. To really understand the role of communication, more or less mediated, in the phenomenon of terrorism we need to be able to see this broader picture. To do so means, first, systematically getting to grips with conceptual issues: beyond the explicit engagement with theory (an explanation of how different variables are causally connected) that has already been highlighted in Chapter 1, what is also required is an elaboration of a statement of how social actors both appropriate the context in which they operate and are shaped by it in their behaviour (social ontology). Second, and more provocatively, that part of the chapter will suggest that to understand the role of communication we need momentarily to "suspend" the use of the "terrorism" category. The very notion of "terrorism," in fact, could be serving as a Kuhnian paradigm. While playing the role of a focal point around which many busy strands of research do actively converge, it also sets limits to what can legitimately be investigated and the kind of explanations that can be produced through the research process. As it will be emphasised in the conclusion, in order to explain the role of communication and the media, we need nothing less than a wholly different view of reality. This will then be developed in Chapter 3.

2.1   What role for communication?

Even without knowing that the term comes from the Latin *communicare* – "to share" – we all understand what communication is about. We have an intuitive notion that it involves an exchange of information, that it can happen face-to-face, but it can also be mediated: it can consist of a written text, it can take place via phone in the shape of a conversation, or through the Internet in sending an email, as well as in setting up a website. It can be one way, as in the broadcasting of a TV programme, or two ways, as in the context of a blog, where there is an exchange between the author who posts an entry and someone who comments on it. What might not be as obvious is that we also engage in communication when we do not explicitly set off to use a communication medium – such as when we pick up the phone, for instance. Voting, for example, is an act of communication in which we express our preference for a candidate and the political manifesto s/he represents. Protesting, whether holding placards or being on a hunger strike, is about expressing support for a cause and letting others know about it. Terrorism, inflicting death and destroying property, is also a way of sending a message.

The analysis here deals with terrorism as a communication phenomenon. As Alex Schmid (1989: 541) phrased it, terrorism can be compared to the proverbial tree falling in the forest, whose sound does not exist until somebody actually hears it: "with the rise of the mass media in the 1880s reporters came to observe the falling of each 'tree' and ... their newspapers brought the story to people who would otherwise never have learned about it." As such the media are essential to terrorists' tactics.

The purpose of the following critical review of the literature is showing that several authors have acknowledged terrorism as an act of communication. They have recognised that terrorists want to send a message; that media are crucial in achieving their objectives; that communication technologies make a difference in the way the message is distributed. While this acknowledgment is one step in the right direction, I argue that it does not go far enough. If we look at the way the literature explains the function of the media, we can see that it presents contradictory statements. As will be explained, this is related to a fundamental misunderstanding of the nature of the "media," but also to the (previously highlighted) absence of causal explanations within which to "fit" them.

2.1.1   Terrorism as communication

Alex Schmid and Janny de Graaf (1982: 14) famously argued that terrorism *is* communication: "For the terrorist the message matters, not the victim." In their words the casualties of a terrorist attacks are "message generators" (ibid.: 29), "the skin on a drum beaten to achieve a calculated impact on a wider audience" (ibid.: 14). This view has been echoed by others. For instance, Ralph Dowling (1986) sees terrorism as a rhetorical genre: "Terrorists seek to change the world, yet they lack the power to do so" (ibid.: 13), "The violent acts required to obtain media access constrain terrorist rhetoric while at the same time achieving rhetorical purposes that ordinary forms of discourse could never achieve" (ibid.: 15). For John Martin (1985: 134) terrorism is "a form of nonverbal communication that the terrorist resorts to when verbal communication fails." The aspects that are most emphasised in the literature are: the way in which violence is used as tool for engaging in political communication with other social actors; the planning behind terrorist attacks, particularly the orchestration of spectacular violent acts that meet newsworthiness criteria, thereby granting terrorists access to the mainstream media. These points will now be illustrated in greater detail.

For Ronald Crelinsten (1987) terrorism's violence is a form of communication that interacts with other forms of social and political communication. More specifically, he interprets terrorism as a struggle over access to, and definition of, meaning within a society's "communication structure" – the communication channels and institutions where political activity is normally conducted (ibid.: 420). According to him:

> Insurgent terrorism can be viewed as a form of political communication or a form of protest in which the terrorist attempts to gain the attention of those in power to promote some cause, via the combined use of threat and violence. The terrorist resorts to violence because he [*sic*] feels – rightly or wrongly – that he has been excluded from the political process. In this view terrorism functions as a form of "propaganda of the deed" in which the terrorist sends messages to those in power, as well as to the general public. On a purely symbolic level, the message is equivalent to shouting "look at me!" or "listen to me!" (Ibid: 419)

Further emphasising the centrality of communication, other authors examine the relationship between terrorism and the media. In this respect, Brigitte Nacos (2002b) approaches terrorism as a "massmediated" phenomenon. The mass media plays a central role in what she calls the "calculus" of perpetrators: terrorists anticipate the consequences of their actions, "the likelihood of gaining media attention" and the possibility of entering, through the media, the "Triangle of Political Communication" (Nacos 2003: 11). In a triangle whose points are constituted by the media, policymakers, and the public, as she explains, the media are not neutral. They are, rather, in a strategic position: they "magnify and minimize, include and exclude" (ibid.). In the global communication system, domestic terrorists can also tap into international media and communicate their message to foreign governments and audiences (ibid.: 12). Access to the media not only grants terrorists the public's attention, but also recognition, and a "degree of respectability" (Nacos 2002b: 14).

Assessing the effectiveness of the terrorists' action on 9/11, she writes, for example:

> There is no doubt ... that the architects of 9–11 had a perfect score with respect to the three media-centered objectives of the calculus of terror: they raked unprecedented media attention, publicized their causes and motives and in the process the grievances of many Muslims, and gained global prominence and notoriety otherwise only accorded to nation-states and their leaders. (Nacos 2003: 8)

Cherif Bassiouni (1981: 17) argues that terrorists "stage" events for obtaining coverage in order "to produce a social impact which would not otherwise exist." "Media-conscious" perpetrators, therefore, "manipulate the instruments of mass communications." What they aim to achieve through their communication strategy is, in his view, to:

(a) demonstrate the vulnerability and impotence of the government;
(b) attract broader public sympathy by the choice of a carefully selected target that may be publicly rationalized;
(c) cause a polarization and radicalisation among the public;
(d) goad the government into repressive action likely to discredit it; or
(e) present the violent acts in a manner that makes them appear heroic. (Ibid.)

Terrorism, due to this aspect of orchestration, is described by Gabriel Weimann and Conrad Winn (1994) as "theatre" (see also Alexander 1978: 112; Weimann 1990; Tsfati and Weimann 2002: 318–319; Burke 2004). Brian Jenkins (1975 in Weimann 1987: 22), in this perspective, writes: "Terrorist attacks are often carefully choreographed to attract the attention of the electronic media and the international press. Taking and holding hostages increases the drama. Terrorism is aimed at the people watching, not at the actual victims. Terrorism is theatre."

The efforts at staging "spectaculars" reflect the attempt to meet what the media regards as newsworthy (Weimann 1987: 23; Viera 1991: 74; Gerrits 1992: 45–49). As Bowyer Bell (1978: 50) put it over 30 years ago: "new transnational gunmen are, in fact, constructing a package so spectacular, so violent, so compelling, that the networks, acting as executives, supplying the cameramen and the audience, cannot refuse the offer."

Robin Gerrits (1992: 32), on the basis of an analysis of terrorists' memoirs, more specifically identifies seven ways in which terrorist groups can maximise their publicity: planning actions for their news value; undertaking supportive propaganda and recruitment activities; choosing the most favourable time and place for their activities; issuing statements; keeping in contact with the press and giving interviews; claiming responsibility for their actions; issuing messages through the meaning or symbolism of the target or the deed.

This point is widely illustrated in the literature by the statement of a Palestinian terrorist after the 1972 Munich Olympics attacks:

> We recognized that sport is the modern religion of the western world. We knew that the people in England and America would switch their television sets from any programme about the plight of the Palestinians if there was a sporting event on another channel. So we decided to use their Olympics, the most sacred ceremony of this religion, to make the world pay attention to us. We offered up human sacrifices to your gods of sport and television. And they answered our prayers. From Munich onwards nobody could ignore the Palestinians or their cause (in Weimann 1990: 16).

Although, as I will further explain in Chapter 3, it is debatable whether it was really the media coverage that placed the Palestinian cause on the international political agenda, this example provides a clear indication of the terrorists' interest in publicity. This has not changed over the years. The impact of the second plane on the North Tower on 11 September 2001, as Shlomo Shpiro (2002: 80) suggests, could have been purposely delayed to make sure that "every television camera in New York would be focused on their murderous activities."

2.1.2 Terrorism and the media: a misunderstood relationship

While there appears to be agreement about the existence of a relationship between media and terrorism, at closer scrutiny the literature reveals a range of different and conflicting claims. Paletz and Boiney (1992: 10), for example, point out that "there are two diametrically opposed camps: those that indict the media as pro-terrorist and those that indict the media as antiterrorist." The "very few works" belonging to the latter camp accuse the media of conspiring with the corporate and/or political power to support a narrow understanding of terrorism, one that is instrumental to pursuing specific interests (ibid.: 12–13). Kevin Barnhurst (1991: 115–119) also identifies "two schools": one which sees the media as "culpable," and instrumental to terrorism; another one arguing that the media are "vulnerable," victims themselves of manipulation by terrorists, yet not directly responsible for terrorists' deeds. Despite this variety of views, the overall understanding of the media role in relation to terrorism in the literature appears overwhelmingly negative.

The dependence of terrorists on the media to publicise their message – one of the most recurrent quotes is by Walter Laqueur (1976: 104): "The media are the terrorist's best friend. The terrorist's act alone is nothing: publicity is all" – has led to establishing, more or less explicitly, a causal link between terrorism and media coverage. Jenkins (1983 in Eke and Alali 1991: 8) goes so far as to say that "terrorism is a product of freedom, particularly, of freedom of the press." For Nacos (1994: 8, my emphasis): "Getting the attention of the mass media, the public, and decision makers is the *raison d'etre* behind modern terrorism's increasing shocking violence."

The relationship between media and terrorists is often described as a "symbiosis" (Bassiouni 1981: 14; Martin 1985: 127; Wilkinson 2006: 145). On the one hand, terrorists need to publicise their motives through the media; on the other hand, media outlets constantly seek compelling stories for their audiences. On this aspect, in her study on the causes of terrorism, Martha Crenshaw (1981: 386) writes: "The most basic reason for terrorism is to gain recognition or attention … . Violence and bloodshed always excite human curiosity, and theatricality, suspense, and threat of danger inherent in terrorism enhance its attention-getting qualities."

The role of the media within the symbiotic relationship with terrorism can vary, however. While the media are always somehow linked to the idea that they support terrorism, the ways in which they can actually aid terrorists in advancing a cause can take different forms. Media can encourage terrorism through "contagion" (Bassiouni 1981: 19): the idea is that the media attention towards terror will encourage further incidents by providing a "model and inspiration" for more attacks (Schmid 1989: 558; see also Alexander 1978: 105). The media can "endorse" terrorism by romanticising or glamourising it. Yonah Alexander (1978), for example, describes how in 1974, in reporting the kidnapping of American newspaper heiress Patricia Hearst by the urban guerrilla group, Symbionese Liberation Army (SLA), the media managed to give a group of "misfits" a modern "'Robin Hood' image" (ibid.: 103). Through their thirst for drama, media are also accused of indulging in disproportionate coverage. Alex Schmid (1989), for instance, compares the volume of *CBS* coverage of the American embassy hostage crisis in Tehran (1979)[1] to reporting of the Vietnam war in 1972. He concludes: 50 US "hostages in Iran received 3,000 times more coverage than 50 G.I.s in Vietnam" (ibid.: 556). Alexander (1978: 112) says that "by providing extensive coverage the media give the impression that they sympathize with the terrorist cause," therefore granting them an aura of legitimacy. Sensationalism, in turn, can easily lead to alarmism and public panic – an outcome British officials often refer to as "doing the terrorists' job for them" (10 Downing Street spokesperson 2003 in Archetti and Taylor 2005: 12 and 13; Straw 2003). Media, in this perspective, can contribute to manufacturing the terrorist threat. The last point is developed by Adam Curtis's documentary *The Power of Nightmares* (2004), in which the media are accomplices in policymakers' deliberate exploitation of fear to support their political agendas. This view is echoed by Nancy Snow (2005: 103), who claims that since 9/11 "we have experienced a coming together of very powerful institutions of information, the federal government and the corporate media, to create a barrier between the American public and the real environment." Along this line John Gray (2005: 16), in the aftermath of the 7/7 London bombings, claimed that they were "an episode in the virtual world that is being continuously manufactured by the media." The media create "collective dreams," "an alternate [*sic*] reality in which insoluble problems [such as terrorism] can be conjured away by displays of goodwill. But the problems never really go away" (ibid.: 17).

Media are not only seen to encourage terrorism indirectly but, through their cameras, they are thought to become co-partners in the terrorist deeds (Schmid 1989: 553; Alexander 1978: 105). They might interfere with governmental crisis management. Martin Bell (2007), for example, writing for the British broadsheet *The Guardian* in relation to the attempted car bombing at Glasgow airport on 30 June 2007,[2] writes that "the government's response to the ... emergency has been measured, welcome and reassuring. The media's, however, has been hysterical beyond belief." Reporters' activities around the locations of terrorist attacks are also found to interfere with police operations (Alexander 1978: 105). Raphael Cohen-Almagor (2005), in this respect, draws a lengthy list of the multiple ways in which "problematic and irresponsible" coverage has placed the media on the side of the terrorists rather than the government's. The "troubling episodes" he describes range from endangering lives in situations in which hostages are taken, indulging in "dangerous speculations," to paying terrorists in order to get interviews, and using irresponsible terminology – for example "freedom fighters" rather than "terrorists" (ibid.: 395).

2.1.3 The demonisation of the Internet

Most of the literature that deals with the role of media tends to focus on the *mainstream* media such as print and TV, at the expense of the Internet and new media. It is only about a decade ago that scholars of terrorism turned their eyes to the role of the Internet. The initial focus was on which terrorist groups had an online presence, their respective websites' function, content, and rhetoric (Tsfati and Weimann 2002; Weimann 2006; Conway 2006). Although contributions are still marginal, they now occasionally extend to the role of social media, like Twitter (US Army 2008: 7–10; Goodman 2011), and YouTube (Conway and McInerney 2008; McInerney 2009; Seib and Janbek 2011). In the following discussion I contrast generalised, and often alarmist, claims about the role of the Internet in supporting terrorism to more balanced and sober assessments. My point is that the former positions are advocated by the loudest voices in the field. Although constituting the majority, they are not as grounded in empirical evidence and analytical engagement with the question of the impact of the Internet on politics and society as the latter. The minority voices are, in fact, wiser, but remain largely unheard.

Terrorists are acknowledged to use the Internet largely for the same reasons as anybody else (Awan 2007b: 390; Stevens and Neumann 2009: 11): because of the low cost and the possibility to communicate virtually instantaneously with wide and often transnational audiences; the anonymity that facilitates engaging in "risky" or "embarrassing" behaviour; the ease of access to information; the lack of censorship; the opportunity to interact with like-minded individuals; the ease with which text, images, and videos can be combined, up- and downloaded, transmitted, and shared between the Internet and other platforms, such as phones.

While all sort of content travels through the Internet, this technology is described as having a crucial role when it comes to supporting terrorist activities, particularly those of Al Qaeda. Alarmist, even sensationalist, statements characterise not only journalistic accounts, but also academic literature and think-tanks' assessments. For instance, journalists at the *Washington Post* Steve Coll and Susan Glasser (2005), wrote that:

Al Qaeda has become the first guerrilla movement in history to migrate from physical space to cyberspace. With laptops and DVDs, in secret hideouts and at neighborhood Internet cafes, young code-writing jihadists have sought to replicate the training, communication, planning and preaching facilities they lost in Afghanistan with countless new locations on the Internet.

In an article published on the journal *International Security* Audrey Cronin (2006: 7) writes that Al Qaeda "is in many ways distinct from its predecessors, especially in its protean ability to transform itself from a physical to a virtual organization." She continues, saying Al Qaeda "has begun to resemble more closely a 'global jihad movement,' increasingly consisting of web-directed and cyber-linked groups and ad hoc cells" (ibid.: 33).

The Internet contributes to several activities of terrorist groups, such as fundraising, networking, and coordination, as well as information gathering (Conway 2006: 283–292; Katz in Committee on Homeland Security 2007: 15–27; Council of the European Union 2007: 1). Literature on the link between terrorism and the Internet is, however, currently absorbed by a focus on the role of this communication technology in information provision – including the production of training manuals and instruction on how to manufacture explosives, propaganda material like videos, communiqués, texts – and recruitment. The Internet, in this last respect, is identified as a platform for the spreading of radical content and extremist ideology particularly targeted at young and vulnerable individuals. The incessant activities of ad hoc media production houses like the Al-Fajr Center (including the more widely known As-Sahab) and propaganda centres like the Global Islamic Media Front (Katz in Committee on Homeland Security 2007: 18–20) are ritually presented as evidence of the threat. The impact of the Internet is thus portrayed in overwhelmingly negative terms, to the point that the technology is often openly blamed for radicalisation, understood not only as the embracing of extremist ideas, but also as their translation into violent action. For instance, a report by the Homeland Security Policy Institute and the Critical Incident Analysis Group entitled "NETworked Radicalization: A Counter-Strategy" (2007: 5–6) states that:

The Internet facilitates radicalization because it is without peer as a tool for both active and passive communication and outreach. Online chat rooms are interactive venues where aberrant attitudes and beliefs may be exchanged, reinforced, hardened and validated (at least in the minds of participants). This mutual affirmation in turn gives rise to a sense of community and belonging – a virtual *ummah* (worldwide Muslim community).

The Commission of the European Communities communication to the European Parliament and the Council on "Terrorist Recruitment: Addressing the Factors Contributing to Violent Radicalization" (2005: 4) also argues that: "the use of the Internet to incite people into becoming violently radical, or as vehicle for terrorist recruitment, is extremely worrying in view of its global reach, real-time nature and effectiveness." As for the availability of material on training and tactics, Rita Katz (in Committee on Homeland Security 2007: 24), director of the Search for International Terrorist Entities Institute (SITE), states that "Using the Internet, jihadist have created a virtual classroom that teaches the online jihadist community how to produce and construct weapons ranging from simple IEDs to nuclear, biological, and chemical weapons."

These assessments come from what might look like official and authoritative sources, yet at closer scrutiny they suffer from being generalised statements that do not appear to rely on solid evidence. Indeed, John Mueller (2012) points out that both policy makers and those who run the "security apparatus" are prone to exaggeration and hyperbole due their constant dealing with worst-case scenarios. Although technically plausible, these scenarios are significantly more catastrophic than what realistically can happen – as Michael Sheehan, New York City's former deputy director for counterterrorism phrased it: "No terrorism expert or government leader wants to appear soft on terrorism. It's always safer to predict the worst; if nothing happens, the exaggerators are rarely held accountable for their nightmare scenarios" (ibid.).

While it is true that considerable amount of instructional content is available on the Internet, it is unclear to which extent it can support actual terrorist plots. Some, in fact, would argue that manufacturing viable explosives requires more than online training.[3] Anne Stenersen (2008: 225), in a thorough investigation of training and instructional material available online (videos and documents covering guerrilla warfare, weapons and explosives, training and preparation for terrorist operations), observes that they convey content "which can in any case be found in open sources." They appear to be targeted at "amateurs" who are most interested in learning the basics (ibid.). Where more sophisticated instruction is provided, in fact, it would not easily be put into practice by viewers. She counters, for example, the suggestion that Iraqi insurgents have allegedly learned how to make EFPs (Explosive

Formed Penetrators) from instruction videos produced by Hizballah. As she explains, by analysing one of these videos, it is possible to see that it "appears to be ... on how to assemble pre-made parts, not how to make an EFP from scratch." She even reports a complaint by a jihadi forum member who commented about it "... the video does not explain a thing, it is for those with advanced skills, who know how to manufacture the detonator, the timer ... and so on" (ibid.: 227). She concludes that "the idea that Internet training material should be used to learn the basics – before moving on to classical jihadi training – makes it perhaps more accurate to talk about the Internet as a 'pre-school of jihad' rather than a 'university'" (ibid.: 231). The incompetence demonstrated even by individuals who attended the proper training, such as Faisal Shahzad, who attempted the 1 May 2010 Times Square car bombing in New York (Keating 2010), casts further doubts on the extent to which online information is really a threat to national security. As for the role of the Internet in radicalising individuals, the Change Institute (2008: 117) writes that "It should be ... noted that whilst a selection of key ideological concepts and narratives are disseminated via propaganda material found on a range of Internet platforms there is a lack of evidence relating to the potential role of the Internet in developing radicalised world views, beyond a facilitation of access to propaganda, operational resources and alternative information sources."

Indeed, Andrew Hoskins and others (2009: 5), drawing on the evidence of an extensive study of virtual jihadist fora, openly challenge the notions of Internet's culpability by pointing out that, rather than tools for the spreading of extremist ideology, extremist websites "are often exclusively closed spaces that seek to reinforce a 'group-think' mentality amongst committed members and thus are often proverbially 'preaching to the converted'." Akil Awan (2007a: 76–77) further stresses that not only many of the jihadi websites function principally as news outlets to counter the perceived bias of "hegemonic" Western mainstream media, but that these fora have actually a positive "cathartic" role by "subsuming diverse strains of political activism, unrest, and dissent, and so providing a conduit and framework for its non-violent expression." The "radicalising effects," in his analysis, have therefore been "vastly over-inflated" (ibid.: 80).

The myth of the radicalising function of the Internet, has nonetheless become deeply entrenched in the current security discourse, as the following example shows. A report by the International Centre for the Study of Radicalisation and Political Violence (Stevens and Neumann 2009: 12, their emphasis) concludes that "there continues to be little evidence to support the contention that the Internet plays a *dominant* role in the process of radicalisation." As they expand:

> Self-radicalisation and self-recruitment via the Internet with little or no relation to the outside world rarely happens, and there is no reason to suppose that this situation will change in the near future. The reason for the absence of self-radicalisation and self-recruitment online is that real-world social relationships continue to be pivotal. (Ibid: 13)[4]

Despite this, the report is called "Countering Online Radicalisation: A Strategy for Action," which implies that the very online radicalisation for which they find little evidence is somehow actually taking place.

The reasons for this trend are documented in detail by Akil Awan, Andrew Hoskins, and Ben O'Loughlin (2011). They meticulously demonstrate how radicalisation has become established as a prominent threat within security discourses in both government circles and the mainstream media. Hoskins and O'Loughlin, in particular (2009: 107–108), point out how the notion of radicalisation conveniently matches both the news and policymakers' agendas: "For security policymakers and journalists alike, 'radicalization' can anchor a news agenda, offering a cast of radicalizers and the vulnerable radicalized, and legitimating a policy response to such danger." It also combines with "that major intangible of 'the Internet'" (ibid.: 108). As they further explain: "It is as if society is endangered by the technology itself, which enables identity theft, the 'grooming' of children by paedophiles or, indeed, 'grooming for jihad'" (ibid.: 109).

The unfortunate outcome is that both the notion of radicalisation and the role of the Internet in promoting it are taken for granted. The fact that unfounded claims become the unchallenged basis of policy, as the following excerpts of official documents illustrate, is particularly worrying. The latest UK *Prevent* strategy (Home Office 2011: 77) states:

> The Internet has transformed the extent to which terrorist organisations and their sympathisers can radicalise people in this country and overseas. It enables a wider range of organisations and individuals to reach a much larger audience with a broader and more dynamic series of messages and narratives. It encourages interaction and facilitates recruitment. The way people use the Internet also appears to be conducive to these processes. Despite the wealth of information available, people often talk to those whose views are

similar to their own, encouraging group thinking and inhibiting external challenge.

A US Presidential Task Force report (2009: 17) further asserts that "The United States should devote far more resources to countering radical extremist messages on the Internet, where the self-radicalization process is spreading and accelerating." The opening sentence of a Congressional Research Service (CRS) report (Theohary and Rollins 2011: 2) reads: "The Internet is used by international insurgents, jihadists, and terrorist organizations as a tool for radicalization and recruitment, a method of propaganda distribution, a means of communication, and ground for training." In a chapter within a volume edited by the US Air Force Research Laboratory and the US Department of State titled, "Countering Violent Extremism," it is even said that "militant jihadi groups are currently highly successful in promulgating their ideological messages and through the skilful use of emotionally manipulative messaging, recruiting, motivating, and equipping men and women all around the world to become highly lethal terrorists" (Speckhard 2011: 166).

2.1.4 Placing the impact of the Internet into perspective

The aim here is not to argue that the Internet does not play any role at all. It can and does play a facilitating function, particularly in terms of organisation, fundraising, distribution and sharing of content, providing an initial meeting place for like-minded individuals, which can then lead to face-to-face contact. These aspects, however, are not characteristics unique to this medium.

The rhetoric revolving around the Internet is clearly technologically deterministic: it assumes that a communication technology is, by its very existence, going to produce certain social and political effects. This is partly related to its association with the popular notion of a "communication revolution" and the idea that the Internet is radically changing our societies. In this respect, Manuel Castells (1996) talks about a "networked society." For sure, the Internet makes a difference. It changes the potential scope of social interaction from locality to a global dimension and affects the dynamics of political processes, from everyday government activities – one can think about the professionalisation of political communication (Chadwick 2006) or "e-democracy" (Coleman and Blumler 2009) – to the conduct of diplomacy and foreign policy (Potter 2002). It is sufficient to take a look back in history, however, to discover that the development of virtually any communication technology – from the introduction of parchment, to the rise of the printing press, telegraph, and radio – was met by the same sense of amazement, uncertainty, and similar alarmed claims that it would forever change the world as it was then known. A statement such as, "It is impossible that old prejudices and hostilities should longer exist, while such an instrument has been created for the exchange of thought between all nations of the earth," might appear to refer to the Internet, but it was written in 1858 and described the development of the telegraph (Briggs and Maverick 1858 in Standage 1998). Marshall McLuhan's experience almost 50 years ago further underlines that the interconnectedness that we think so much characterises our present time is nothing really new: "Today, after more than a century of electronic technology, we have extended our central nervous system itself in a global embrace, abolishing both space and time as far as our planet is concerned. As electronically contracted, the globe is no more than a village" (McLuhan 1994 [1964]: 3).

The impact of the Internet on contemporary society is largely overestimated. The characteristics of the medium, such as the speed and low cost at which information can be exchanged, do encourage the transmission of unprecedented volumes of information across wide distances and the exploitation of the tool for organisational purposes. Let us not forget, however, that the first global and virtually instantaneous communication technology was, again, the telegraph. The literature on social movements also reminds us that transnational mobilisation took place well before the Internet: one can think about the anti-slavery movement (Tarrow 1998: 47) or the International Workers Association whose slogan, since its foundation in the nineteenth century has been "Workers of the world unite!" Studies of riots and protests over the seventeenth and eighteenth centuries also confirm that news was still able to travel, if certainly not instantaneously, then surprisingly quickly, even across wide distances:

> A glance back at 1789 or 1848 will indicate how closely Europe's political centers connected with each other well before television or mass journalism provided their publicity. In 1789, English radicals and conservatives alike followed Parisian events day by day. The construction of "Parisian" barricades became standard practice in the Germany of 1848. (Tilly 2002: 109)

The idea that the Internet's synchronous communication almost naturally leads to greater bonding among individuals (Sageman 2004; Gupta 2011: 51) is challenged by online activism literature, where there is a whole debate about whether the exchanges among strangers in cyberspace can support the constitution of real communities or simply a superficial involvement – what is referred to as "armchair activism" (Karpf 2010).[5] If individuals committed to, let us say, environmental issues could become less involved in their cause when only interacting online, why should individuals with an interest in jihad through the same mechanisms necessarily become more fixated in their beliefs and even reach the point where they are ready to take lethal action in the real world?[6]

Questionable assumptions further relate to the effects of audiovisual messages. They are generally assumed to have a greater impact than simple text. Anne Speckhard (2011: 167), for example, writes that "Any emotionally vulnerable person watching these [terrorist propaganda] videos [who] is swept up in the provocative imagery and emotional language can find it relatively easy to accept the false statements and be led down a path of logic that emotionally manipulates them into supporting the militant jihad." A US government report recommends: "The United States should focus its efforts on the extremist chat rooms, since these types of two-way interactions are far more dangerous as recruiting tools than websites, where propaganda can merely be downloaded" (Presidential Task Force 2009: 17). In this respect Awan, Hoskins and O'Loughlin (2011) challenge the points made by US government advisor Evan Kohlmann, who took part in the 2005 *BBC* documentary "London under attack." Kohlmann stated: "[W]hile a picture may be worth a thousand words, a video, uploaded to an Internet site, is worth 10,000"[7] (ibid.: 75):

> Attacks are recorded and sent "spinning around the world," but most aspects of social life are now recorded – think of family events, or even routine uploadings – so why remark that the attacks are? It would be more surprising that they are not, and it seems like Taylor [Peter Taylor, presenter of the documentary] is part of a generation of journalists, policymakers and "experts" who find remarkable a media ecology which to younger generations is taken for granted. Is a video "worth 10,000" words? Is there any evidence that moving images have a quantifiably measurable impact on, say, potential supporters or terrorised publics? And then, after have a 10,000-word impact, the viewer is told such videos have "an incalculable effect."

The fact that extremist content is online and *potentially* available to worldwide audiences does not necessarily mean that these publics are actually accessing it, let alone being influenced, if not driven to violent action by it. In relation to the British case, Awan (2007a: 76) writes that "the overwhelming majority of virtual jihadist forums are published in Arabic alone and so inaccessible to a large proportion of Muslims as well as other Internet users. British Muslims audiences are predominantly (74 per cent) South Asian and are therefore more likely to speak Urdu, Punjabi, or Bengali, than Arabic."

Even if audiences were actually accessing the extremist material, the question of its effects would still need to be ascertained. It could appear that the Internet figured in the build up of extremist beliefs in a range of plots, from the 2004 Madrid train bombings to London 7/7 in 2005, to radical plots being developed in the Netherlands, Canada, and Morocco (HSPI/CIAG 2007: 3–5). However, at a closer look the Internet tended to provide the "initial impetus," which was then followed by the more ordinary real-world planning, meetings, and training (Awan 2007a: 78).

In fact, it is not at all clear why content available on the Internet should be more responsible for radicalisation than content accessible through alternative formats. This is especially puzzling considering that what is available online, despite the much-emphasised interactivity of the Internet, is still text. Daniel Kimmage (2008a), in an analysis of online jihadi media (press releases, statements, essays, books, video clips, and films) he conducted in 2007, found that Al Qaeda was still "stuck" in Internet 1.0 – that is the use of the Internet for old fashioned "broadcasting" purposes rather than two-way communication. If one can argue that the use of the Internet might have developed since then, again Hoskins and others (2009: 5) more recently show that, even sites where multimedia material is uploaded, do not really lead to significant interactivity: "Contrary to the established view that jihadist websites/forums [*sic*] seek to radicalise, most virtual fora exert no considerable or sustained effort in persuasion or legitimation of the ideology or culture of Jihadism[;] ... there is little ostensive or meaningful debate, discussion, or dialogue amongst members of most jihadi forums observed. For example, a statement by Al-Zawahiri or a new militant video would be lauded with a string of support, praise, and prayers by members, without any critical engagement with the material in question."

Besides, jihadist material has long been available through videos and publications since well before the Internet (Awan 2007a: 78–79). Osama bin Laden, Ayman Al-Zawahiri, as all the individuals who first joined Al Qaeda in the late 1980s, certainly did not belong to the Internet generation. Ed Husain recalls in *The Islamist* (2007: 20–21) how, as a young boy growing up in London's East End, he became interested in a political interpretation of Islam by reading a school textbook about religion. To find a contemporary example of extremism beyond that inspired by Al Qaeda one can additionally look at the case of Norwegian Anders Breivik. In his over 1,500-page manifesto (Breivik 2011), he discusses at length the ideological reasons for his bombing of the Oslo city centre (which caused eight fatalities) and the killing on Utøya Island of 68 young political activists in the summer of 2011. The sources he cites, particularly "the cultural Marxists" who gathered around the "Frankfurt School" – he specifically mentions Georg Lukacs, Antonio Gramsci, Wilhelm Reich, Erich Fromm, Herbert Marcuse, and Theodor Adorno (ibid.: 26–30, 40–45 for "Further readings on the Frankfurt School") – produced texts that are not normally regarded as "extremist" and that are widely available in ordinary libraries.

Finally, why criminalise the Internet, when there are other portable and interactive platforms that can equally well be used for exchanging and sharing information? On this point, Hoskins and O'Loughlin (2009: 109) write that "there is a need to research 'convergence' – the seamlessness through which extremist materials can be sent, by Bluetooth, for example, and consumed on mobile media including phones – without the Internet coming into play at all." The British summer riots of 2011, in this respect, have brought to the fore the potential role of Blackberry Messenger, Twitter, and Facebook (Hallyday 2011) in the organisation of violent public disorder. While, again, these technological platforms were the target of extreme initial claims about their function as "drivers" of violent collective action, their role has subsequently been re-dimensioned (Ball and Lewis 2011; Mackenzie 2011), not least by the acknowledgment that, so far, they have not been subject to rigorous examination, mostly as a result of the inaccessibility of the information exchanged, especially in the case of Blackberry Messenger (Ball and Brown 2011).

This discussion was not to deny the relevance of the Internet, but to demonstrate that its role is widely misunderstood. This is largely due, as seen, to two reasons. The first is the lack of perspective that could be provided by a greater engagement with the development of communication over history and an appreciation of the complexity involved in assessing media effects on audiences. The second is the lack of empirical research that characterises Terrorism Studies. The Internet makes a difference in all domains of Western society, not just in the pursuit of terrorist activity. What counts, in the end, are not the technical characteristics of the medium, but the way in which they are appropriated by social actors to mobilise support and resources.

2.1.5   The problems with the "media"

As it emerges from the review of the literature, the "media" tend to be understood as a monolithic and homogenous entity which, when it is not subservient to political power or simply a victim of the terrorists' manipulation strategy – a "conveyor belt" for the messages of either the government or the terrorists – has a will of its own and masters full control over the coverage it produces. These views amount to gross generalisations concerning the nature of the media, what they produce, and their role in society. Such views would appear naive to researchers from fields of study engaged with research on communication. Let us first, however, clarify what considerations and distinctions should be made when using the term "media."

What is the "media"?

The term "media" in the terrorism literature is used as self-evident. This, in practice, means that it ends up referring to completely different sets of phenomena and processes. In fact, there are at least three meanings of "media" that need to be distinguished. First, "media" refers to communication technologies. In this sense "media" is simply the plural of communication *medium*: beyond the already mentioned Internet, telephone, telegraph, communication platforms like Facebook or Twitter, a communication medium is also a sheet of paper or a clay tablet on which something is written. This is literally the medium that allows a message to be conveyed, transmitted, and shared. Second, "media" can refer to the content of a communication process or the "message." When in everyday language we say that "the media" are "saying" something, what we are referring to is actually their content. We are referring to the media coverage – what is written in an article or said in a news report. The term, media, however, has a third meaning: that of an organisation. There are, for example, news organisations like newspapers, TV broadcast companies, and news agencies. These "media" are made up of journalists, editors, producers, cameramen, technicians ... . Each individual has a unique background shaped, among the things, by gender, educational experiences, previous career, ethnic origin, religion, political orientation, and class. These individuals work for an employer. They might be at the service of an organisation that delivers a public service, like the *BBC*, but most of the time they work for a commercial organisation. The drive to make a profit might be less pronounced in the former kind of organisation rather than in the latter, but both need revenue to survive financially. As any organisation, also media organisations have rules about what can and cannot be done. This also applies to what can and cannot be reported, as well as how it should be covered – a set of rules embodied by editorial guidelines (see Paletz and Tawney 1992 for a discussion of terrorism-related editorial guidelines). What is reported and how also depends on the target audience, particularly its interests and expectations, which is again related to the fact that the organisation, whether or not of a commercial nature, needs to be relevant.

One could argue that distinguishing these different meanings of "media" is pedantic hairsplitting and that terrorism researchers cannot be blamed for a little inaccuracy and generalisation. The study of media and communication is not their main concern – and why should it be? Media researchers would perhaps be far more inaccurate if they started talking about terrorism. What has this to do with terrorism anyway, which in practice consists in killing people and "blowing things up"? The problem, as this book points out, is that the inability to approach the communication components of the terrorism phenomenon is an obstacle to understanding the real nature of the phenomenon. In fact, although the exchange of information and mediation – both in terms of how we communicate with other people, but also in the way we make sense of the information we receive about what happens around us – have always been part of the way social reality works, they are absolutely crucial to anything we do in an interconnected world in which information is potentially available in all places at all times.

To further explain the relevance of the distinctions between the meanings of "media" and the understanding of terrorism, let us use an example. If somebody said (as researchers actually do, as previously seen) that "the media contribute to radicalization" – where radicalisation is the embracing of extremist views that might lead to violence – what is this statement actually implying? Is the researcher behind the claim suggesting that it is the availability of communication platforms (i.e. the technology) that allows, for example, radical individuals to exchange and further cultivate extreme ideas? Or is it what media are reporting (i.e. the content), for instance the focus in the coverage on collateral civilian victims at the expense of progress in development of security in Afghanistan, that fuels resentment and therefore extremism? In yet another of the many possibilities, it could be suggested that it is journalists who, under the pressure of tight deadlines, do not use language as accurately as they could. In this case they could be contributing, through a rhetoric that encourages Islamophobia and the identification of Muslims as "the enemy," to fuelling resentment and, consequently, radicalisation. These scenarios not only describe very different causal processes. Each of them implies a very different strategy to address the problem at hand. While there are always multiple solutions to the same problem, a plausible reaction to the first situation could be, for a fictional governmental actor, monitoring access to certain websites, perhaps restricting access to extremist content. In the second case, a course of action could be for the International Security Assistance Force (ISAF) mission in Afghanistan to attempt balancing the negative stories in the coverage with more positive ones, perhaps by actively producing press releases, pictures, and footage of good news from the theatre of operation or having a Twitter account directly promoting positive news bites. In the third case, training courses for journalists could be organised in collaboration with news organisations. An alternative could be developing editorial guidelines about the use of language (*BBC* Editorial Guidelines n.d.).

Comparing views

The idea that media can be easily manipulated by governments when it comes to reporting about terrorism would be troubling to any researcher from Political Communications. The very issue of the relationship between media (more specifically understood as journalists and editors operating within organisations) and officials, particularly the extent of media independence vis-à-vis the political establishment, has been for decades one of the thorniest topics of debate in the field (Esser and Pfetsch 2004). The notion that journalists can be used as mouthpieces, either by terrorists or by governments, dismisses an entire tradition of sociological studies of news organisations' norms, journalistic practices, and newsgathering routines (for an overview of the different perspectives see Tumber [1999]). A scholar in Media Studies would be puzzled by the fact that these assessments are generally applied to "media" without distinguishing between print, TV, Internet, radio, "new," or "mass" media. The suggestion that media content can have a direct effect on potential terrorists, leading them to engage in violent behaviour – the "contagion hypothesis" – would be recognised by a researcher in communications as closely resembling the "silver bullet" or "hypodermic needle" theory of media effects (Brooker and Jermyn 2003: 6). This is based on the belief that the media can trigger an immediate, virtually identical, and predictable response in a public exposed to their messages, as if the audience had been "injected" with those contents. The theory was developed in the 1920s and 1930s, initially as an attempt to explain how British propaganda had contributed to defeating Germany during World War I (ibid.: 5). The rise of European dictators appeared to support the idea that masses could be manipulated by leaders who were able to exploit modern communication technologies, such as radio at that time. Despite this, the theory was quickly deemed unsatisfactory to explain media effects and was replaced by more nuanced models. Paul Lazarsfeld's "two-step-flow," for example, later hypothesised, rather than a direct influence of the media on the public, but a process in two stages in which media messages were filtered to the masses through the interpretations of opinion leaders (Lazarsfeld, Berelson and Gaudet 1944). Within the "reception studies" tradition, the "uses and gratification" theory (Blumler and Katz 1974), instead, emphasised the way in which each individual "uses" media messages to satisfy psychological or social needs. These are just early conceptualisations. The description of how they evolved to this day, for instance by entirely abandoning the notion of a "mass public" or incorporating ethnic readings of media texts, could be lengthy (see Miller 2008 for a critical review of research approaches to media audiences over time). These examples are nonetheless more than sufficient to show that a substantial part of the literature on terrorism and the media does not know much about the media and their effects. The way media are seen by most of research on terrorism is stuck in the early twentieth century.

The inadequacy of theoretical frameworks within the literature on terrorism and the media becomes strident when compared to the explanatory sophistication produced by other branches of research analysing the role of media in the construction of social problems. Let us consider, for instance, sociological research on the relationship between media and crime.

A range of studies about media coverage of crime point at the way this is defined – not by criminals, or by authorities, or by the media themselves – but by sources' interaction. Stuart Hall and others (1978: 58, their emphasis) emphasise the role of authorities as "primary definers" of topics in the news: "the practical pressures [on journalists] of constantly working against the clock and the professional demands of impartiality and objectivity ... combine to produce a systematically structured *over-accessing* to the media of those in powerful and privileged institutional positions." The "primary definition," in turn *"sets the limit* for all subsequent discussion by *framing what the problem is.* The initial framework then provides the criteria by which all subsequent contributions are labelled as 'relevant' to the debate, or 'irrelevant' – beside the point" (ibid.: 59, their emphases). As they continue "the media are frequently not the 'primary definers' of news events at all; but their structured relationship to power has the effect of making them play a crucial but secondary role in *reproducing* the definitions of

those who have privileged access ... to the media as 'accredited sources'"
(ibid., their emphasis).

Philip Schlesinger (1990) criticises the structuralist view of Hall and
his colleagues by applying a Bourdieuan perspective. "Primary definition" for him is *an achievement rather than a wholly structurally predeter-
mined outcome*" (ibid.: 79, his emphasis). In the news, meaning is still
shaped by competition among different sources: they are actors with
different interests, resources, and forms of social capital who struggle to
achieve symbolic dominance (ibid.: 78). The consideration of this literature – which could include Chibnall (1977: especially 7 and 105–106);
Ericson, Baranek and Chan (1989); Miller (1993); Sacco (1995); Chermak
(1997) – raises the question of why the coverage of terrorism, a particular form of crime, should be explained in radically different (and much
simpler) terms than the more general reporting of crime. While it is true
that ordinary criminals do not normally seek publicity in the media, as
terrorists do, in many instances their activities are as much newsworthy.
Coverage of crime has also raised concerns similar to those which can
be found in the literature on terrorism. They involve the issues of over-
reporting and the effects of sensational coverage, especially in relation
to public anxiety (Sacco 1995: 149 and 151; Reiner 2007: 302, 316, 321).

2.2   The need for a new framework

Although the previous section has shown that input from communication studies would help to make better sense of the very nature of the
media and to place into context their impact on society, it is not possible to fully place them into the terrorism picture if there is no overall theory (causal explanation) of the way the phenomenon actually
occurs, particularly one that spans the individual (micro) dimension to
the level of society-wide (macro) factors. At an even deeper level, it is
not possible to fit communication and the media into any theoretical
framework if they are not even acknowledged as relevant and legitimate
subjects of investigation. Beyond the theoretical gaps within the field
of Terrorism Studies, the set of assumptions that define the world in
which terrorism takes place – what we might call the "terrorism paradigm" – are not suitable to detecting the role of either communication
or the media.

2.2.1   What's missing?

To continue with the example made earlier of the process of radicalisation, it is not possible to find out the role of the media – understood

either as communication technologies, as the contents carried by media platforms, or as organisations – within it, if not simply "where" they fit, if there is no overall explanation of how radicalisation occurs in the first place. In fact, what are the causal mechanisms between the stage in which an individual comes into contact with extremist ideas and becomes engaged in actual terrorist activities? How does the combination of messages conveyed through the media and personal interpretation of those messages generate extremism? How do the social connections of an individual affect his/her interpretation of extremist ideas? What is the role of communication technologies in creating those social ties? Under what circumstances does the process accelerate or break down? And how does the holding of extremist views – not a characteristic unique to terrorists – degenerate into violent behaviour? If communications are to be used against terrorism, for example to promote a message – or "narrative" (Home Office 2011: 50–51; National Coordinator for Counterterrorism 2010) – that serves as an alternative to the one advocated by the terrorists, what effects are such messages expected to produce? How are they going to produce such results? How can we measure the effectiveness of "our" narrative and, ultimately, progress in opposing terrorism?

What is largely missing at the moment from the literature, which would better equip us answering these questions and which has already been discussed in Chapter 1, is an explicit engagement with theory. Beyond theory, what is absent from research is also an underlying ontology of the world or "a general statement of the manner in which agents are believed to appropriate their context and the consequences of that appropriation for their development as agents and for that of the context itself" (Hay 2002: 113). A social ontology establishes the proportion of individual agency and structural influences that explain what happens in reality. In the case of the relationship between media and terrorism, both agents and structures need to be identified. Who are "the media?" What can the "media" do? Who uses them? Who are the agents? And what are the constraints (structures) influencing agents' actions? How do terrorists, journalists, policymakers and the public interact? Who influences whom? What is the role of information exchange in their interactions? How is information produced, shared, and processed, in a globalised world? Where do communication technologies fit?

2.2.2 Terrorism as a paradigm

The well known mantra in Terrorism Studies that terrorism is "in the eye of the beholder" is problematic because it means that the researcher is constantly wading through sensitivities about the use of the term and de facto taking a political stand whenever applying it. Further, it also has deeper epistemological implications in terms of what we can *know* about it. If terrorism is a specific category of violent, politically motivated acts, directed at innocent people, conducted to generate fear among a wider audience, anything that does not fit this conceptual category is outside the legitimate boundary of investigation. Either political acts that are non-violent or violent political acts that are not addressed at "innocents" would be excluded on the ground that they are not relevant. Authors placing their research within the conceptual territory of Critical Terrorism Studies, in this respect, criticise what they call Orthodox Terrorism Studies (mainstream terrorism studies) for tending not to address violence perpetrated by states – "state terrorism." As Jason Franks (2009: 154–155) puts it: "Orthodox terrorism theory is essentially a Western model of understanding terrorism rooted in Western freedoms, the rule of law and the liberal democratic Westphalian state." The fact that terrorism targets "innocents" and is morally reprehensible has also led, as Joseba Zulaika and William Douglass (2008) point out, to ignoring the "terrorist subjectivity." By this the authors mean a systematic neglect of the terrorists' point of view as a valid source of understanding for the acts they commit:

> The *will* of the terrorist does not figure in our discourse. Some experts might know, of course, that what enraged bin Laden is the US military presence in his native Saudi Arabia, which for him amounts to occupation of sacred lands by an invader. But these are footnotes to a public debate overwhelmed by the perception of utterly senseless nihilism on the part of the terrorists. It is the all present logic of taboo obtaining here: since terrorism is unspeakable Evil, you must avoid any contact with it or even contemplation of it, let alone projecting yourself into the terrorist's subjectivity. The mere act of paying attention to what the terrorists have to say is a fateful step towards perhaps making an effort to understand their motives, something that might lead to somehow "justifying" what is unjustifiable. (Ibid.: 32)

The notion of "terrorism" appears to be based on a series of assumptions that de facto have guided research within firmly established boundaries. Some of these assumptions are: terrorism is practiced by individuals who are very different from "us"; terrorism falls outside the boundaries of "normal politics"; it should therefore be kept separate from non-violent political mobilisation. Additionally, the researchers who engage in the study of terrorism might come from a range of disciplines, but they tend to share the idea that there is a society, often divided along the lines of nation states, and it is made up by individuals who associate in various ways to pursue certain objectives.

Although widespread, this is by no means the only way to conceive social reality. The prevailing conceptual perspective in Terrorism Studies largely matches what, in Relational Sociology, is called "substantialism." In the words of one of its key theorists, Mustafa Emirbayer (1997: 282): "The key question confronting sociologists in the present day is not 'material versus ideal,' 'structure versus agency,' 'individual versus society,' or any of the other dualisms so often noted; rather, it is the choice between substantialism and relationalism." Substantialism is based on the notion that the social consists of "*substances* of various kinds (things, beings, essences) that constitute the fundamental units of all enquiry" (ibid.). Any study, within this perspective, starts with these entities coming "preformed" and only then becoming engaged in processes (ibid.: 282–283). As Emirbayer points out, this approach is even shared by research traditions that would appear very far from each other, such as Rational Choice Theory on the one hand and Constructivism on the other hand. Rational choice approaches notoriously assume that actors have fixed preferences, interests, and objectives (ibid.: 283). The constructivist approach, despite having developed as a reaction to rational choice and explaining behaviour through an individual's desire to act in conformity with certain norms rather than selfish rational calculation, still "depicts individuals as self-propelling, self-subsistent entities that pursue internalized norms given in advance and fixed for the duration of the action sequence under investigation" (ibid.: 284). To relate this to terrorism, even studies that do not focus exclusively on material factors, like those that, instead, consider the relevance of extremist ideology as a driver for action, assume that a "preformed" way of thinking is embraced by "preformed" individuals who then start behaving fairly predictably by engaging in violent politically motivated action. Relationalism, on the contrary, conceives reality in "dynamic, continuous, and processual terms" (ibid.: 281). Within this view, individual identities are incessantly being constituted and re-constituted through relations. Social action is the outcome of who we are and what we know (the way we interpret reality from our "corner" of the social world) as a result of these shifting relationships. This approach would conceive the rise of violent extremism in terms of individuals whose identities are shaped by the constellations of relationships they are involved with, developing a vision of the world that matches the one promoted by a terrorist group. Violent extremism is an outcome of both individuals' sense of identity and the information they process as result of their position within the social universe. I am going to return to relationalism in greater depth in Chapter 3, where I will also show more in detail how it applies to terrorism.

Substantialism is not exclusive to Terrorism Studies.[8] Together with the defining features of "terrorism," however, the assumptions that characterise it contribute to drawing the limits within which terrorism research is being conducted. Indeed, it could be argued that the very notion of "terrorism" works as a paradigm. For Kuhn (1962: 6) a paradigm sets "the standards by which the profession [we can think of it as a field of study] determine[s] what should count as an admissible problem or as a legitimate problem-solution." Paradigms "specify not only what sorts of entities the universe does contain, but also, by implication, those that it does not" (ibid.: 7). By defining both what should be investigated and according to which method, the paradigm also narrows the range of possible findings of the scientific enterprise: "the range of anticipated, and thus assimilable, results is always small compared with the range that imagination can conceive" (ibid.: 35). What does not fall within the paradigm's range of expectation is either a mistake – "the project whose outcome does not fall in the narrower range is usually just a research failure, one which reflects not on nature [or society, in our case] but on the scientist" (ibid.) – or they are unimportant facts: results that cannot articulate a paradigm "are *mere* facts, unrelated and unrelatable" to the continuing progress of research (ibid., Kuhn's emphasis).

What I argue is that, not only are there no broad sociological explanations for the phenomenon of terrorism – a theoretical scaffolding on which to "fit" both communication and the media – but the very notion of "terrorism" as a paradigm does not enable registering the deeper, social role of communication. Recognising that terrorism is an act of communication – that it is about sending a message, that communication technologies can support terrorist groups in spreading their ideology or organising terrorist plots, or that wide coverage of terrorism might contribute to giving extremists an aura of legitimacy – is, in fact, not sufficient to explain the role of communication and the media. Focusing on communication only when it becomes "relevant" to a terrorist operation can be compared to attempting to predict an earthquake by focusing exclusively on what happens during a major tremor, without considering the seismic stresses that preceded it.[9]

Whether media are understood as communication technologies, the content carried by media platforms, or media organisations, they are all-pervasive and entrenched in the very fabric of society. Communication technologies like the Internet, for instance, should not just become relevant when they are used for the organisation of a terrorist plot. They are *always* relevant. They allow us to live the way we do in developed societies. The technology that enables terrorists to communicate with each other is the same that allows friends to organise a party, companies to trade more quickly, and police to track down criminals. The coverage produced by media organisations is relevant not just at times of terrorist attacks, but is there 24/7. This is not only applicable to today's globalised world. Although communication tools have changed throughout history – ranging from cave paintings to the iPhone – media have always been part of social life. Beyond all this, communication, meant in its simplest form as the sharing and processing of information, is the very enabler of any form of social interaction. According to Niklas Luhmann (2007: 302) "it is not action but rather communication that is an unavoidably social operation and at the same time an operation that necessarily comes into play whenever social situations arise." It is what leads to the formation of our very sense of identity and what allows citizens both to form groups and mobilise around a cause. If we want to understand the role of communication and the media, it is therefore necessary to change the very way we conceive reality.

Chapter 3 will address this issue by suggesting a relational understanding of the social world (social ontology) to make sense of the role of communication in society and support an explanation for the role of the media and communication technologies in the terrorism phenomenon.

3
A Communication Approach

Chapter 2 has established that terrorism is inextricably linked to communication. There are, however, two major obstacles to understanding the role of communication. On the one hand is the lack of solid explanatory frameworks in the field of terrorism studies within which to "place" the exchange, sharing, and processing of information. On the other hand is the existence of assumptions shaped by the way terrorism has been studied over decades. They do not even allow us to register communication as relevant to the study of terrorism – what has been called in the previous chapter the "terrorism paradigm." The combination of these aspects is an hindrance to understanding the role of communication technologies, media organisations, and the effects that messages carried by the media can have, for instance, in the individual development of radical views, mobilisation of terrorist groups across borders, or the weaving of a terrorist plot.

The purpose of this chapter is to develop a theoretical framework (or model) to explain how processes of communication, more or less mediated by technology, are key to explaining the construction of identity and political mobilisation.[1] The first part of the analysis establishes the conceptual foundations of the framework. They are rooted in Relational Sociology, particularly in the work of Harrison White (2008). While relational sociology considers *communication* crucial to the very functioning of society, to more fully make sense of the role of *communication technologies* the model also incorporates elements of Actor Network Theory (ANT), particularly drawing on the work of Bruno Latour (2005). Relational Sociology and ANT provide together an explanation of how the social universe works – a social ontology. In order to more specifically explain political mobilisation, however, the model further combines social movement theories, especially borrowing from the work of Charles Tilly (2002) and Sidney Tarrow (1998).

The newly assembled framework is then presented in the second part of this chapter. That section contains an explanation of the social mechanisms that underpin the arguments presented in the rest of the book. The new framework brings together and redefines notions that are already used in talking about terrorism: "networks," "narrative," "identity," "groups," "perceptions," "media," and "communication technologies." As the following chapters will show, these concepts are often used loosely, inaccurately, inconsistently, and in isolated contexts. For example, those who talk about the terrorist narrative, are a different set of researchers than those who talk about networks, despite the fact that narratives, as I will show, are essential to the formation of networks. Narratives are also approached as mere "messages" that can be sent, just like packages, from sender A to receiver B. Instead, as will be explained more in detail in Chapter 5, they should be examined as collectively constructed interpretations. As such, they are constantly reworked and change both shape and meaning depending on which social actor's perspective the researcher decides to consider. The model not only pins down the meaning of these widely used concepts, but also grounds them in a broader explanatory framework. It thus shows that these terms describe different aspects of the same connected reality. The analytical benefits of the model – particularly the fact that it can be used as a lens to read current accounts of terrorism in a radically different way – will be illustrated through examples in the last part of the chapter.

3.1 Assembling a new theoretical framework

3.1.1 Relational sociology

The building of the theoretical framework starts from a review of the way Relational Sociology conceives the very notion of the "social." Relational Sociology has developed through the research of a cluster of scholars who started to converge around the Paul Lazarsfeld Centre for Social Sciences at Columbia University in the 1990s and who tend to be referred to, collectively, as the "New York School." Harrison White, director of the centre at that time, is one of the main figures in that school.

Relational Sociology approaches the social universe as entirely made up of relationships constantly being negotiated. In this process communication is "central" (White 2008: 3). The extent to which relationships are subject to incessant reworking is captured by White's comparison of social reality to a shapeless matter that never sets: "There is no tidy atom and no embracing world, only complex striations, long strings reptating as in a polymer goo" (ibid.: 18). This way of understanding the nature of the social is useful to the purposes of this book in two immediate respects. First, it allows the researcher to "see" communication – the very activity that enables the establishment of relationships – as pivotal to the very fabric of the world we inhabit. Second, it grounds in a solid conceptual framework that seamlessly spans the micro and macro dimensions concepts that are key to explaining political mobilisation: identity (both individual and collective), networks, stories, narratives. I am going to illustrate these aspects further by getting into the details of White's understanding of society.

The relational nature of the social[2]

The approach of relational sociology has been called a "comprehensive paradigmatic way of taking social structure seriously by studying *directly* how patterns of ties allocate resources in a social system" (Wellman 1988 in Mische 2010: 1, my emphasis). In fact, it takes relations, rather than abstract categories such as "class," "gender," "age," or for the purpose of this book, "terrorist," to be the basic unit of analysis. The focus on relations involves not just the explanation of interactions among individuals, but extends to the very generation of identity. Identity, in this perspective, is constituted in and through social ties. Social action, too, is the outcome of the opportunities and constraints embedded in an individual's constellation of relationships. This is important to understand that relationships do not only exist where people perceive themselves to be part of a group – as with the members of a curling club or a terrorist cell – but relations exist everywhere. This perspective also allows tracing the causes and motives of social action more broadly than the immediate circle of like-minded individuals that surrounds an actor.

White's approach stems from his rejection of "conventional survey analysis as the scientific method proper" (Azarian 2005: 18). For him, scientific enquiry is about *explaining* relationships between cause and effect and not, as in traditional survey analysis, *describing* reality through abstract and (inevitably) arbitrarily chosen categories (ibid.). Without an insight into causal processes, in fact, it would not be possible to demonstrate that these abstract categories are actually related, no matter how precisely and broadly measured the phenomena they refer to can be. White turns to network analysis as an unmediated and direct way to capture social processes in their complexities. He takes distance, however, from the mostly quantitative approach of traditional network analysis to integrate a concern for perception and cognition: "White often speaks of the need of research designs that can venture directly into the micro-space of the actual experience, *perception* and *comprehension* of the real business people [one of his early studies focused on job mobility processes] who, having only partial views and accounts of what takes place around them, try to manage their daily tasks" (ibid.: 17, my emphasis).

In the book *Identity and Control* (2008), White sets off to completely rewrite the understanding of society by rejecting, on the one hand, the idea of society as "an all-embracing whole or totality, as a real and concrete entity which has an independent, self-contained existence and which is clearly separated and demarcated from its surroundings" (Azarian 2005: 114); and, on the other hand, the idea of individual as a "distinct, autonomous, self-contained and self-directing being who possesses a set of unique characteristics" (ibid.: 115). Instead, social reality is for him "a huge, dense, and impenetrable texture of interlocking and overlapping networks that emerge as ties of various kinds concatenate into numerous strings without any clear-cut boundaries or stable forms" (ibid.: 117). The social world, in this perspective, is in constant movement and is incessantly negotiated by the actors who constitute it (White 2008: xxi). In fact, what looks like "normality," according to White, is only a "gloss on the reality of turbulent efforts at control by identities as they seek footings" (ibid.: 1).

Identity

All identities, in this perspective, are "produced and sustained within interacting relational networks" (Bearman and Stovel 2000: 74). The concept of identity is neither only related to human agents – people – nor restricted exclusively to the notions of the self and consciousness. Instead identity is "any entity to which observers can attribute meaning" (ibid.: 2). Identities arise out of communication situations (White 2008: 21). As White phrases it: they "trigger out of events," they are "switches in surroundings" (ibid.: 1): "A firm, a community, a crowd, oneself on the tennis court, encounters of strangers on a sidewalk – each may be identities" (ibid.: 2). As such there cannot be just one identity, but each of us has multiple ones. An individual might be a husband, but also a brother, a journalist, and a member of a bird watching association; just as a teacher can also be a friend, a son, and a terrorist. These are identities triggered by different sets of relationships organised in overlapping networks (which White calls "networks domains" or "netdoms"). To illustrate the way individuals have multiple identities and just "switch" from one identity to another when navigating across sets of relationships, White uses the analogy of an Internet forum (ibid.: 2–3). One can create an account on a discussion forum (about sociology, for instance) and his identity is not created by the mere act of subscribing, but by the participation, that is by the engagement in the discussion through postings that link him through stories to other users. The fictional user can log out from that account and participate in another discussion (on a football forum, for example). Although the user has logged out of the sociology forum the postings are not deleted: "the activity has left a social trace consisting of the ties to other identities in the forum. But the interaction has just switched from one netdom to another" (ibid.: 3). In relation to the study of terrorism, this helps in contextualising – if not rejecting – statements about individuals' vulnerability to extremist messages because of their alleged sense of "alienation" and "lack of identity." For example, a report by the UK Department for Communities and Local Government (Choudhury 2007) suggests that individuals are particularly susceptible to radicalisation when they are experiencing an "identity crisis" (ibid.: 6) and are involved in a "search for identity" (ibid.: 5). A Chatham House report about the role of strategic communication in countering radicalisation similarly argues that those "who feel split in their identity ... seek to find meaning and a sense of identity through a radical narrative" (Cornish, Lindley-French and Yorke 2011: 34). In a social relational perspective these statements do not make any sense: since individuals always have multiple identities they cannot possibly lack a sense of it.

Social ties, stories, and networks

Saying that social reality consists of networks of relationships also means that it is made of the *stories* that are attached to these relationships. In this respect, communities regulated by traditions are, effectively, networks of relationships underpinned by stories that persist through time by being constantly re-enacted. In a similar way, individuals belonging to a terrorist organisation are brought together by their sharing of a founding myth: one can think, for example, about the symbolic significance of the "Lion's Den." This was a military base established by Osama bin Laden in the late 1980s in Afghanistan. The story of a handful of mujahedeen who managed to repulse a Soviet attack would later inspire volunteers to join the organisation (Kepel and Milelli 2008: 41–46; Inkster 2011: 5). This last example suggests that relationships are not only real – based on an actual contact – but also imagined. Although what I am going to discuss next about the nature of social ties, their constitution and management, might appear rather far from terrorism, it is important to understand the reality in which all social action – violent extremism included – takes place.

For White (2008: 20), any relation between pairs of identities is a tie. This is a "theoretical construction, abstracted by the analyst from the bulk of largely erratic streams of affections, encounters and interactions between a pair of actors, be they human beings, informal groups, formal organizations, or others" (Azarian 2005: 37). Ties exist wherever there is a perception by one of the identities being paired, or by an external observer, that the tie exists:

> a relationship may be perceived by the connected actors and/or it can be defined by the observer. On the basis of the existence of some sentiments and attitudes between the actors. It might also be perceived on the basis of some ongoing activity, making the actors and/or observer to conceive the tie as a channel of exchange and/or diffusion, through which anything material or non-material like directional streams of goods, capital, information, rumours, and so on can flow. (Ibid.: 38)

White calls the perceptions of the parties involved in a relationship – particularly the "accounts developed and reported by each part about the nature, character, and state of the relationship" (ibid.: 51) – "stories." In his words: "a story is a tie placed in context" (White 2008: 20). Put another way, a relationship exists wherever there is a story. As examples to further illustrate these notions, a conversation with a stranger at a bus stop does not constitute a tie (ibid.: 25), while a relationship to a cousin, even if one does not perceive that tie, still exists because that person "remains known socially as your cousin" (ibid.).

Indirect social ties "are no less real" than direct ones (Azarian 2005: 41). It is interesting to notice that identities can emerge "independent of tangible social relations, constituting forms of imagined communities" (Bearman and Stovel 2000: 74, n. 8). For Peter Bearman and Katherine Stovel (2000) this helps in explaining, for instance, the emergence of nationalism, where ties between people are replaced by ties "between persons and symbols" (ibid.). On this point, Mustafa Emirbayer (1997: 296) further writes that individual identities are constituted within "circles of recognition." They do not only include "circles of interpersonal, social relationships," but also "'virtual' circles with cultural ideals and fantasized objects" (296–297). An example of belonging to an "imagined community" that supports engagement in terrorist activity is offered by self-proclaimed affiliates of Al Qaeda. As Edwin Bakker and Leen Boer (2007: 20) point out, several groups like Abu Sayyaf in the Philippines; Lashkar Al-Toiba, Jaysh Muhammad, and Harakat Al-Ansar in India; Al-Itkihad Al-Islami in Somalia, and Al-Jama'a Al Islamiya in Indonesia, either consider themselves (or are seen by others) to operate under the Al Qaeda name. They can be more or less autonomous, but their link to Al Qaeda central is only indirect. As the researchers put it: "in some cases both sides may not even be aware of any connection between individuals within their network" (ibid.).

A pattern of ties constitutes a network (White 2008: 20). Every social agent can be conceived of as a node that is "located at the intersection of several distinct, often heterogenous networks" (Azarian 2005: 60). This defines the unique position of each social actor within the social universe. Such position is defined by the content of the ties – which might be goods, information, capital, rumours – but also by expectations that other identities are imposing on the actor. As Reza Azarian (ibid.: 61) describes this: "Since each relationship brings along a bundle of particular expectations and obligations, this embeddedness means being simultaneously subjected to a number of specific constraining forces."

Identity and the management of social ties

The social ties shape our cognitive horizon, our scope of action, and whether such action is going to be more or less constrained (in this perspective no action can truly be independent). As such, ties affect what we know and how we are going to interpret both the world around us and incoming information. Although social ties shape who we are, what we know, and ultimately what we do, as social actors we are not passive, but we purposely manage social ties. This point is crucial to understand that the behaviour of terrorists, as that of all social actors, is not the almost-mechanical product of either the environment in which they live (e.g., political situation of a country, economic deprivation, social discrimination), or of their own decisions (e.g., individual sense of alienation, personal grievance or trauma, psychological stress). Instead, social action results from the incessant negotiation – and relative ever-changing outcomes – between these two aspects over time.

White's book is entitled *Identity and Control* because identity is a byproduct of the attempt at controlling the sets of relationships that trigger it. The expectations placed on an actor by the constellation of relationship the actor is embedded in make the social environment resemble an ever-shifting terrain that appears very uncertain. Control, in this respect, is an attempt at "managing the ties": "control is used to designate the whole array of attempts undertaken by the actor to reduce the uncertainties and contingencies in his [*sic*] social environment" (ibid.: 65). Examples of ways an actor can use to exercise control on relationships, according to White, are: ambiguity; social *ambage* (i.e., "proceeding indirectly"); and decoupling. The first refers to leaving the description of a relationship open, so that it can lend itself to redefinition. The second is about social manipulation and indirectly influencing a target through the chain of ties that connect to that target. The third is about cutting off undesirable relationships, which includes the obligations, information flows, and goods that come with them (ibid.: 69–75). All these strategies are examples of control activities in which all actors are simultaneously involved:

> a social tie is conceived best as a locus of the ongoing dynamic control processes that are launched by its participants. Any social relationship should, in other words, be viewed as a battle field where the participants struggle ceaselessly for control and mutual constraint, and where each participant gives his account of such struggles in the form of stories. (Ibid.: 76)

The extent to which "fresh action" is constrained by network obligations is the outcome of the actor's greater or lesser success at managing the ties and of moving beyond what White calls the "Sargasso Sea of social obligation" (White 2008: 4).

Identity, within this struggle against uncertainty, provides principles on how to deal with the flows of obligations, information, and expectations that come from the ties. Identity is

> the specific behaviour profile that is particular to an actor and that grows out of his [*sic*] attempts to handle the unique and erratic bombardments [of contents, constraints, etc. from social ties] to which he is subjected. It refers to the certain fashion and style that the actor develops to handle these bombardments and create some degree of order and regularity in his [*sic*] habitat." (Azarian 2005: 80)

In other words, it is a "mode of conduct that is stable and reoccurring enough to make him predictable and recognizable by others" (ibid.: 81).

The position of every social actor, which can be actively changed through tie-management strategies, is unique and defines the social horizon of that actor. In fact, as ties consist in flows of information, the unique constellation in which the actor is embedded shapes his/her knowledge (ibid.: 67). As White states: "Identity becomes a point of reference from which information can be processed, evaluated" (White 2008: 1–2) and ties are "prisms for meaning" (ibid.: 20).

Narratives

In White's relational understanding of society, communication is central, not only as in the sharing and exchange of information, but also as its processing: "Human social process typically orients around meanings of events and interpretations of relations among identities" (ibid.: 3). The importance of communication is further underlined by the key role of stories and narratives as, respectively, accounts produced by actors about the relationships in which they are involved and ordering principles of social action. Again, this is relevant to the purposes of this book to understand that narratives are not "tales" or "messages" that can simply be "made up" by social actors – for instance, for the purpose of political mobilisation or to radicalise new followers in the case of an extremist organisation. Instead, narratives are at the same time the product of a broader context than one's single imagination and a flexible guide to social action. Once more, the following discussion might seem to diverge from the topic at hand, but it is actually useful to grasp the social depth of narratives and to realise that terrorist groups are organised exactly like other units in the social universe.

Narratives, according to White, differ from stories because they are organised around values. To understand where values come from we need to take a step back and examine the idea of "disciplines." Disciplines are defined by Azarian (2005: 101) as "tiny islands or enclaves of order, regularity and predictability in a world that is otherwise chaotic, disorienting and confusing." A discipline is constituted by a limited number of actors and is perceived as a distinct whole (ibid.: 100). It has its own collective identity and an externally "recognizable mode of action" (ibid.: 101). Examples of disciplines are companies, institutions, or political parties. A terrorist group can also be conceived as a discipline.

Disciplines are characterised by internal organising schemes or rules that provide guidance to actors who might want to "join" them. These rules contribute to keeping the identities of the members "on track" with the collective identity (ibid.: 104–105). They are called "valuation order." They could be compared to the specific "idiom" of a discipline (ibid.: 105) and can vary according to the nature of the discipline itself. White distinguishes three kinds of disciplines and three corresponding valuation orders. "Quality" is the valuation order that regulates disciplines involved in production (White 2008: 64), such as commercial enterprises (although the "goods" produced could be of any nature, from baked beans to research reports). "Prestige," "in the sense of the perceived capacity to influence corporate action," is what organises institutions concerned with regulating "the flow of people and resources" from the external environment "into the control of the local system" (ibid.: 65). These kinds of disciplines, which can range from a government department to a university, are called "councils" (ibid.). "Purity," related to a system of inclusion and exclusion (for example being baptised or being enrolled on a professional register) is, instead, what defines the boundaries of "arenas," yet another social unit that could span churches and fraternities. A terrorist cell, whose boundaries are defined by an individual commitment to the ideology of the group, could also be regarded as an arena.

What we would normally call "values," arise from the valuation orders of each collective social unit (or discipline). Narratives are sets of stories organised around a value: "Accounts by multiple sources, strung together over time around a value, yield a narrative of events" (ibid.: 222). Narratives perform an ordering function by creating what White calls a "regime." This, in turn, can span different domains of social life – "realms" (ibid.).

A realm can exist at different levels: we can talk, for example, about the "realm of law" or "the realm of science," or art, but we can also identify realms at a smaller scale. White mentions "American theatre" as an example of the latter (ibid.: 178). The separation of realms is explained through the switching of identities among different network domains (ibid.: 238). For instance, we can think about the separation in everyday life between "work" and "play." That is the switching between the network constituted, on the one hand, by colleagues and superiors at the office and, on the other hand, by the network of friends and acquaintances at the boxing club.

To both draw the last few points together and provide clarification, story sets from networks and valuation orders from disciplines contribute to building a narrative which establishes, in turn, a regime that becomes the "grammar of right and wrong" (ibid.: 224). One could think of the way in which, within a Western country like the United Kingdom, both the stories generated by citizens' networks and the valuation orders of disciplines (for example political parties, churches, NGOs, citizens associations) contribute to the generalisation of values like respect for the law, for human rights, and for individual freedoms. They are the values embedded in the narrative of a democratic country. This, in turn, acts as an ordering principle over the many realms contained in British society. In this sense the current idea that Western governments should build a narrative ("our" narrative) to counter the terrorists' narrative (Presidential Task Force 2009, for instance) is misleading. "Our" narrative already exists and is solidly rooted in the processes that have been described.

3.1.2   Actor Network Theory

In Relational Sociology communication is acknowledged to be the essence of social interaction. Within this approach what matters are the constitutions and constant reworkings of relationships, and it makes no difference whether they are constituted face-to-face, over the phone, online, or even if they are imagined. The fact that communication is virtually – and indistinctly – everywhere, however, can turn into a hurdle on a researcher's way to making sense of mediated communication, particularly of the role of communication technologies. The analysis turns, therefore, to Actor Network Theory (ANT), which more explicitly addresses the question of the nature of technology and its role in society.

The social nature of technology

ANT develops from the field of Science and Technology Studies. It is particularly associated with the work of the anthropologist Bruno Latour. Together with Steve Woolgar, in *Laboratory Life,* he examined the way in which scientific facts are not discovered, but *constructed* in a research setting: "Argument between scientists transforms some statements into figments' of one's subjective imagination, and others into facts of nature ... reality [in the study they conducted] was the *consequence* of the settlement of a dispute rather than its *cause*" (Latour and Woolgar 1979: 236, emphasis in original). The manufacture of scientific facts involves human interaction, but also the identification and creation of "objects" of study, as well as the reliance on technical infrastructure. Throughout that investigation, Latour started developing the radical notion – which he further expanded in later works – of a networked social reality in which there is no distinction between the "technical" and the "social." This means, in practice, that society is made up of networks – a view entirely compatible with that of Relational Sociology. These networks, however, include not only humans, but also non-humans: objects, technologies, and ideas.

Latour developed this approach to overcome the "methodological individualism" that, despite stretching its roots to Aristotle and medieval philosophy, is still at the core of contemporary sociological explanations of reality (Emirbayer 1997: 283–284). John Dewey and Arthur Bentley (1949 in Emirbayer 1997: 284), although writing over 60 years ago, still capture the present-day tendency to see individuals as the ultimate source of social action:

> All the spooks, fairies, essences, and entities that once [during the Middle Ages] had inhabited portions of matter now [take] flight to new homes, mostly in or at the human body ... . The "mind" as "actor," still in use in present day psychologies and sociologies, is the old self-acting "soul" with its immortality stripped off.

The puzzling result for Latour is that, albeit Sociology developed mostly after the Industrial Revolution, in an era of profound technical advances, the role of objects in our society is largely ignored. As he lyrically phrases it, they "remain asleep like servants of some enchanted castle" (Latour 2005: 73). In reality, as John Law, another influential voice within the ANT camp, points out, objects like machines are an integral part of our very identity:

> we are all heterogeneous networks, the products of confused overlaps. Did you really find your way through last week without machines? Of course not! *You are part machine.* And if you pretend otherwise, then this is presumably because you (like me) prefer to think otherwise. For in polite company ... it is not generally considered to be a good thing to allow oneself to be "dehumanised." (Law 1991b: 17, his emphasis)

As Law (1991b: 16) continues: "Structures do not simply reside in the actions of people, or in memory traces. They exist in a network of heterogeneous material arrangements." In fact, as Latour (1991: 110) writes:

> we are never faced with objects or social relations, we are faced with chains which are association of human (H) and non-humans (NH). No one has ever seen a social relation by itself ... nor a technical relation ... . Instead we are always faced by chains which look like this H-NH-H-NH-NH-NH-H-H-H-H-HN.

Objects – technologies and, among them, communication technologies – in this perspective, do not just enable establishing networks, but they change the actors themselves. Technologies are not just tools or intermediaries, but are "mediators" (Latour 2005: 128). In this respect ANT makes objects "participants" in social action by overcoming the very definition of actors and agencies most adopted in Sociology:

> If action is limited a priori to what "intentional", "meaningful" humans do, it is hard to see how a hammer, a basket, a door closer, a cat, a rug, a mug, a list, or a tag could act. They might exist in the domain of "material" "causal" relations, but not in the "reflexive" "symbolic" domain of social relations. (Ibid.: 71)

To "break away from the influence of what could be called 'figurative sociology' [the tendency to attribute 'faces' to social action], ANT uses the technical word *actant*" (ibid.: 54, his emphasis).

Actants have agency, which means that they "make a difference": "hitting a nail with and without hammer, boiling water with and without a kettle, fetching provisions with or without a basket" (ibid.: 71) do make a difference, which makes the hammer, kettle, and basket participants in the course of action. In the actions of a terrorist group, the same could be said for explosives, cars, computers.

This, however, does not mean that an object *determines* the action. The object *participates* in the action through what Latour (1999: 178–80) calls "interference" and "composition" (ibid.: 180–183). In the case of interference, a technology can change an actor's "programme of action," which can be thought of as the attempt to achieve a certain goal. A person holding a gun is not the same as a person not holding a gun. The man with a gun is a new "composite actor." This does not necessarily mean that the man with the gun will use it, but while an initial goal might have been just to cause injury, the fact that a gun is in the hand of the actor can lead to a different goal – killing. The transformation of the person once s/he holds a gun, is symmetrical with that of the object:

> You are different with a gun in your hand; the gun is different with you holding it. You are another subject because you hold the gun; the gun is another object because it has entered into a relationship with you. The gun is no longer the gun-in-the-armory or the gun-in-the-drawer or the gun-in-the-pocket but the gun-in-your-hand, aimed at someone who is screaming. What is true of the subject, of the gunman, is true of the object, of the gun that is held. A good

citizen becomes a criminal [or a terrorist], a bad guy becomes a worse guy; a silent gun becomes a fired gun; a new gun becomes a used gun, a sporting gun becomes a weapon. (Ibid.: 179–180)

The second way in which objects participate in social action is "composition."[3] This refers to the fact that if, in order to achieve a goal, an actor uses an object, then the reaching of the goal is a "common achievement" (ibid.: 181) of both actants: "The chimp plus the sharp stick reach (not reaches) the banana" (ibid.: 182). To apply this to terrorism one could think that an extremist individual plus planes, cars, telephones, Internet, and buildings lead to an act of terrorism. Action is therefore not the property of humans only but of "associations of actants" (ibid.). Given the extent to which human action is delegated to machines (ibid.: 190), social action is the result of increasingly long associations of human and non-human actants.

The process through which the nature of all actants is transformed by the very fact of entering into a relationship (man + gun; chimp + stick; extremist + planes + cars + telephones + Internet + buildings) is called "translation": "Translation does not mean a shift from one vocabulary to another, from one French word to an English word, for instance, as if the two languages existed independently. I use translation to mean displacement, drift, invention, mediation, the creation of a link that did not exist before and that to some degree modifies the original two" (ibid.: 179). In this sense, as for White, entities are "produced in relations" (Law 1999: 4) and social actors are "network effects" (ibid.: 5).

The role of communication technologies

This understanding of the social and the role of technologies within it is useful for conceptualising the role of communication technologies in the phenomenon of violent extremism for three reasons. First, it underlines that communication technologies are not just a passive infrastructure whose role is enabling the establishment of relationships or, in other words, allowing the transmission of messages from actor A to actor B. Instead, they are actants in the social actions being performed. As such, in the process of translation, they transform both their own nature and the identity of those being connected. A terrorist with access to a technology that has global reach, like the Internet, is not the same as a terrorist without that technology.

At the same time, as a second point, ANT allows the researcher to place technology into perspective. This particularly refers to avoiding the demonisation of communication technologies, especially the Internet.

Terrorists are who they are and manage to do what they do not only because of the Internet or because of the use of a particular communication technology, but because they are actor-networks – the outcome of constellations of relationships they are involved in, which include like-minded individuals, mothers, brothers, ordinary citizens, computers, mobile phones, cars, roads, explosives, washing machines, and guns … . "We" are who "we" are because of different constellations of networks still including similarly minded individuals, mothers, brothers, ordinary citizens, computers, mobile phones, cars, roads, washing machines … .

Thirdly, ANT warns against the limitations of comparisons, either historical or across cases in understanding social phenomena – terrorism in our context. In fact, in an ANT's perspective, there is absolutely no point in establishing comparisons to further our understanding because the action of every actant is embedded within a specific constellation of relationships at a particular time and place. This makes every actor network unique. Latour (1999: 150) takes this point to the limit by arguing that even material substances, which our common sense would suggest cannot possibly change across time or space (Are not chemical substances always made by the same configurations of atoms?) are still the product of specific networks: "A lactic acid ferment grown in a culture in Pasteur's laboratory in Lille in 1858 is not the same thing as the residue of an alcoholic fermentation in Liebig's laboratory in 1852." The very way of categorising as a yeast in 1858 what was an inert substance in 1852 reveals a shift in the two scientists' views of the world: respectively "a world in which the relation between organic matter and ferments is one of contact and decay" ("yeast is … an unwelcome impurity that would hinder and spoil the fermentation") and "a world in which a ferment is as active as any other already identified life form, so much that it now feeds on the organic material, which instead of being its cause, has become its food ("the yeast has become a full-blown entity") (ibid.: 116–117).

By taking White's and Latour's social embeddedness to its logical end, nothing could ever be learned outside the uniqueness of the network configuration at any given time and place. This is why, as explained in Chapter 1, while rejecting the belief that causality can be inferred through comparative research design only, in this book I take a more moderate stance and support the role of comparison in *sensitising* the researcher to difference and variation.

How to conceptualise change?

Both Relational Sociology and ANT are useful to establish the foundations of an alternative perspective about the way social reality works to the one that is at the moment de facto prevailing within the field of Terrorism Studies. Relational Sociology and ANT can be regarded as social ontologies in which the traditional agency and structure debate has been overcome. Indeed, for both there is neither distinction between micro and macro levels of analysis, nor regional, national, or international dimensions: everything is connected. As Latour puts it: the global is local at every single point (1993: 117; 2005: 173–190). This is a fruitful springboard for understanding political mobilisation in an age of interconnectedness: relationships are established and communication develops in myriad networks that bypass national borders one interaction at a time. It also supports a deeper understanding of a central concept in politics: power. Power, in a relational perspective, is not something one "owns," but it is embedded within changing patterns of relationships, as well as distribution of resources, exchange of information, and building of expectations attached to them (Emirbayer 1997: 291–292). As Latour writes (1991: 110): power is the property of a chain of associations.

Neither approach, however, gets into the details of why and how political mobilisation actually occurs: why and how do network arrangements change? In both accounts no actor, whether human or non-human, can behave truly independently of the networks it is part of. For White (2008: 4), "fresh action" depends on the relative balance between identity affirmation (that is control of social ties) and demands, expectations, and constraints placed on the actor by those ties. But when and under which circumstances does "fresh action" arise? What is it that leads social actors to want to cut through the constraints of social obligations in the first place? Similarly, for Latour (2005: 46, his emphasis) an actor is that which "is *made* to act by many others." For ANT it is even more uncertain how new action is generated, since "we never know for sure who and what is making us act" (ibid.: 52), "No one knows how many people are simultaneously at work in any given individual; conversely, no one knows how much individuality there can be in a cloud of statistical data points" (ibid.: 54). While both Relational Sociology and ANT provide an account of the way social reality works, it is ultimately their inability to explain contingent change and action that has led some (Collins 1988; Scott 2000) to call the relational approach a *method* at best rather than a *theory* of the social. The method consists in the application of network analysis. For Latour (2005: 12), this translates into the identification and mapping of the networks of actants and the technique of "following them" wherever they might lead. To further grasp mobilisation around a political cause, which is relevant to understanding the spur to action of extremists and terrorist groups, I am therefore now turning to social movement theory.

3.1.3 Social movement theory

Social movement theory is concerned with the way political identities are formed, how they become the basis for making claims in the public arena, and how collective action is achieved through mobilisation of both symbolic and material resources. An approach that is particularly useful to explaining identity construction and mobilisation in a world in which relationships and the interpretations of those relationships – stories – matter, is that developed by Charles Tilly (2002). In his analysis, stories are crucial both to the constitution of political identity and as a rationale for action. Social action, in turn, takes place within changing structures of opportunity. They are not only material, but also constituted by perceptions. As such, they can be altered through the communication of new information and the establishment of "imagined" ties.

Stories, identities and politics

In *Stories, Identities, and Political Change* Tilly (ibid.: 5–6) examines the role of stories in "contentious politics" – the making of public claims on each other by "politically constituted actors." As in White, stories reside in social ties: "Rather than living inside the human bodies, true identities invariably live in ties among persons" (ibid.: 48). In fact, as Tilly writes: "Skinheads become skinheads in relation to and distinction from other people – skinheads, nonskinheads, and antiskinheads" (ibid.: 76).

Stories are essential in political mobilisation in two respects. First, they are crucial to the constitution of the political identity of the actors: "Every social relation includes a boundary between the sites involved. At the individual level, the boundary falls somewhere between you and me. At the collective level, it falls between us and them. Boundary construction is fundamental to social process. That process is crucial to the production of identities" (ibid.: 11). Second, stories also have the function of channelling social action. They do so by providing a compelling motive for it:

> [stories] pop up everywhere. They lend themselves to vivid, compelling accounts of what has happened, what will happen, or what should happen. They do essential work in social life, cementing people's commitments to common projects, helping people make sense

of what's going on, channelling collective decisions and judgements, spurring people to action they would otherwise be reluctant to pursue. (Ibid.: 27)

But stories also provide boundaries to the modality of social action and are continuously modified as a result of it. As Tilly continues:

> Stories emerge from active social interchange, modify as a result of social interchange, but in their turn constrain social interchange as well. They embody ideas concerning what forms of action and interaction are possible, feasible, desirable, and efficacious, hence at least by implication what forms of action and interaction would be impossible, impracticable, undesirable, or ineffectual. Even if the individuals involved harbour other ideas, the embedding of stories in social networks seriously constrains interactions, hence collective actions, of which people in those networks are capable. (Ibid.: 8–9)

Stories appear extremely important to the mobilisation of terrorist groups. Khachig Tololyan (1988: 222–226), for instance, emphasises the role of three stories that provided Armenian terrorism with a frame for heroism and sacrifice: the story of the Armenian genocide that took place between 1915 and 1923 and that is believed to have led to one and a half million deaths (The Armenian National Institute, n.d.); the story of Vartan and his followers, who became martyrs in a battle against the Persians dating to the second half of the fifth century; a set of stories about the Armenian killers who, in the early 1920s, attacked the members of the Young Turk junta responsible for the genocide. We can also think about the notion of oppression of Muslim lands over centuries at the hands of Western powers as the story underpinning action against those who are perceived as enemies and attackers of Islam: the United States and its allies involved in Iraq and Afghanistan.

Social movements and mobilisation

Terrorism could, indeed, be regarded as a form of collective action. In fact, it could fit the description of a social movement insofar as it is a form of mobilisation around a political claim by people who do not have regular access to institutions, who make new or unaccepted claims and who, by doing so, challenge authorities (Tarrow 1998: 3).[4]

The mobilisation of a social movement takes place when there is an opening in the "political opportunity structure." This term is borrowed from Sidney Tarrow (1995) and refers to both the opportunities and constraints that either encourage or discourage political action. For instance, they could be, respectively, external support for the movement or authorities' repression of protesters (ibid.: 19–20). For Tarrow, more specifically, in the context of a window of political opportunity, a social movement is produced through: access to known and flexible repertoires of contention; the development of collective action frames; and the establishment of structures for mobilisation around social networks and organisations. I am going to briefly explain how these aspects are going to be interpreted for the purposes of the theoretical framework developed in this book.

In terms of repertoires of contention, mobilisation translates into creative action within some predictable boundaries.[5] They are the "conventional" means through which protest is communicated. As Tilly (2002: 118) points out, claim makers, tend to use a narrow range of actions:

> Demonstrators often march in ranks, display banners, shout slogans, and present petitions, but rarely carry machine guns, defecate in the street, strip naked, strangle spectators, sing nursery rhymes, stop to buy the day's groceries … . If participants in contentious conversation did not adopt recognizable idioms, they would undercut their own efforts to coordinate actions, convey messages, and influence objects of their claims.

Petitions, building barricades, and organising peaceful demonstrations might be the more or less acceptable means of protesting in democratic societies. The repertoire of terrorist organisations is extreme violence.

Framing is related to constructing meaning and, from the point of view of a social movement, consists in presenting an issue in a way that can resonate with a desired audience. Framing can be defined in many different ways (for a review of literature see König, n.d.). For David Snow and Robert Benford (1992: 137) a frame is an "interpretative schemata that simplifies and condenses the 'world out there' by selectively punctuating and encoding objects, situations, events, experiences, and sequences of actions within one's present or past environments."

I take on board Tarrow's understanding of framing, particularly the idea that specific interpretations of reality – frames – can be planned, manufactured, and promoted to fit a political agenda. As I will explain in the next section, however, I prefer to refer to them as (collective) "narratives" because frames do not just portray issues in ways that can appeal to a desired constituency. They also contain a whole projection of what is the problem a movement is trying to tackle, what the solutions are, what the role of the movement and its members should be, who the opponents are, what the struggle is going to be like ... . In the view I present here, the "resonance" of frames (or collective narratives) – in other words the degree to which they are going to be understood and embraced to constitute the basis for the development of a common identity – does not only depend on an "alignment" of a social movement's frame either with "sentiment pools" of "aggregates of individuals who share common grievances" (Snow et al. 1986: 467) or with the "existing culture" (Tarrow 1998: 110). In fact, if a culture is "a collective mode of life," a "repertoire of beliefs, styles, values and symbols" (Smith 1990: 171) that characterises a community, a nation, an ethnic minority, then the "alignment" of a frame with it should lead to a joining of a movement en masse. That is not at all the case. In addition, if frames really connect with already existing grievances within a group, why do they resonate only with some of the individuals who hold those grievances and not with all of them?[6] Especially in a world where collective narratives can be communicated across national and cultural lines, the degree to which frames are going to be understood and possibly embraced by followers who apparently live in different cultures needs to be addressed. The same applies to the fact that even individuals who appear to share similar interests still react differently to the same political call.

As for the aspect of organisation, this is crucial to ensuring the survival of the organisation beyond the act of protest. Tarrow (1995: 124–125) talks about three different aspects of a movement's organisation: a formal hierarchical organisation, which can be regarded as the internal structure of a movement; the organisation of collective action in communicating grievances to the political opponents, such as "informal social networks, ... formal branches, clubs, and even military-like cells" (ibid.); the connective structures that link leaders to followers and allow the organisation and coordination among the members. While they can all apply to terrorist organisations, I take this further by adding the existence of indirect and imagined relationships between the terrorist organisation and followers who might feel inspired by the group and act in its name, but are not formally and directly related to it. I will come back to this aspect shortly.

Opportunity structure and communication

The opportunity structure is not only material and shaped by political alliances and support networks. It is also shaped by perceptions. This has implications for the role of communication technologies and media coverage within the process of political mobilisation.

In relation to the importance of perceptions, as Tilly (2002: 108) writes referring to the revolutionary movements that developed across Europe between 1847 and 1849: "The rapidity of the movement between nonrevolutionary and revolutionary situations, between inaction and action, between low and high levels of movement activity generally does not result from quick changes in state capacity, but from the rapid diffusion of new information, beliefs, and evaluation of action's probable consequences." He continues: "Communication and shared belief play significant parts in such revolutionary processes. Three elements change as they advance: (1) common readings of state capacity, (2) shared beliefs concerning the likely consequences of different claims and collective actions, and (3) relative capabilities of different actors to mobilize and act collectively" (ibid.).

He is particularly referring to the fact that the diffusion of information changes the "political opportunity structure." He further illustrates the point through the example of the 1989 Eastern European revolutions:

> the common experience of Soviet hegemony created communication networks among Poland, East Germany, Czechoslovakia, and Hungary. Those networks reinforced the extreme sensitivity of those states to change in relations of any one of them to the Soviet Union. The absence of Soviet reaction to the flight of East Germans to the West through Hungary and Czechoslovakia in 1989 rapidly lowered estimates of the probability of Soviet military interventions in that zone. (Ibid.: 109)

Tilly underlines that what circulates across countries is not simply an image of what is happening, thereby leading to some sort of "imitation," but information that supports a reassessment of the political structure: "what actually spread [in the period 1789 to 1848] from place to place: not so much shared interests, awareness of oppression, or even models of collective action, rather information concerning changes in the vulnerability of authorities, the likelihood of international support, and the effectiveness of different forms of collective action. If internationalization occurs, we should not imagine a wave of imitation, but a change in the connection between the political situations of spatially separated actors" (ibid.).

This can help us reflect on the role of communication technologies in contemporary politics, particularly in placing into perspective the extent to which communication technologies "cause" change, whether it is the shift from authoritarian governments to democracy, as in the "Arab Awakening" of 2011,[7] or terrorism.

3.2 An alternative understanding of terrorism

The theoretical framework presented in this section brings together the elements of Relational Sociology, ANT, and social movement theory approaches that have been described in the first part of the chapter. The suggested model allows a radically different interpretation of the phenomenon of violent extremism. After having laid out the basics of the model, I will illustrate more in detail its analytical implications, followed by an examination of the way the new framework challenges a set of current assumptions about the relationship between terrorism and the media, and what it all means for the study of violent extremism.

3.2.1 A communication model

The phenomenon of violent extremism takes place in a social world that is constituted by overlapping networks of relationships. They shape who we are – our identity. The model is fundamentally based on a tight inter-relation among identity, knowledge, and action. In other words, who we are, shapes what we know – including the interpretation of incoming information – and this, in turn, shapes our behaviour (action). Each single relationship we have exists on the basis of a "story." This means that we are able to provide an account of who the person we have a relationship with is, what is the nature of our relationship, and how it developed. Exchanges of information, goods, and resources might be attached to the relationship. They are part of the story. In fact, they constitute it and, or over time, can also change it. The combination of all of these stories, together with the view of the world we develop as a result of the constellation of relationships, the interpretation of incoming information through the perspective resulting from our position in the social space at any given time, our account of what we do (including why we do it) as a result, constitute our *individual narrative*. This could be described as the unique perspective that an individual has on the world from his/her "corner" of the social reality (Figure 3.1).

It is important to understand that the individual narrative is *not* the same as the sum of relationships, information received and exchanged, and actions taken. Relationships, information, and actions exist onto-logically on a different level. The individual narrative is an *account*, an interpretation that we create about who we are, what our place in society (or circle of friends, workplace, professional field ...) is, what happens around us and in the world, what we do, and for what purposes. As Tilly (2002) observes, individuals' accounts of their own lives (which he calls "standard stories") are characterised by

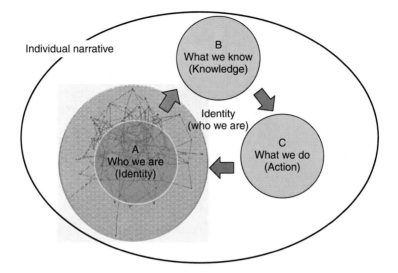

Figure 3.1   The social construction of the individual narrative

independent, self-motivated and conscious characters that interact within a limited space and time horizon. These accounts, as he puts it "do a wide variety of important social work. That work certainly includes accounting for skinheads and counterrevolutions, but it also includes autobiography, self-justification, social movement mobilisation, jury deliberation, moral condemnation, cementing of agreements, and documentation of nationalist claims" (ibid.: 74). These stories shape our world. They do not, however, reflect the way the social world actually works. We are not self-propelled and independent actors, but are enmeshed in so much broader networks of relationships than we are ever able to realise. These networks do offer us opportunities for relatively "freer" action, but also tie us in nets of obligations. The challenge for the social scientist is thus being able to see through the inevitably short-sighted individual stories to construct what Tilly calls a "superior story" – that is a scientific explanation of events and social phenomena (ibid.: 25–42).[8]

Where do communication as the sharing and transmitting of information, communication technologies, media organisations, and media coverage fit within this perspective? They all contribute to the formation of identity (Figure 3.1, area A). Communication is the very enabler of the formation of any relationship. Social ties do not just exist with people we are in contact with but are also indirect and articulated through the sense of belonging to imagined communities.

Craig Calhoun (1991a), in this respect, argues that the proliferation of "indirect relationships" and the production of "imagined communities" are two features that fundamentally characterise modernity. He distinguishes four kinds of indirect relationships: (a) direct interpersonal relations (face-to-face); (b) imagined personal connections that can exist, for instance, with political representatives, TV personalities, but also through tradition; (c) one-directional relationships that are only known to one of the parties: examples are surveillance, phone tapping, but also census data (which reveals information about individual spending patterns, for instance, without the population even knowing it); (d) "the world of systemic integration or coordination by impersonal ... steering media ... which gives the illusion of not involving human interaction" exemplified by "capitalism" or "the market" (ibid.: 96–105). The first two kinds of relationships are particularly relevant to the model presented here. Communication technologies can extend our social reach in forming direct relationships (through emails, for example, or by having a chat over the phone) but they can also contribute to indirect relationships. For instance, an activist can develop an indirect relationship with an admired political figure one comes to know through television or through speeches available online.

The "imagined communities," to borrow the term used by Benedict Anderson (1983),[9] are based on the "politics of identification" (Calhoun 1991a: 108). As Calhoun (ibid.) explains: "People without direct interpersonal relations with each other are led by the mediation of the world of political symbols to imagine themselves as members of communities defined by common ascriptive characteristics, personal tastes, habits, concerns." These communities are "imagined" because they are not based on either direct or indirect relationships, but rather on "categorical identities." In this respect, there can be imagined communities of interest like those constituted by environmental activists, gay marriage campaigners, radical Muslims who aspire to live in a society regulated by Sharia law, people with a passion for ballroom dancing or creative writing, communities of consumers of Ikea furniture or Mac cosmetics, Lady Gaga's fans ... . Although it is possible for a person belonging to any of these communities to actually know like-minded individuals, the sense of shared identity and "fellow-feeling" extends well beyond the direct relationship.

The sense of imagined community can be supported in a variety of ways. Media can be directly involved. Anderson (1983: 29), for instance, explains the rise of nationalism through the daily ritual of reading the newspaper: "The mass ceremony ... is performed in silent privacy ... .

Yet each communicant is well aware that the ceremony he performs is being replicated simultaneously by thousands (or millions) of others of those whose existence he is confident, yet of whose identity he has not the slightest notion." The same could be said for contemporary viewers of and listeners to globally covered events. Daniel Dayan and Elihu Katz (1992: 1) call "media events" those "historic occasions ... that are televised as they take place and transfix a nation or the world." Among the examples of media events they present are the funeral of Egypt's president, Anwar el Sadat, and that of John Fitzgerald Kennedy; and the wedding of Prince Charles and Lady Diana. During media events the barriers to total and unmediated communication – normally represented by the fact that there are multiple messages, that audiences are selective, and that the diffusion of information takes time – are momentarily overcome. Media events, in the analysis of Dayan and Katz, are able to create communities of vast audiences (ibid.: 15). Their being broadcast live, the ceremony and ritual that accompany them, the focus on a central value, and the interruption they bring to daily life contribute to an experience of communion among members of the audience that the authors describe as "reminiscent of holy days" (ibid.: 16). The same principle could apply more recently to the witnessing of events such as 9/11 or the British royal wedding in 2011. The live coverage of these events, this time on multiple platforms, might have led to a sense (albeit perhaps only fleeting) of connection among global members of the audience who knew other people around the world were experiencing the same scenes at the very same moment.

But a sense of community can also be supported by objects as material as a building, like a temple in the case of a religious community (Calhoun 1991a: 112), or as immaterial as memories of events. An example of the latter is the very name chosen by the Greek terrorist organisation, 17 November. The date, evoking the authorities' bloody repression of student protests that took place in 1973 at the Athens polytechnic, also serves as a powerful reminder of the common ideological commitment of the group's members, both within the organisation and externally (Council on Foreign Relations, n.d.).

Face-to-face communication, communication technologies, and media coverage, however, occupy another place on the social map (Figure 3.1, area B). They allow the acquisition of new information (through conversation, surfing the Internet, reading the newspaper, watching TV ...), which will be interpreted via the relational perspective occupied by the individual at any specific time. It is at this point that an individual can come into contact with other narratives.

They might be other actors' individual narratives (belonging to our friends and acquaintances, for instance), but also collective narratives (related to the sense of belonging of a democratic society, for example, or sustained by the traditions of an ethnic minority, the rituals of a religious group, and so on). The collective narratives might be promoted, as in the case of political movements (including terrorist organisations), for specific mobilisation purposes. I will come back to this in a moment in discussing collective narratives.

Any incoming information, including other actors' narratives, will never be absorbed as it is but filtered and appropriated through the prism of the individual narrative. This might, over time, lead to a change in the vision of the world of the individual, reflected in his/ her changing patterns of social relationships, development of a revised identity, individual narrative, behaviour, and so forth in a continuous cycle. Partly as a result of our action, partly as the outcome of the simultaneous action by all the actors within our networks, the relationships' maps are constantly changing. This leads to our identity being continuously evolving, together with the way we interpret the world around us and the way we act. Such evolving of our interpretation also includes a continuous reworking of the past, as well as of our projections of future action trajectories (Emirbayer and Mische 1998). This is reflected in a continuously and progressively changing individual narrative. Figure 3.2 shows the way in which different networks lead to different identities, interpretations of the world, and consequent behaviour.[10]

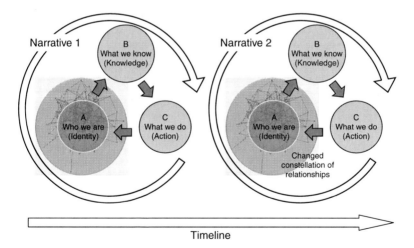

Figure 3.2 Evolution of the individual narrative over time

As identities exist at both individual and collective levels, so do narratives. Collective identities are at the same time constructed out of individual identities and constitute the context within which such individual identities are formed. As Sciolla (1983 in Schlesinger 1991: 152) explains it:

> There is ... the possibility of conceiving collective identity as a result of complex processes, that is as constituted by an autonomous drawing up of boundaries and construction of symbols which nevertheless interacts with the expectations and projections of given individuals and with which it might also come into conflict, in a sort of unstable equilibrium whose outcomes could be either the modification of individual identity (in the extreme case, quitting the group) or the modification of the group's own identity (in the extreme case, the dissolution of its collective identity).

Being a member of a group means sharing a common collective narrative while at the same time having an individual narrative that is compatible with it (Figure 3.3).

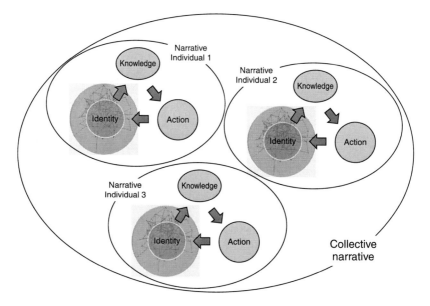

Figure 3.3   Compatibility between individual narratives and collective narrative within a group

In this perspective, according to Alberto Melucci, social movements (including terrorist groups) "offer individuals the collective possibility of affirming themselves as actors and of finding an equilibrium between self-recognition and hetero-recognition" (Melucci 1982 in Schlesinger 1991: 154). If, over time, the collective and individual narratives, in their continuous evolution, come to diverge, the dissonance between them will lead the individual to not identify any longer with the group (Figure 3.4).

Those who develop an individual politically extremist narrative as a result of a time- and place-specific constellation of relationships can either interact face-to-face in a group or indirectly through the phone or the Internet. Alternatively, or in addition to this, they might just feel part of a broader community of extremists they have never met and which coalesces around political symbols. It is important to understand that sharing a common collective narrative with a group does not mean deleting the peculiar features that uniquely characterise the individual narrative of each of the members of the group. In this respect, Anna Cento Bull, in analysing the self-narratives of three Italian neo-fascists

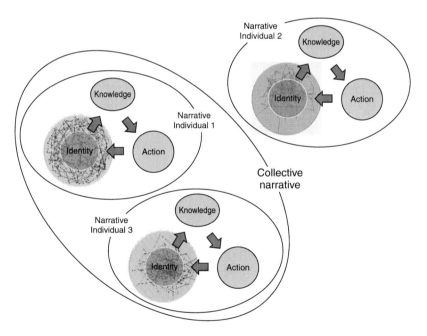

Figure 3.4 Changing membership of a group over time: compatibility/dissonance of individual narratives with a collective narrative

in the 1960s and 1970s, demonstrates that the narratives of the three individuals maintain their own uniqueness, even if they embrace the same radical ideology – which we might think of as a collective narrative. She points out, for example, the differences between the self-narratives of Vincenzo Vinciguerra and Luigi Ciavardini. Vinciguerra's narrative is highly ideological and characterised by three "myths": "the myth of the hero overcoming adversity; the myth of the martyr, ready to die in defence of his faith; and finally, the myth of Christ, who was betrayed by his disciples and died to show the way to the whole humankind" (ibid.: 191). Ciavardini, instead, strongly downplays ideology as a motivation for engaging in terrorist activity:

> We [Ciavardini and Vale, another neo-fascist] did not have a political project[;] ... we are [*sic*] taking the distance from politics. I was getting close to being spontaneous [*spontaneismo*]. To get armed, to attack, to steal. Living my own way against all and everybody. Together with a group, cemented, united certainly by its being a group of the Right, but above all by the common life experiences, of bravery, displayed day by day. Between myself and Drake [Vale] there was a relationship that went beyond ... extremism. (Semprini 2003 in Cento Bull 2009: 193, my translation)

A terrorist group is here approached as a social movement which operates within opportunity structures that are not only shaped by material reality (the availability of explosives for instance, or the fall of a government), but also by perceptions about relationships both real and imagined. Audrey Cronin (2006), in explaining the reasons why terrorism ends, presents the example of the Red Army Faction (RAF) as a case in which there was a failure to transition the terrorist "cause" to the next generation. She mentions *in passim*, in a footnote, that "the dissolution of the Soviet Union severely undermined its [the group's] ideology" (ibid.: 23, n.50). In the framework presented here the explanation for the decline of terrorism is not the failure to pass the cause to the next generation (what would explain that, by the way?), but what must have been perceived as the loss of credibility of the symbols that had thus far brought together and motivated the armed struggle of an imagined community of communism supporters.

Terrorist groups, as individuals, also undergo a continuous evolution of their identity, vision of the world, and political action as an outcome of changing relationships with other actors in the political arena. The relevant "others" of a terrorist group's relationships are authorities, other terrorist groups, institutions, individuals, publics, ideas, and symbols. This is well illustrated by the shifts in the self-identity and corresponding political action of the Red Brigades in Italy between the early 1970s and the early 1980s. Alison Jamieson (2007) in this respect identifies first a "social period" (1970–74) in which the *Brigatisti* saw themselves as "the torch-bearers of the partisan revolutionary tradition, champions of a working class abandoned by the PCI [Partito Comunista Italiano – Italian Communist Party] to the mercies of rampant capitalism, and the front line of defence against an enemy which was both fascist and institutional" (ibid.: 512). The group's identity evolves then through the 1975–79 "existential phase" in which, according to Jamieson, the gap between the insiders of the organisations ("us") and the wider society ("them") has widened so much that there are "no longer men and women with everyday emotions but a series of 'functions' operating within an inimical homogeneous mass which was 'the enemy'" (ibid.: 514). The third "survivalist" phase (1980s onwards) sees the extension of the terrorist group's cause to "calls of support for the Palestinian cause, criticism of militarization of land and space, of labour legislation and of environmental neglect" (ibid.: 517). Jamieson develops this chronology in detail and explains these shifts through a progressively decaying moral identity within the group. My analysis would both distance itself from taking a moral stance on what was "heroic" or "criminal" and take a further step back: what was leading to the change in identity? An alternative interpretation of the same events involves reading such changes as a reflection of the Red Brigades' shifting political alliances: the kidnap and later release of Fiat personnel director Ettore Amerio in 1973, the first phase, led to the revocation of 400 redundancies at Fiat. This "triumph" (ibid.: 512) proved the bargaining power of the terrorist group and led to the perception of widespread support among the workers. As Jamieson writes "kidnap requests flooded in daily from factories all over the country" (ibid.). During the second period, however, "many extraparliamentary groups of the 'new left' had dissolved and their members mostly re-absorbed into conventional politics. Others felt stranded and directionless, and looked on in dismay as the PCI's reformism brought in huge electoral gains" (ibid.: 515). In the second half of the 1970s the Red Brigades started to realise that they were losing their popular support. This was further confirmed by the fact that the appeal for the workers to rise in their support issued in occasion of the kidnapping of Prime Minister Aldo Moro in 1978 fell on deaf ears (ibid.: 516). On this point also Michel Wieviorka (1992: 165) argues that "measuring" the distance between the working class and the Italian far left is essential to understanding the Moro kidnapping and assassination. Authorities also pursued a firm non-negotiation strategy. The move, in the early 1980s, to incorporate international issues in the terrorist group's political manifesto can finally be seen as an attempt to tap into alternative networks of support.

This outline of a communication model to read the phenomenon of terrorism in an alternative way has several analytical repercussions. It also affects the way the relationship between media and terrorism should be conceived. They will be tackled next.

3.2.2   The practical implications of a communication approach

There are six major implications of a relational understanding of terrorism. The first is that no prediction of the eruption of terrorism can be made on the basis of either individual characteristics and structural factors alone. When Andrew Silke (2004a: 23, his emphasis), writing about the achievements and failures of terrorism research, states that "good science is fundamentally all about prediction. Good science *allows* reliable prediction. Terrorism research has generally been very poor when it comes to predicting future trends," and when Martha Crenshaw (1981: 379) suggests that a "comparison of different cases of terrorism" can lead to identifying "a common pattern of causation from the historically unique," they assume the social world to be much simpler and predictable than it actually is. By no means alone in their belief, they are well-known representatives of the methodological influence of (American) political science within terrorism studies. As Tololyan (1988: 217) notes, "political science seems all too eager for a model, or at best a few models, that will enable generalizations suitable to its empirical discourse and instrumental aims." But the very belief that the social world is predictable and that comparison can be used to infer causes is, in itself, a paradigm based on a positivist view of reality. Far from being a statement about the truth or objectivity of the social world, it is a conceptual construction that took place in Western Europe at the time of Cartesium in the seventeenth century (Joas and Knöbl 2009: 125–126). As Margaret Somers and Gloria Gibson (1994: 45–52) further demonstrate, even the distinction between individual agency on the one hand and structural constraints on the other, which characterises all modern Sociology, is part of a broader, constructed metanarrative of modernity. As they explain the point:

> Sociology's discovery of the social actor emerged from a convergence of mushrooms, reason, and revolution. In the first case, the

Hobbesian abstraction ("Let us ... consider men ... as if but even now sprung out of the earth ... like mushrooms ... without all kinds of engagement to each other") celebrated the emancipator vision contained in the idea of the self-interested individual free to create his/her world anew. Second, the Kantian critique positing reason over the naturalism of Hobbes's ontology appealed to progressive minds and lodged the idea of the morally autonomous modern individual on firm grounds. Finally the French Enlightenment sealed the amalgamation: Voltaire's, Diderot's, and Rousseau's free self was driven naturally to repel the force of political authority, tradition, custom, and institutional bonds – all in the name of freedom from domination (ibid.: 48).

The dominant aspect within society, which the individual – the sociological "agent" – was trying to free itself from, would be taken on by the concept of "structure" (ibid.: 49–52).

If, however, one understands identity as relationally constructed through a set of relationships and corresponding evolving narratives, it becomes apparent that "there is no reason to assume a priori that people with similar attributes will share a common experience of social life unless they share narrative identities and relational settings" (ibid.: 79). In other words – which helps in explaining the failure of terrorism research to find a definite set of "causes" for terrorism – there are no individual characteristics that define the profile of the terrorist (Gartenstein-Ross and Grossman 2009: 56–57), and there are no given structural conditions in which terrorism will arise. As it has been noted, individuals who turn to terrorism might be the unemployed, excluded, alienated, vulnerable young people, but they could equally well be the educated, middle class, and even well-off (Bjørgo 2005a: 256; Sageman 2008: 48–50; Presidential Task Force 2009: 4; Beski-Chafiq et al. 2010b: 12). Extremism can develop in closed societies (Bonanate 1979), in democratic ones (Eubank and Weinberg 1994; Weinberg and Eubank 1998), or in both (Eyerman 1998; Bjørgo 2005a: 257). What matters is that terrorist action is the outcome of the constitution of an identity and a corresponding narrative that legitimises violent action. Where and when the constellation of relationships – both real and imagined – that will support the formation of that violence-based identity will materialise simply cannot be anticipated with mathematical certainty without reference to the specific milieu in which it develops.

The second implication is that radicalisation is not a state of mind only, but the temporal- and context-specific outcome of a constellation of relationships. As a study on radicalisation in Denmark notes, radicalisation is increasingly approached as an individual "problem" (Kühle and Lindekilde 2010: 26–27). This is the result of erroneously believing that individuals – they are also referred to as "lone wolves" (Pantucci 2011) – can radicalise "on their own," especially by interacting online and communicating with like-minded individuals over the Internet, or coming across extremist content and messages. An individual does not, however, act as an extremist because a message of extremism, as a form of virus, has taken hold of him/her. Acting out as an extremist is, again, the reflection of having developed the identity of an extremist: "people act in particular ways because not to do so would fundamentally violate their sense of being at that particular time and place" (Somers and Gibson 1994: 67). Calhoun (1991b), in an example that could easily apply to young individuals who decide to become "martyrs" for a terrorist cause, examines the way in which the political identity of Chinese students changed over the six weeks of protest leading to the events of Tiananmen Square in 1989. He is particularly interested in understanding how individuals who were not habitual risk-takers came to "be brave to the point of apparent foolishness" (ibid.: 53) and even risked (and indeed lost) their lives as a result of such behaviour. He explains how, through the very act of protest, the students came to see themselves as intellectuals with a responsibility towards the nation. As such, they understood their actions within a history of protest going far back in time: "when Chinese students in 1989 said that they were acting as 'the conscience of the nation,' and that this was not just a simple choice but a responsibility they had to live up to, they were speaking in line with a long tradition" (ibid.: 55).

The further and third implication is that there are no radicalising messages. It is often argued that videos are more "radicalising" than text. For instance, Rita Katz, Director of the Search for Internet Terrorist Entities Institute (SITE) in a statement prepared for the US Congress in 2007 (Committee on Homeland Security 2007: 21) stated that "the propaganda in jihadi videos is compelling, convincing, and able to be accessed in a growing number of languages." More recently, Anthony Lemieux and Robert Nill (2011: 144) underlined the role of music in jihadi propaganda, particularly its role in leading individuals exposed to the lyrics to "engage in deeper processing and consideration." But no message, in and of itself, is either "convincing" or able to connect at a deeper emotional level with an individual. Whichever information and messages one receives will be filtered through the lenses of an individual's identity and point of view from a specific "corner" of the social world. The very fact of being "convincing" or "moving" is relative and depends on the relationship between the message and the individual narrative. Individuals who have become extremists do not necessarily need to be exposed to extremist material to reinforce their conviction and perhaps take violent action. They can just watch the news and find confirmation of their interpretation of what happens in the world around them. For example Nizar Trabelsi, accused of plotting to bomb a military base in Belgium in the name of Al Qaeda, stated during his trial that he had decided to carry out the attack after seeing pictures of a Palestinian baby girl who was killed in the Gaza Strip in 2001 (*BBC News* 2003). It is not clear exactly where Trabelsi saw those pictures. Yet, it is very likely that many more people (perhaps even tens of thousands if the images had been broadcast over the daily news) must have been exposed to the same images and did not become "radicalised" by them. The extent to which what one might consider the "objective" content of a message can change when filtered through a personal narrative, is illustrated by Tololyan (1988: 218), who emphasises how images and information can be projected into a whole new world in which even spatial and temporal coordinates are different: "It can be a revanchist's vision of a land that he has never seen or the aspiration of the alienated ecologist seeking a land unmarked by society. Not only the time and place that are immediate, but absent times and places, as well as projected times and places, provide the context which is the domain in which a cultural vision can produce terrorists."

The fourth point: there are no radicalising technologies. This applies in two respects: in relation to the content carried by communication technologies and in relation to the role of technologies in establishing links among individuals. Let us examine them in turn. First, despite the idea that content over the Internet is somehow more dangerous and potentially radicalising due to its multi media nature, the extent to which any content, whether video, images, text on a screen or written on paper, will have any effect on the way of thinking of an individual, again, depends on the individual's identity and position within a constellation of networks. Who one is, which is shaped by the constellation of relationships one has established, affects what one knows and one's interpretation of any incoming information. This will affect what one does (one's behaviour) which, in turn, will change one's identity and view of the world in a continuous cycle. So the new incoming information might well, over time, affect the behaviour of a person, but the individual is always the ultimate gatekeeper. In relation to the second aspect, the Internet, indeed, allows individuals to establish connections across distances, possibly with a large number of people. From the point of view of the framework presented here, there is no distinction between the online and offline dimensions. Both domains are just social space. In fact relationships do not have to be "real" and necessarily based on contact, whether constituted by an email, a chat over the phone, or face-to-face conversation. One can feel connected with individuals and collective publics without the need of any actual exchange. As an example we can think about the inspiring role that previous "martyrs" can have on an extremist, even if one has never met them, or the sense of acting in defence of the ummah. This consideration leads to a fifth point.

In the understanding of social reality outlined by this chapter there is no distinction between "real" and "imagined" relationships. This is important to remind us that there are not only direct relationships among extremists, as they could exist within the "bunches of guys" described by Sageman in his *Leaderless Jihad* (2008: 69–70), but also indirect relationships: we can think about the followers, online and offline, of extremist preachers. An example is offered by the case of Britain's Roshanara Choudhry. According to what she said in a police interview, the online sermons of Yemeni extremist cleric Anwar Al-Awlaki contributed to her decision to stab MP Steven Timms in May 2010 to punish him for supporting the Iraq War (Dodd 2010).

That is why, as a last implication, there are no "lone wolves" or "independent" cells. Even where direct or indirect exchanges are missing, individuals might not be alone in their minds. In fact, actions committed by single individuals, including their justifications, do not take place in a vacuum (COT 2007: 87). They can still belong to imagined communities of like-minded extremists. The Norwegian Anders Breivik, although having had contact with the British English Defence League (Hughes and Rayner 2011), appears to have planned and carried out on his own the Oslo city centre bombing and Utøya island killings in July 2011. Despite this, he opened his statement at the first public hearing of his trial in November 2011 by saying that he was the "commander in the Norwegian resistance movement" (Day 2011). While from a physical point of view he does not belong to a material network (even further stressed by his solitary confinement since the day of his arrest) his identity appears to be defined by imagined relationships with a range of "resistance fighters" he believes exist across his country and, according to his manifesto (Breivik 2011), Europe. True, one could say that his *2083: European Declaration of Independence* was simply delusional. The xenophobic ideas illustrated at length in it, however, are nonetheless very real and, indeed, shared by far right groups on both sides of the Atlantic (Shane 2011; Towsend and Traynor 2011).

3.2.3 Redefining the relationship between terrorism and the media

There is widespread recognition that terrorists depend on the media for achieving their objectives. There is merit to this statement. Publicity is extremely important to what violent extremists do. However, publicity is not the real cause of a group's increased political visibility. In fact, while high tension and human drama might secure a few immediate headlines, the very fact of getting access to the news in the longer term is not only the result of spilling blood. Newsworthiness, far from consisting in the mere actualisation of the maxim that "if it bleeds, it leads," should also be understood as a relational outcome. I am now going to explain these counterintuitive aspects by using the example of the PLO (Palestinian Liberation Organization).

Access to the media as the outcome, not the cause of increased political visibility

Bruce Hoffman (2006: 61), in what is regarded as a seminal text about terrorism, writes that "the advent of ... modern, international terrorism occurred on July 22, 1968." Hoffman is referring to the hijacking of an Israeli El Al flight en route from Rome to Tel Aviv by the Popular Front for the Liberation of Palestine (PFLP), one of the six groups that then constituted the PLO. He describes this event as a "bold political statement" (ibid.: 61) that radically departed from previous terrorist conduct insofar as the events were designed to involve symbolic targets and to address broader international audiences. This shift, according to Hoffman, was facilitated by improved TV and air transportation technologies:

> These dramatic tactical changes in terrorism were facilitated by the technological advances of the time that had transformed the speed and ease of international commercial air travel and vastly improved both the quality of television news footage and the promptness with which that footage could be broadcast around the globe. Accordingly, terrorists rapidly came to appreciate that operations perpetrated in countries other than their own and directly involving or affecting foreign nationals were a reliable means of attracting attention to themselves and their cause. (Ibid.: 64)

Hoffman further writes that this change was indeed "revolutionary," especially if one looks at the "depths of obscurity and international neglect from which the PLO emerged" (ibid.: 65). If, however, one closely examines the very analysis he proceeds to present, then the extent to which this statement reflects reality becomes rather dubious. In fact, as proof of the "obscurity" and "neglect," he lists the following (ibid.: 65–66):

- After the first Arab-Israeli war in 1949 between 700,000 and 950,000 Palestinians had left the Jewish State of Israel and relocated as displaced people across Jordan, Syria, Lebanon and Egypt. They lived in "wretched conditions" in refugee camps.
- A reference to their precarious situation was often strategically deployed by leaders in those neighbouring countries: "the Palestinian cause was a useful means by which to marshal international opprobrium against Israel and also to generate support among Arab states for greater regional unity against the common Zionist enemy." In addition to this their cause also "offered a convenient way to deflect attention from domestic problems by focusing popular discontent outward, against Israel, for the injustice done to the Palestinians."
- Within the refugee camps political movements and associations were established and groups of fedayeen (commandos) started to "carry out cross-border hit-and-run attacks on Israel."
- Egypt was both training and arming the fedayeen.
- By 1953 these attacks "had become sufficiently frequent and sufficiently lethal to attract Israeli military reprisals."
- Israel's interventions culminated in the 1956 Suez crisis, which gave Israel the opportunity to "invade the Sinai peninsula and eliminate the Egyptian bases supporting the fedayeen operations."
- Almost ten years later a similar pattern of attacks and Israel reprisals led to the 1967 Six Days War.

Hoffman's argument is that, despite the central role of Palestinian refugees in the politics of the whole Middle East, one major international crisis, and another war, "few outside the region took notice of, much less cared about, the Palestinians" (ibid.: 66). According to him, it was really the hijacking and the following murder of 11 Israeli athletes at the 1972 Olympic Games in Munich, both heavily covered by international media, that placed the Palestinian cause on the world's agenda.

This interpretation disproportionately emphasises the role of technology in shaping terrorist tactics. Hoffman is not alone in doing this. Another example is offered by David Rapoport (1988b) who, before him, argued that "terrorist groups developed an international dimension in the 1960s": "Weapons were cheaper, more destructive, easier to obtain and conceal .... Modern communications and transport allowed hitherto insignificant persons to coordinate activity quickly over vast spaces. Finally, by giving unusual events extensive coverage, the mass media completed this picture" (ibid.: 33). Exactly as did Hoffman, Rapoport (1988b) then presents an analysis of terrorist memoirs in which it is very clear than terrorism had had a strong international dimension well before the 1960s.

Both accounts can be challenged by examining the networks of political alliances that developed around the terrorist organisations over time. In Hoffman's chronology of events, such networks (including relationships of support, but also of opposition) grew and progressively enlarged their scope, culminating and becoming extreme through two outright conflicts. In this perspective the 1962 hijacking reflects both the grown political stature of the Palestinian activists – their acquired identity as a political player in the Middle East – over 20 years and the wider networks of support – including the state of Egypt – and relative resources behind the group. The fact that "few outside the region had taken notice" of the Palestinian cause is hard to believe, considering that the 1956 Suez crisis had directly involved France, the United Kingdom, Israel, and Egypt and had been subject to strong pressures from the United States, the Soviet Union, and the United Nations. Historical accounts of the crisis also identify the fedayeen attacks and retaliations as "significant factors in the outbreak of hostilities" (Tucker and Roberts 2008: 364, for instance).

The oxygen of publicity is in short supply

Although the 1972 Munich events in particular did generate headlines across the world due to the strong concentration of journalists at the Olympic Games, it is difficult to assess the effects that the images of the terrorists could have produced across the world. Hoffman (2006: 69) writes that "an estimated 900 million people in at least a hundred different countries saw the crisis unfold on their television screens .... Henceforth, those people throughout the world who before the games had neither known the Palestinians nor been familiar with their cause were no longer as ignorant or dismissive". The extent to which those audiences really became interested in the plight of the Palestinians is questionable. How much background about the terrorist organisation and the rationale for the killings did the coverage actually provide to the audiences of the different countries and media outlets? Even a brief glance at the coverage of the time is sufficient to reveal variations in the volume of coverage, as well as in focus, particularly the greater inter-est of some countries and media outlets in the human drama of the athletes rather than in the political aspects of the attack. For example, an American *ABC News* broadcast aired on 6 September and anchored by Howard Smith[11] opens by reporting about the political implication of the events: "[B]oth houses of Congress by unanimous vote adopt a resolution calling for world isolation of any nation encouraging ter-rorism" following the events in Munich. The further seven minutes of footage, however, focus on the changed atmosphere at the Olympics and do not even mention the motives of the terrorists. The gunmen are actually consistently called "guerrillas" by Peter Jennings reporting from the German city. By contrast, the Italian press does report the motives of "Black September," but the rationale for the attack appears secondary to the human drama that has taken place: the motives are covered across several outlets in short paragraphs on pages three to six of the newspaper editions,[12] while fuller articles stressing how the tragic events represented a betrayal of the spirit of brotherhood among nations that should have been celebrated through sport occupy either the front page[13] or the comments section.[14]

An alternative explanation to Hoffman's is that the sustained media interest in the Palestinian issue was not the result of the publicity stunt, but a reflection of the increasingly broader set of political alliances in which the PLO has become enmeshed over time. This argument is sup-ported by the fact that news is not a mirror to reality, but the result of a construction process. More specifically, although journalists are the ones who physically report about what happens in the world, the cri-teria they use to select what to report, how much space to give to each issue, and which sources to "let speak" within their stories, originate far beyond the newsroom. In this respect, a comparative study of the cover-age of 9/11 across the United States, Italy, France, and Pakistan (Archetti 2010) has led to, among other things, the identification of foreign policy – understood as the extent to which a country is involved in international alliances – as a major news shaper. In the specific case of the 9/11 coverage, the level of international involvement of a country – one can compare the multilateral foreign policy of France against the unilateral policy of the United States – influenced the cover-age by affecting the ratio of international rather than national sources reported in the stories. In this respect the French coverage was shaped by sources ranging from European Union, Middle Eastern and Asian leaders, to foreign media and Afghan resistance groups opposing the Taliban, while the US coverage presented sources mainly from within the country and the theatres of operations in Afghanistan and Pakistan. One can, with good reason, hypothesise that foreign policy orientation and alliances within international relations are also bound to have had an effect on the coverage of the Palestinian issue. In fact, as Hillel Nossek (2004) suggests, media outlets within countries that both support or oppose the Palestinian political project would find the issue more newsworthy than media outlets within countries that have no clear stance on the matter.

Alex Schmid (2004: 208, my emphasis) is therefore wrong in writing that:

> The media and the terrorists interact in a peculiar way. While it is true that everybody tries to use the media, the terrorists do so by spilling people's blood, mostly the blood of innocents. *The purposeful creation of bad events by means of terroristic violence can assure them free access to the news system.*

There is no such thing as "free access to the media." Newsworthiness depends on a journalist's (and a media organisation's) assessment of expected audience interest. It might appear that drama always sells in the short term. This outcome, however, is relative. There are terrorist actions being carried out every day, but we do not learn about all of them in the media. Those happening in obscure African countries or Latin America rarely make it into mainstream Western news unless they can be linked to Al Qaeda. The reason for the Islamist groups still being in the news is not so much the spectacularness of 9/11 or even the lethality of the organisation, which could indeed be questioned: John Mueller (2005: 220), in this respect, points out that "the total number of people worldwide who die at the hands of international terrorists is not much more than the number who drown in bathtubs in the United States." It is, instead, the political mobilisation that followed 11 September 2011, including a war that involved a coalition of over 60 countries.[15] It is this mobilisation and the consequent outpouring of substantial military, financial, and legal resources in the "war on terror" that has made Al Qaeda an international political player, not the group's alleged technological worldwide reach, or even its access to the Internet.

3.2.4   How, then, to study terrorism?

The fact that it is not possible to foresee with positivist certainty when and where a terrorist attack will take place does not mean that terrorism cannot be studied or that indicators of the development of an extremist identity cannot be identified and triangulated to assemble at least a grainy picture of the narrative of specific individuals or groups.

The framework presented suggests that the development of an extremist identity can be detected through the content of narratives. They can be examined at either individual or group level: for instance, in the case of individual narratives of terrorist suspects, through personal communications or blog postings; in the case of group narratives, through political manifestos or leaders' public statements. At either level what a researcher should find out is: Who is the actor in question (either the individual or the group)? What is his/her/its place in society? Who are the "others?" What is the world like (players, significant events ...)? Which political, social boundaries are relevant? The narrative also gives an idea of the actors, real or imagined, with whom either the individual or the group's members have relationships with. The network, in turn, can provide clues about the sources from whom either the individual or the group members receive information, which helps explaining their understanding of the world and consequent behaviour.[16]

All of this, however, is dynamic and should be studied over time. Particularly the changes over time are significant. A change of identity might be signalled by a shift in the content of the narrative and/or an evolving pattern in the network of relationships. Such a network is not only made up of the people with whom either an individual or the members of a group are in contact, but also by indirect relationships and the sense of belonging to imagined communities. The pattern of relationships cannot, therefore, be mapped only through surveillance, but needs to include an analysis of the extremist worldview. The relationship between the (ever changing) network of relationships and the (continuously evolving) resulting narrative within specific time and social contexts further emphasises the importance of local and community approaches to both examining the phenomenon of terrorism and countering it. These aspects are going to be further developed in the following pages.

These three initial chapters have focused on conceptual issues. In the rest of the book I am moving closer to practical matters by showing the utility of the framework presented. I will apply it to understanding radicalisation (Chapter 4), particularly through demonstrating the key role of narratives in better explaining the process of becoming an extremist (Chapter 5). In the last part of the book (Chapter 6) I will show how the alternative way of understanding terrorism presented in this chapter can support the empirical analysis of the content of narratives, the measurement of the strength of a group's identity, and an assessment of progress in counterterrorism.

4
Explaining Radicalisation

Why do people join terrorist groups? This chapter discusses current analyses of the process through which apparently ordinary individuals come to embrace extremist beliefs – radicalisation. The purpose here is twofold: to show the weaknesses of current analyses of radicalisation and to demonstrate the applicability of the communication model outlined in Chapter 3. To these ends, I will first briefly discuss the concept of radicalisation and the crucial role played by communication, regardless of how the process of becoming an extremist is defined. I then critically examine two main strands of research: the point of the analysis is to demonstrate that the communication model synthesizes in a holistic framework notions and arguments that are already developed, but which, on their own, only explain part of the story.[1]

The first strand of research to be discussed directly tackles the role of the media in spreading the terrorists' message. While it provides insights into the mechanisms of information distribution in a global communication environment, this literature tends to limit itself to identifying the "message" – the "ideology," the "narrative," or the "extremist content" – as the psychological trigger to radicalisation. In some approaches simple exposure to extremist content is regarded as a sufficient condition for radicalisation. This set of studies tends to neglect the fact that individuals actively select and appropriate external information (they do not simply receive it), and that group interactions affect its subsequent interpretation. Such approaches appear, from a sociological point of view, rather shallow. The second strand, instead, provides sociologically more sophisticated explanations of how individuals become involved in political action. This literature addresses the formation of collective identities and mobilisation. Yet, as it does not explicitly engage with communication and the role of the media, it cannot satisfactorily account for the creation of group identities and collective action on a cross-national and global scale.

The discussion highlights the shortcomings of both approaches and argues that the concept of "narrative" – a relationally constructed interpretation of the world that can exist both at an individual and at a collective level – can help providing an analytical bridge between them. The chapter closes with an assessment of the implications that a narrative-based explanation of radicalisation means both for the understanding of extremism and for counterterrorism.

4.1 Radicalisation and communication

The notion of "radicalisation," and the associated terms of "counter-radicalisation" and "de-radicalisation," have become so widespread in official circles, journalistic jargon, and think tank reports that one could be forgiven for thinking that a "radicalisation process" must have an objective existence; that, as such, it can be identified; and that there must be sufficient knowledge about it to inform targeted policies to prevent it. These reasonable inferences, however, are not at all supported by the state of research on radicalisation. A closer look at official documents and current studies reveals a lack of agreement, not only on what radicalisation actually consists of, but also on its causes. Regardless of what radicalisation involves, there is also a general failure to acknowledge communication as a fundamental aspect in both the adoption of extremist beliefs and their translation into violent action.

The problem of finding a consensus on what radicalisation exactly refers to can be better illustrated by an anecdote. In March 2010, I participated, together with other researchers, in a Prevent Research Seminar organised by UK Home Office, Office for Security and Counter-terrorism (OSCT) in London. The purpose of the event was to share expertise and encourage networking between academia and government to help understand the way in which extremist views develop and lead to terrorist violence. A speaker from the OSCT told the participants that what causes radicalisation is "well known" to authorities. Indeed, the academics were later invited to take part in a tabletop exercise in which they were provided with a list of 43 factors that could lead to terrorism violence. These factors had been compiled by the Counter-terrorism Office by consulting existing terrorism studies and through interviews with experts. They ranged from an "identity crisis" (of second generation immigrants, for example), a "breakdown of the relationship with the father" (lack of a protective figure, which makes individuals more vulnerable to violent extremism), to a "lack of housing" (inadequate provision of physical security, fuelling a sense of relative deprivation), to perceptions of a country's "foreign policy" (the notion that the United Kingdom or the United States, together with political allies, are attacking Muslim countries, for instance). As the spokesman continued, authorities "knew" what the causes of terrorism were. What they did not know was which factors were "more important" than others and "how they were connected." From the point of view of the arguments presented in this book, this means not having an explanation (or theory) of radicalisation. The academics, divided into groups, were then asked to pick the five factors they thought were most important, and to arrange them in causal order. The complete diversity of the charts I saw by looking across the tables suggests that anything even remotely resembling an agreement is still very far from being reached. A review of the literature confirms that there are myriad different suggestions, not only in terms of defining what radicalisation is, but also how it actually takes place.

The current UK government's *Prevent* strategy (Home Office 2011: 108) defines radicalisation in general terms as "the process by which a person comes to support terrorism and forms of extremism leading to terrorism." This phrasing closely reflects the European Commission's: radicalisation is "the phenomenon of people embracing opinions, views and ideas which could lead to acts of terrorism" (European Commission 2008 in Kühle and Lindekilde 2010: 24). The London think tank, International Centre for the Study of Radicalisation and Political Violence (ICSR), provides only a slightly more nuanced suggestion, which distinguishes between the adoption of radical ideas and their actual implementation through acts of violence: "the process (or processes) whereby individuals or groups come to approve of and (ultimately) participate in the use of violence for political aims. Some authors refer to 'violent radicalisation' in order to emphasise the violent outcome and distinguish the process from non-violent forms of 'radical' thinking" (Stevens and Neumann 2009: 10).[2] From the other side of the Atlantic, a report of the Foundation for Defense of Democracies (FDD) (Gartenstein-Ross and Grossman 2009: 7) argues that radicalisation "implies not only extreme beliefs, but extreme action." The latter does not just involve violence, such as turning into a suicide bomber, but also "it refers to the process of adopting for oneself or inculcating in others a commitment not only to a system of beliefs, but to their imposition on the rest of society" (ibid.).

In continental Europe some definitions incorporate the mention of democratic values. The Municipality of Amsterdam (2007: 18), for instance, talks about the phenomenon as "the growing preparedness to strive for and/or support deep interventional changes in society that are at odds with the democratic legal order and/or whereby undemocratic means are employed." The Danish government, which tends to use the term "extremism" to refer to radicalisation, expresses similar views. They extend beyond the religiously inspired radicalism:

> Extremism is characterized by totalitarian and anti-democratic ideologies, intolerance of others' views, enemy images, and divisions into "them and us." Extremist ideas can be expressed in different ways and may, in the extreme, lead to individuals or groups using violent or undemocratic methods to achieve a specific political purpose, seeking to undermine the democratic order or engage threats, violence and degrading harassment of groups of people because of, for example, their skin colour, sexuality, or belief. (Regeringen 2009 in Kühle and Lindekilde 2010: 23–24)

The real object of contention is the way in which processes described by these definitions actually translate into action – in other words the causal mechanisms of radicalisation. Why would any individual support terrorism? More specifically, why would an ordinary citizen adopt radical ideas? Why would one approve of violence? The explanations vary. A widely quoted report by the New York Police Department (NYPD), *Radicalization in the West: The Homegrown Threat* (Silber and Bhatt 2007), for example, suggests a four-stage model of radicalisation. Although, as the report states, the model is "sequential," individuals do not necessarily have to follow it in a "linear progression" (ibid.: 6). The stages are: (a) Pre-radicalisation: the life situation before adopting a "jihadi–Salafist" ideology; (b) self-identification: the state in which "individuals, influenced by both internal and external factors, begin to explore Salafi Islam, gradually gravitate away from their old identity and begin to associate themselves with like-minded individuals and adopt this ideology as their own"; (c) indoctrination: the progressive intensification of an individual's radical believes and the conviction that "militant jihad" is required to further pursue the ideological cause; (d) jihadisation: the self-designation as "holy warrior" that, in practice, consists of planning, preparing, and carrying out a terrorist attack (ibid.: 6–7) (Figure 4.1).

A "Radicalisation and Mobilisation Dynamics Framework" elaborated by the US National Counterterrorism Centre (NCTC) (n.d.), provides a

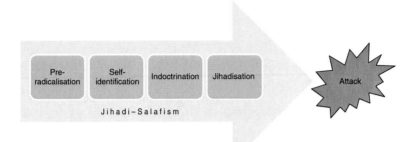

Figure 4.1 "Radicalisation process" (New York Police Department)

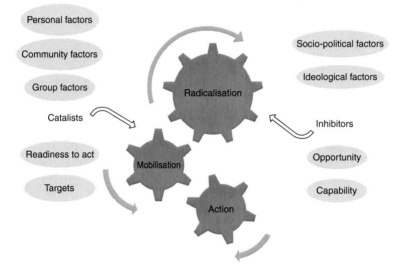

Figure 4.2 "Radicalisation and mobilisation dynamics framework" (US National Counterterrorism Centre)

more "fluid" model which involves "a dynamic and multi-layered process involving several factors that interact with one another to influence an individual. There is no single factor that explains radicalization and mobilization." In this perspective, "personal," "community," "group," "socio-political," and "ideological" factors lead to "radicalisation." This, in turn, leads to "mobilisation" (to which "readiness to act," "opportunity," "capability," and "targets" further contribute). All aspects eventually lead to "action" (Figure 4.2).

In sharp contrast with these models is the explanation of radicalisation elaborated by Selma Belaala (2008) in a comparative study of radicalisation in France, Spain, and the United Kingdom.[3] The previous suggestions consider radicalisation as a process that might involve different factors and "paths," but the final outcome is, essentially, the same. Belaala's approach, instead, ties the phenomenon of radicalisation to the combination of historical, political, and cultural circumstances within a specific local context. As such, it can produce different outcomes. Belaala's stance, deeply rooted in ethnography, is inspired by the "interactionist school of the European cultural anthropology," particularly by the work of Frederich Barth (1970). She describes the utility of his approach in "enabling the examination of the cultural identity of social groups not as an immutable entity but as a transformation process based on the relationships with the world outside and the interactions with other groups" (Belaala 2008: 19, n. 23). She explains radicalisation, within the context of the town and regions (across France, Spain, and the UK) used as her case studies, as the outcome of a "double rupture": a process that involves detachment from the family but also from the national community. Radicalisation, in this perspective, essentially consists in a reworking of the individual's *political* rather than religious identity. As Belaala writes:

> radicalisation is both an individual and collective process of identity construction that involves a social rupture in the relationship of the individual with his/her fellow citizens. The radicalized young people reject others on a cultural and political basis. They oppose their values and even develop antagonism towards their own families and local communities. They equally reject other cultural groups both locally and in the rest of society: Jews, Hindu, or moderate Muslims. (Ibid: 18)

In practice, depending on the context, radicalisation can translate into different thinking and behaviour. Belaala shows, for instance, that radicalisation in the "micro-local" isolation of small towns (like the Parisian *banlieu* or a town like Crawley [4,000 inhabitants] in Britain) and larger centres (like the Spanish Ceuta and Melilla [around 70,000 inhabitants]) can consist in the development, by individuals and groups, of a deformed interpretation of the armed conflicts taking place in the Muslim world. For individuals involved in criminality, however, radicalisation can also mean providing a political justification for theft, aggression, and social violence. As part of the process, these individuals tend to attribute to their victims the label of "political enemy." In this case, as the author puts it: "radicalisation becomes the ideological and political justification for the control [by the radicals] of a local area and its resources" (ibid.: 7).

The comparison among different explanations of radicalisation shows two important points that will be further developed in the rest of the chapter. The first is that understanding radicalisation involves the combination of different perspectives: not only examining psychological changes at the level of the individual, but also the broader constellation of relationships in which an individual is located in the specificity of a geographical and temporal context. The second point is the relevance of communication across the board: the models presented show the relevance of the transmission of ideas and beliefs (in the NYPD's "self-identification" and "jihadisation" phases, for example) as well as perceptions (in the NCTC's "mobilisation" phase). Communication is also key in the implementation of extremist ideologies, particularly in the planning and organisation of a terrorist plot (NYPD's "jihadisation," or the NCTC's "action"). Most importantly, communication – or the lack of it, in the case of the isolated youths in French, British, and Spanish small towns – leads to interpretations of the outside world that can support the development of a distinct individual and collective identity.

The purpose of the following analysis is to stress further the limitations of current approaches by reviewing two main lines of research. The individual and collective levels of analysis they respectively represent should not be taken too strictly as mutually exclusive categories, but as the extreme ends of a continuum within which research about radicalisation can be positioned. Some studies (like Sageman 2004, 2008; Horgan 2009, for instance), in fact, attempt to integrate both dimensions and would stand close to the middle ground. The point is not that the arguments are wrong or that they do not throw light on the phenomenon of violent extremism. Simply they are, on their own, incomplete. The final part of the chapter will suggest a synthesis.

4.2 Explaining extremism I: persuasion, and the terrorist message

When it comes to explaining radicalisation, a first line of research concentrates on the individual level of analysis – perhaps only extending to include those who, in close proximity to the individual, belong to a terrorist cell – at the expense of an examination of the broader relationships and collective identities in which a person is entangled.

This strand does not necessarily use the language of psychology, but de facto tends to address the cognitive effects of the terrorist message on the individual. Because of this focus on the "delivery" of radical ideas, the studies at this end of the spectrum of explanations about radicalisation involve several claims about the role of communication, either face-to-face or mediated. I am going to illustrate them by referring to the aspects that are identified as key drivers of radicalisation: the resonance of a message of grievance promoted by terrorist organisations with vulnerable audiences; establishing relationships with like-minded individuals (or becoming part of a terrorist network); the exposure to extremist ideologies through global media, particularly through the Internet; and the perception of belonging to a discriminated community.

The impact of a "narrative of grievance" on impressionable targets is emphasised, for instance, by *The United Kingdom's Strategy for Countering International Terrorism* (Home Office 2009: 35). The document states that Al Qaeda has "a detailed public narrative that claims to justify the killing of civilians and the means to disseminate that narrative quickly and widely into homes in this country": "vulnerable institutions and public places ... provide a platform for their [terrorist] propaganda." There are numerous references throughout the document to the "grievances" that Al Qaeda "ideologues" are exploiting in order to target "vulnerable" individuals (ibid.: 14). The US Department of State Country Report on Terrorism (2008: 11) also underlines the "increasing evidence of terrorists and extremists manipulating the grievances of alienated youth or immigrant populations." The idea of vulnerability and alienation, especially in young people, is widespread (Homeland Security Institute 2009; Alexander 2010; Royal Canadian Mounted Police 2011; Thompson 2011).

Marc Sageman (2004), the most visible representative of the network approach, talks about the spontaneous self-organisation of informal groups of trusted individuals from the bottom up as the fabric of a "leaderless jihad" (2008: 69). Sageman's work is not limited to the individual level of analysis insofar as he refers to the global Salafi jihad as a "social movement" (2004: 137). In his *Understanding Terror Networks*, the author states that: "Participants in the global jihad are not atomized individuals but actors linked to each other through complex webs of direct or mediated exchanges" (ibid.). As he explains, while face-to-face communication and personal contacts are important, small local and self-organised groups are able to link to a "disconnected global network" (Sageman 2008: 143) through new communication technologies – what he calls a "leaderless Jihad." The Internet, particularly, he continues, has made "possible a new type of relationship between an individual and a virtual community" (Sageman 2004: 160). He writes, as an example: "E-mail was routine among the members of the Hamburg clique [where some of the 9/11 hijackers began their extremist activities] and helped them sustain emotional closeness and common beliefs despite physical separation by communicating shared meanings, past events, and internal jokes. In the past, letters fulfilled the same function. Through its speed of expression and response, e-mail goes a step further by reducing time spent waiting for the intimate partner's reply" (ibid.: 159).

Exposure to extremist ideologies is another of the alleged causes that can lead to the development of extremism. This aspect is particularly stressed by studies about online radicalisation. The Internet is suitable to the spreading of radical content for the same reasons that have led to this technology's popularity with civil society organisations and the general public: it makes the exchange and dissemination of content "virtually free"; it enables access to knowledge and know-how; it facilitates networking with like-minded individuals across distances and national borders; and it lowers the threshold for engaging in risky behaviour because of its anonymity (Stevens and Neumann 2009: 11). The extent of the "culpability" of the Internet in promoting extremism varies across the literature. A report about "Countering Internet Radicalisation in Southeast Asia" by the Australian Strategic Policy Institute, for example, drawing on Maura Conway and Lisa McInerney (2008), emphasises the role of technology in the phenomenon of "auto-radicalisation" (Bergin et al. 2009: 4). The idea, elsewhere referred to as "self-radicalisation," is often linked to cases of extremists who appear not to have had any obvious link to Al Qaeda, but who have accessed extremist material online. A widely cited example of the use of the Internet to radicalise new followers is that of British citizen, Younis Tsoulis ("Irhabi007"), who was arrested and convicted in 2007 under the Terrorism Act for inciting terrorism. His activities, although confined to cyberspace, consisted of setting up jihadi websites, distributing video content, and "inciting others to follow an extreme ideology of violent holy war against so-called disbelievers" (Crown prosecutor Ellison in Dodd 2007). The more recent case of the American major Nidal Malik Hasan, who killed 13 people at Fort Hood in Texas on 5 November 2009, has raised the issue of the effects of mediated content on "lone wolves" (COT 2007; Pantucci 2011). Evan Kohlmann (2009), for instance, writes: "The cleric's [Anwar Al-Awlaki] recurring presence again in the Ft. Hood case seems to be powerful and disturbing evidence of how fringe extremist – who otherwise might remain in obscurity with no real means of living out their private jihadi fantasies – are quite literally being equipped for battle by so-called 'theological' advisors known only to them through the Internet. In short, it is a reminder of how real online terrorism networks have become". What makes the Internet especially suitable to recruitment, from the point of view of these studies, tends to be its multimediality. In an example of how simplistic this interpretation can be, Anne Speckhard (2011: 166) writes that: "the emotion-packed imagery in their [Al Qaeda's] Internet 'products' is enough to cause secondary traumatisation in viewers, galvanizing them to action."

News media, according to Farhad Khosrokhavar (2005), play a central role in the perception of belonging to a discriminated community. As he writes: "the media become a spokesman for the downtrodden Muslims whose sufferings are shown on television day in, day out" in what he terms "humiliation by proxy" (ibid.: 157). The fact that the coverage of conflicts in Palestine, Chechnya, Bosnia, and Iraq has contributed to building this perception is confirmed by statements made by terrorists and radicalised individuals. One of the 7/7 London bombers, Mohammed Siddique Khan, for example, said in a video recorded before his death: "Your democratically elected governments continuously perpetuate atrocities against my people all over the world" (*BBC News* 2005a). In a recent BBC2 documentary, "Generation Jihad" (Taylor 2010), an extremist from Halifax (West Yorkshire, UK) recalls the shooting, captured on camera, of Mohammed Al-Durrah by Israeli soldiers in September 2000:

> Mohamed Al-Durrah is a blatant example. It's, like, if you can't see what's happening now you might then well go back to sleep or you are living in zombieland because this is blatant for you to see. When a father is protecting his son, and he is telling them [soldiers] to back off, and you now see the sniper shooting blatantly at him ... I know that Mohamed Al-Durrah is shot every day. Mohamed Al-Durrah is all over the place. Just one got caught on camera. (Ibid.)

These perceptions also appear to resonate with individual experiences of social discrimination (Sageman 2008: 99–106).

Although there is widespread agreement that all these drivers of extremism are somehow related, it is not clear how they are connected and, most importantly, how they produce actual engagement with terrorist activities. Joining a terrorist network also means sharing ideas and a whole vision of the world. Sageman (2004: 158), for example, says: "Social networks are complex communicative networks that create shared worlds of meaning and feelings, which in turn shape identity, perceptions, and preferences." Exposure to extremist content, some-times through actual social interaction, sometimes only through the mediation of technologies, appears to be able to lead, in some cases whose circumstances are not well defined, to extremist behaviour. What is precisely the link between the "message" and the action?

4.3   Explaining extremism II: theories of mobilisation

A second strand of terrorism-related literature attempts to explain how individuals become engaged with terrorist groups through social move-ments and mobilisation theories. These accounts are more sophisti-cated, as the following examples will show.

Donatella della Porta (1995) compares political violence in Italy and Germany between the 1960s and 1990s. She presents a multi-level explanation of political radicalisation that integrates theories of conflict, mobilisation, and activism, and spans external conditions (macro-level), organised group dynamics (meso-level), and individual motivations (micro-level) (ibid.: 187). She explains that at the macro-level of political opportunities the initial reluctance of both Italian and German authorities to integrate the demands for reform of the political regime (ibid.: 189) allowed the diffusion of "radical frames of meaning" (ibid.: 201). Especially the hard-line policing styles, based on a restric-tive understanding of protest rights (ibid.: 190), led to the creation of "martyrs and myths": examples are the figure of Benno Ohnesorg, a student killed by police during a protest against the Shah of Iran's visit to Berlin, or the "battle" with the police by student protesters in Valle Giulia in Rome, "which took on a legendary quality for Italian activists" (ibid.: 191).[4] The fact that neither country was a consolidated democracy influenced "the frames of meaning elites used to define the 'dangers' of protest." It also affected the radical movements in adopting frames of meaning that referred to previous historical events:

> The Italian movements claimed they had to carry on their fathers' Partisan movement against a "fascist state" – a movement, according to them, the Old Left had sold out. The German activists asserted that they had to resist with all means the new "Nazi" state to avoid repeating their fathers' mistakes and redeem their shame. (Ibid.: 194)

Within this context, at the meso-level, the movements became them-selves "entrepreneurs of violence": the small radical organisations supporting the use of violence broke away from larger non-violent movements. As della Porta continues, they "underwent further radicalisation and eventually created new resources and occasions for violence" (ibid.: 195). This was fostered by a political culture that was receptive to violence (ibid.: 197). Especially the immigrant workers from the South of Italy and alienated young people in large towns in Germany were accustomed to radical conflict and saw "violence as a cohesive force" (ibid.: 198). Political violence in the two countries could not, however, be explained without considering how the political opportunities and the radical organisations affected the activists' lives in terms of building a "radical collective identity" (individual micro-level): "One's chance of being recruited into a movement increased with participation in specific personal networks connected with movement activists" (ibid.: 202). The radical groups were characterised by such close relationships that "the members believed it was impossible to live outside it [the group]" (ibid.: 204). This strong sense of solidarity affected the way radicals interpreted reality: it intensified "the 'us' versus 'them' mentality" and "all the information individuals received was filtered through the group, which defined the external reality by providing master frames of meaning" (ibid.). The result was that members adopted "the values and goals of the movement as their own," developed a sense of belonging and came "to define themselves first of all as movement activists" (ibid.: 205–206).

Other researchers suggest the application of social movement theory (Wiktorowicz 2004, 2007; Dalgaard-Nielsen 2008; Change Institute 2008: 120–130). Quintan Wiktorowicz (2007), in particular, explains the applicability of Resource Mobilisation Theory (RMT), the concept of opportunity structures, and framing to understand Islamist movements. According to Wiktorowicz, most studies of Islamist movements are trapped in very early approaches to political mobilisation. More specifically, they are based in functionalist social psychology that assumes the natural status of society to be equilibrium: demands by social actors tend to be accommodated by institutions; political disorder is the result of institutions not satisfying these demands. Mass mobilisation, in this context, happens as a result of psychological discomfort (ibid.: 191). Such a framework tends to be applied to Islamist movements because they are seen as an expression of frustration. The situation in which the movements take place is the general crisis produced by the failure of secular modernisation in several Middle Eastern countries: Western models of modernisation are adopted; rapid economic development leads to wealth remaining confined among elites and corrupted officials;

urban infrastructures are inadequate to house the heavy influx of immigrants looking for jobs, thereby supporting the rise of shanty towns and oversized urban centres like Cairo, Tehran, and Algiers (ibid.: 192). Reviewing existing studies, Wiktorowicz identifies three main sources of stress associated with these political and social circumstances – stress that that leads to Islamic activism. The first is the sense of alienation experienced by the newly arrived immigrants, cut off from their families and rural environments and relocated in an urban milieu that has different values. The second is the perception of (Western) cultural imperialism and the urge to protect Muslim societies. The third is the inability to gain political access (political stress) to counter the negative impact of modernisation (ibid.: 191–195). Indeed, one can see how these arguments resonate in the widespread sense of alienation felt by young Muslims when addressing the problem of home-grown radicalisation (US Department of State 2008: 11, for example). While these suggestions appear convincing, Wiktorowicz points out that they disregard two aspects: they "ignore the innumerous instances where stress did not actually engender movement mobilization," and they also dismiss "the purposive, political, and organized dimensions of movement contestation." In other words, "Movements are not merely psychological coping mechanisms: they are explicitly focused and directed toward the political arena" (Wiktorowicz 2007: 195).

The approach of RMT, instead, starts from the acknowledgement that social movements are not as widespread as grievances. What enables the rise of a movement are the mechanisms through which resources are mobilised to support the collective action over time. Wiktorowicz, in this respect, explains the key role played by organisations. Among them – Islamic non-governmental organisations (NGOs), student associations, political parties, and informal social networks such as charities or nadwas (Qur'an study groups) – one of the most effective institutions is the mosque:

> The mosque ... is frequently utilized as a religio-spatial mobilizing structure by various Islamist groups ... . Within the physical structure of the mosque, Islamists offer sermons, lessons, and study groups to propagate the movement message, organize collective action, and recruit new joiners. Mosques also provide an organic, national network that connects communities of activists across space. (Ibid.: 196)

The concept of "political opportunity structure" further supports making sense of the effectiveness of social movements: despite the existence of grievances and the availability of mobilising resources, in fact, the scope for action of social movements, as well as its actual form, are constrained by external factors. Among them are, for instance, the extent of state repression, the level of access to political institutions, the availability of allies (but also the presence of opponents), and the stability of ruling elites (ibid.: 200). This helps explain why even Islamist movements that are seen to rigidly adhere to their ideology can shift their stance over time as a result of changing political circumstances. An example Wiktorowicz offers is that of Hamas. Before the Intifada that began in 2000, the organisation was categorically against a peace process. The growing popular support for peace (in the hope that this would put an end to the hardships of occupation), however, threatened Hamas's political survival. As a result, the group adjusted its position regarding the issue: peace was framed as a temporary pause in the jihad that would strengthen the Muslim forces before a final attack (ibid.: 201).

This brings up the last analytical contribution of social movement theory: framing as a tool to make sense of the way meaning and identity are constructed, but also as a device to convince bystanders to become members of a movement and participate in it (ibid.: 202). In this respect, Wiktorowicz explains that Islamist movements are heavily involved in "struggles over meaning and values" (ibid.: 203). As with any political movement, they engage in three "framing tasks." The first is the elaboration of "diagnostic frames": interpretations of the causes of political problems, such as the identification of the adoption of Western practices as a source of crisis (ibid.). The second is the production of "prognostic frames": these relate to the suggestion of a solution for the problem, as it could be a break with the West and the choice of Islam as the way ahead (ibid.: 204). The third is providing a rationale to sustain support for the movement: this involves a competition with alternative frames, such as "official frames" (ibid.: 205).

Moving on to a different explanation of extremist mobilisation, Terrorism Studies literature focuses on, among other things, explaining why individuals join terrorist organisations. Jerrold Post (2007), for example, specialises in psychological factors. Despite his attention to the "terrorist's mind," he argues that "explanations at the level of the individual psychology are insufficient": "the importance of collective identity and the process of forming and transforming collective identities cannot be overemphasized. This fact, in turn, highlights the role of the sociocultural context, which determines the balance between collective identity and individual identity" (ibid.: 8). The ethnographic work of John Horgan (2009), in this respect, has particularly focused on integrating the individual perspective with group dynamics. The author's argument is that terrorism operates at multiple levels. Horgan writes: "there is the individual terrorist, but there is also the group and the broader network to which he or she belongs, the community being represented by the terrorist, and the broader social, cultural and other issues that can impinge upon the individual terrorist at any time and at any phase of their involvement" (ibid.: xx).

What the studies that have been discussed so far do not appear to acknowledge is that all these processes of mobilisation are related to communication: mobilising resources and opinion means that a group has coalesced around an idea and agreed on a course of action to achieve a specific objective. This implies the transmission of that idea, as well as the goals to be accomplished. Action also requires coordination and organisation, which again rely on exchange of information. Through the excerpts of interviews conducted by Horgan with former members of extremist organisations, it is possible to identify a role for the media and communication in both providing information about radical organisations, but also in the consolidation of extreme beliefs. To provide an example of how "older media" and face-to-face communication combined in an individual's quest for engagement, a former member of the Norwegian right-wing extremist group Nasjonalt Folkeparti recalls how he came across the address of the group on "a sticker on a car window" and later decided to write its members a letter. The group then replied and invited him to a social gathering – an occasion which marked the beginning of his involvement with the organisation (Horgan 2009: 41). A former member of Al Qaeda, instead, remembers his growing willingness to become more directly involved with the terrorist organisation while watching TV:

> after seeing the kinds of images, the damage that was done, some of the images coming from Western media ... [hearing] about the way in which an American fighter pilot struck his bomb on a village because he didn't want go back to his base empty, you know, with his weapon intact. [T]hat's ... what *really* struck a chord[;] it really touched on an emotional thing. (Ibid.: 65–66, his emphasis)

The approaches that have been described revolve around concepts of identity, community, the way a shared collective identity affects individual interpretations of events and incoming information. Within the appropriate structural conditions and group dynamics, they further lead to mobilisation. However, because these accounts tend not to engage *explicitly* with communications and the media, they cannot overall account for identity construction and social mobilisation on a global scale. The next section argues that the concept of narrative, grounded in the communication model presented in Chapter 3, can effectively synthesise the two branches of literature so far outlined.

4.4   Explaining extremism III: a narrative bridge?

What comes out of this brief look into the studies attempting to explain extremism is that research which deals more explicitly with the role of the media tends to be sociologically superficial. Sociology-oriented literature about terrorism – theoretically more substantial and which tackles issues of mobilisation, identity construction, and the way in which individual agency and social structures are mutually interdependent – does not really engage (at least directly) with media and communication.

Bridging the two approaches means explaining extremism more comprehensively by covering the way the terrorist message is promoted by an extremist group and its sympathisers through global media, how it is appropriated by audiences, and how it is exactly translated into social action. The concept of narrative – understood, as explained in the communication model presented in Chapter 3, as the outcome of a collective process of social construction – is a useful analytical tool in this respect. It brings together the concepts of "network," "message," "story," "identity," "community," and "mobilisation" and allows overcoming the distinction between individual and collective levels of analysis. It seamlessly integrates the online and offline dimensions and, besides taking into account the promotion of extremist ideas by terrorist organisations (top-down), it also envisages an active role by individuals (grassroots) in appropriating and "retelling" those ideas within their own network of relationships.

4.4.1   A narrative approach

Individual narratives reflect the set of stories embedded in the constellation of relationships (elsewhere called "networks") to which the individual belongs. As Margaret Somers (1994: 616) explains, narratives define our identity and are relationally constructed: they are "constellations of relationships (connected parts) embedded in time and space, constituted by causal emplotment." By shaping who we are – our identity – they also affect what we know – our knowledge – including the way we interpret incoming information, and what we do – our actions. As she puts it, "People act, or do not act, in part according to how they understand their place in any number of given narratives – however fragmented, contradictory, or partial" (ibid.: 618). This action, in turn, will produce new constellations of relationships, reflected in new narratives, which will affect subsequent action.

Somers argues that explaining social conflict through narratives is more effective than using traditional categories offered by "interest politics" (such as class) or the new labels of "identity politics" (like gender): "While a social identity or categorical approach presumes internally stable concepts, such that under normal conditions entities within that category will act uniformly and predictably, the narrative identity approach embeds the actor within relationships and stories that shift over time and space" (ibid.: 621).

This approach allows the overcoming of the categories and identity labels that are currently used in terrorism-related research, such as the notions of "terrorist" and "Muslim." It has often been noticed that terrorists do not have typical profiles (Horgan 2009: xxii; Fenstermacher 2011: 7): some are more educated than others; some have been trained in foreign countries; others have come across radical content simply while surfing on the Internet; some might become engaged with terrorist groups because of their sense of religious duty, others because of a (perceived) lack of meaning in their life or a feeling of being marginalised in society. Not all Muslims experience a sense of social injustice or grievance. They live their religion in very different ways. As Chahla Beski-Chafiq and others (2010b: 11), for instance, in a study of radicalisation in Lille, point out, there is a "plurality of Islam experienced by young people" in France. They write: "adherence to Islam among youths ... relates to a dynamic of identity construction which is in conformity with the ideas they develop through interactions with their environment: themselves, others, and society" (ibid.: 12). Further to this, Muslim communities in some countries, like the United Kingdom, have experienced home-grown terrorism to a relatively greater extent than other Muslim communities in continental Europe. How can we account for all these variations?

The labels currently used tend to conflate and homogenise: the very use of the term "radicalisation" misleadingly supports the impression that it refers to a stable process that manifests itself virtually identically across cases and contexts. Yet, as ethnographic studies confirm through a wealth of details, this is not at all the case (Institute for Change 2008; Beski-Chafiq et al. 2010a; Beski-Chafiq et al. 2010b; della Porta and Bosi 2010; Githens-Mazer et al. 2010; Kühle and Lindekilde 2010). According to Somers (1994: 624), a "narrative identity approach ... assumes that social action can only be intelligible if we recognise that people are guided to act by the structural and cultural relationships in which they are embedded and by the stories through which they constitute their identities – and less because of interests we impute to them." The communication model developed in this book suggests a conceptual distinction between the individual narrative, which is unique to every social actor, and the collective narrative shared by members of a group. In practice, however, they are tightly interrelated. While the collective narrative is itself constructed through the contributions of the individual narratives, it is also the context within which individual narratives further develop and find their grounding. Being part of a group or not being part of a group, in this perspective, is the outcome of, respectively, consonance and dissonance of the individual narrative with the collective one.

This argument is in line with the findings of Horgan (2009: 8, his emphasis) about the psychology of terrorists: "the [individual] mindset should be considered a *product* of the terrorist group: expressed more formally, it is a reflection of a repeated social and psychological interactions with an ideology (however diffuse or unstructured), the community of practice it engenders and the meaning that is derived by the individual terrorist from sustained involvement and engagement with the group and activity." The deep interrelation between social relationships, identity, interpretation of the external world and of incoming information, as well as behaviour, further explains another observation of Tore Bjørgo and John Horgan (2009). In studying disengagement from extremist groups they find that "individuals do not necessarily join extremist groups because they hold extremist views; they sometimes acquire extremist views because they have joined such a group for other reasons" (ibid.: 3).

4.4.2 The crucial role of context and time

The narrative approach is space- and time-contingent. Such embeddedness in specific contexts helps in understanding that one cannot assume that similar sets of individual characteristics and structural factors will produce the same radicalisation outcome irrespective of the relational context in which they are situated. If we compare the experiences of Muslims across countries, or even across regional and urban settings, it becomes clear that radicalisation (when it actually exists in its violent manifestation) can take completely different forms and arise in totally different environments, for equally different reasons.

For a start, ethnographic studies show that radicalisation does not always consist in a simple and utter rejection of "our" values. Kühle and

Lindekilde (2010), for example, find that the development of radical views can well fit within a democratic setting and does not necessarily need to translate into violence. They demonstrate that the support by young Muslims in Aarhus (Denmark) for organisations that are labelled "terrorist" by Western authorities is "overwhelming" (ibid.: 47). This, however, does not mean that they advocate terrorism in Denmark. The youths' logic is that some organisations, albeit being internationally regarded as "terrorist," are actually engaged in a "resistance war" against invading forces. It is acceptable to kill in war, but absolutely intolerable in the context of a peaceful society (ibid.: 47–60). Even those who would want to see the development of an Islamic state show that, even though they hold these potentially radical personal views, they also share collective democratic values with fellow Danes. As an interviewee put it: "One cannot implement sharia in Denmark unless there are Muslims who want sharia – a majority. We can never be ten people who want it – it is very unrealistic" (ibid.: 66).[5]

The social and political circumstances in which Muslim communities live and might develop radical views – not necessarily violent – vary widely. In Lille a sizable Muslim community[6] of mainly Moroccan and Algerian descent is geographically concentrated in 4 out of the 10 districts that constitute the municipality (Beski-Chafiq et al. 2010a: 25–26). The community has firmly established itself through, among other things, the first Muslim university institute in France (Institut Avicenne des Sciences Humaines), the property of seven mosques that have been active since the 1970s, the activities of a cultural centre (Centre culturel de Lille-Sud) that organises (besides religious celebrations) a wealth of activities: the teaching of Arab and Islamic culture, educational seminars, welfare support, a centre of activities for women. The centre also has a library, a newsletter, and the second private Muslim educational institution in France: the Averroe grammar school (ibid.: 26–28). Muslims in Italy, instead, are immigrants who have only very recently arrived in the country. They are diverse in terms of ethnic origin, language, and cultural practices, and are geographically dispersed (della Porta and Bosi 2010: 16). Islam is not yet recognised as an official religion in Italy: Muslims cannot allocate a quota of their personal income tax to the Muslim community; deduct donations to the Muslim community from their taxes; do not have the right to abstain from work on religious holidays, or easily establish places of worship (Zincone 2006 in della Porta and Bosi 2010: 17). Even within Italy, Donatella della Porta and Lorenzo Bosi (2010: 18–20) demonstrate the sharp difference related to the experience of living in Parma, a town with a long tradition of left-wing politics, and Verona, an urban centre of similar size whose historical background includes 40 years of Christian Democratic rule and at least 20 years of administration by the strongly anti-immigrant Northern League. While there is evidence of across-the-board informal discrimination against young Muslims in both educational and employment environments – a phenomenon related to their status of immigrants rather than any religious-based hostility (ibid.: 20–25) – the Muslim community in Parma enjoys a good relationship with authorities thanks to regular interfaith initiatives (ibid.: 19). In Verona, on the contrary, "migrants have been considered a problem" and Muslims are often "victims of manifestation of prejudice" (ibid.: 20).

The examination of local circumstances is crucial to understanding the development of both personal narratives and collective ones. Again della Porta and Bosi (2010: 28) demonstrate that the perception of having a stigmatised identity (deriving from experiences of discrimination and negative images in the national mainstream media) leads some young Italian Muslims in Parma and Verona to develop a deeper religious commitment. Religious identity becomes a bridge that enables them to feel a connection with the dispersed and ethnically diverse communities of first generation immigrants in the country. In Lille, where Muslim communities are more organised, religious commitment has a different meaning: for some it consists in supporting the "sociopolitical project" related to the development of a Muslim community united and governed by Islamic values (Beski-Chafiq et al. 2010a: 36). Neither of these processes of identity building necessarily involves the legitimation of violence.

These examples show how the construction of identity is the outcome of broad social interactions. The way in which identity evolves over time leads, in turn, to changes in the way those who share that identity can at any given time mobilise further resources and political allies – the management of the political opportunity structure. Beyond the possible material facilitating factors and constraints – such as the presence of local consultative bodies on integration policy in Parma and the lack thereof in Verona – the imagined communities of allies play an important role. More specifically, the way political groups position themselves in relation to others in their own collective narrative affects the degree to which they will provide support (both ideological and material) for sister causes. Della Porta and Bosi (2010: 13), in this respect, note that after 9/11 the political conflicts in which Muslims have been involved in Italy have evolved "from those oriented around identities as migrants to those around identities as Muslims." This has affected the extent to which the support of trade unions, Catholic NGOs, and left-wing social movements which have been campaigning for the economic and social rights of migrants can be mobilised: "[T]he construction of religious identities and demands for their [communities of Muslim immigrants] recognition seems to have displaced these potential allies" (ibid.).

Once a "narrative" is conceived as a relational product that is constructed by the individual as a result of changing sets of relationship-based stories that define his/her identity, it becomes apparent that it is not possible to talk about a "single narrative" (Schmid 2010; Home Office 2011: 108). A report by the Change Institute (2008) about ideologies and narratives of extremism across the United Kingdom, Germany, Denmark, and France shows that there can be shared narrative "themes" across countries. These are, for example: the notion of living in a hostile society; a sense of disenfranchisement coexisting with a heightened political consciousness; and the ideas of anti-imperialism and social justice (ibid.: 97–103). These, however, arise from very different local experiences. For instance the study, through a series of interviews with Muslim residents in different countries (Denmark, France, Germany, the UK), finds that the theme "living in a hostile society" is shared by participants in both France and Britain. Yet, even the same theme is explained in widely diverging terms. The French participants lived negatively the experience of being immigrants because of the "cultural hegemony" denying their difference (ibid.: 100). One of the interviewees living in France put it this way: "I felt even more Algerian because there was racism, they put us all together amongst ourselves in corners, they did not look after us, there was no support. Whether it was sport or education they could have supported us better, they know very well that we were from immigrant families, that we had differences and that we aren't like the others" (ibid.). On the other hand, one of the British interviewees emphasised the way in which the diversity of young Muslims was constantly highlighted: "I am really sick of the reporting going on in the media representing young Muslims. It's so negative and in the news so much" (ibid.).

In addition, the Change Institute report shows that what leads the individual to act in a certain way is not a "narrative" per se, but the appropriation and articulation of that narrative by the individual in the first place. The previously mentioned narrative themes are, in fact, found to be shared by both radical and non-radical Muslims. They are interpreted and acted upon differently depending on whether an individual is an extremist or a moderate. As the institute's researcher writes, "These narratives may have a radical representation in the hands of 'angry young men' or be articulated in a thoughtful and cohesive manner by those with 'moderate' or 'progressive' views" (ibid.: 98, see also 113). And beyond all this, narratives continuously evolve over time as a result of shifting patterns of relationships.

Communication is an integral part of the social world and, as such, is also crucial in the radicalisation process. It is wrong, however, to think that face-to-face interaction and communication technologies like the Internet are simply opportunities for radical messages to be "delivered" to vulnerable individuals. Both direct and mediated communications contribute to multiplying the relationships that shape the individual identity, narrative and, in turn, action. From this point of view there is no distinction between the online and offline dimensions, as they are both part of the changeable geometry of social space. Indeed, face-to-face contacts, mediated interaction, as well as symbolic interaction in imagined communities are all shaping an individual's identity and behaviour. This is why Tim Stevens (2010) challenges the myth of the "lone wolf," the self-radicalised individual who allegedly acts "independently." While it is true that some individuals might not be formally members of an active organisation, they are not alone in their minds. As he phrases it: "they have the love of Allah, solidarity with the ummah, and the ideological and psychological support of online, and other, communities that may or may not be aware of their intentions.'

Face-to-face-interaction, communication technologies, and media coverage do provide the individual with a continuous flow of information. Indeed, they also convey other actor's individual and collective narratives. The latter might well be promoted by groups such as terrorist organisations. These external narratives, however, are not simply "absorbed" but, again, are interpreted through the lens of the individual narrative.

4.5   Conclusion: how to tackle radicalisation?

As has been discussed, communication approach to explaining extremism can support an alternative way of conceiving the process of becoming a violent radical. In turn, this leads to four practical implications in tackling radicalisation.

The first is that the availability of extremist content – also the existence of a terrorist "narrative" – is not the problem per se. The fact that jihadi videos or terrorist websites are potentially available to worldwide audiences does not mean that these publics are necessarily going to access them, let alone embrace the radical ideas such outlets advocate: reach is not impact. Even if extremist messages are accessed, the key issue is the individual *appropriation* of those contents through the interpretative prism of the beliefs and worldview that result from the individual's constellation of relationships – the individual narrative.[7] This explains, among other things, why many readers will have watched terrorist propaganda videos or consulted extremist manifestos without becoming radicalised. The proposed communication model of radicalisation offers an insight into how social ties shape the way individuals interpret external information and events: for example the extent to which they will either appropriate, reinterpret, or reject extremist ideas they might have come across on the Internet, by watching the news, or reading a book. This point leads to a second implication.

What is "extremist" is relative. The very understanding of what constitutes "extremist" ideas or content depends, in the first place, on the parameters established by the individual narrative at any given time. What law-abiding citizens of a democratic country might normally regard as excessively violent and extremist might appear entirely acceptable within a relational setting – and relative view of the world – that regards violence as legitimate. Conversely, even ideas that are not regarded as a threat to society, like the views of theorists from the Frankfurt School, can be used as a rationale for violence, as in the case of the Norwegian killer, Anders Breivik.

This shows, as a third point, that focusing on eliminating extremist online content is not the best use of resources in countering violent extremism. Beyond the fact that this practice only has limited effectiveness – given that the material can easily be copied and transferred elsewhere before being removed by censors (Theohary and Rollins 2011: 14) – it also targets what Western counterterrorists see as "extremist" from the perspective of *their own* network of relationships. In principle, any content (text, video, image, audio recording) across any communication platform (Internet, VHS tape, mobile phone, audio cassette, photocopied leaflet, wall graffiti), could be contributing to reinforcing a violent extremist interpretation of the world. What should "we" be doing about that, then?

The time- and context-specific combination of circumstances that leads to the development of violent extremist action makes community-based and local approaches the most effective in dealing with radicalisation. Trying to identify the individual characteristics (such as personality traits) and structural conditions that lead to radicalisation in general and abstract terms – most existing literature talks about radicalisation as if it occurred in the same way on a national, even international level – is meaningless, for two reasons. One is that individual characteristics and structural factors do not exist independent of each other. The second is that, in the social world, timing and sequence are of essence, as are the continuous re-arrangement and re-negotiation of relationships that come from responding to unfolding events. Reality never sits still. Police forces engaging with local communities on a regular basis are the best assessors of whether radical ideas that could sustain violent action are developing in their respective contexts because they are part of the same networks in which radical individuals are also, eventually, enmeshed. As much as violent extremists might want to avoid contact with the external world, they are in fact still living in somebody else's neighbourhood, buying food, paying bills, and renting accommodations. As Robert Lambert, former head of the Muslim Contact Unit in the Metropolitan Police, recently pointed out, the most useful intelligence is gathered in the United Kingdom through collaboration with community members who volunteer information as part of what they see as their civic duty (Lambert 2011). The fact that, since 9/11, 9 major plots have been foiled in the United Kingdom (Home Office OSCT 2011: 7) and 40 in the United States (Carafano and Zuckerman 2011) – not counting the successful minor antiterrorist operations – should be seen as a confirmation of the fact that information related to terrorist activities does circulate and, in doing so, it gets systematically picked up along the law enforcement networks.

5
The Role of Narratives

The previous chapter has shown that it is unfounded to assert that the terrorists' narrative has the power to cause a law-abiding citizen to turn to extreme acts of violence. Not only that, the chapter also exposed the lack of explanations in current literature about the way narratives (whether individual or collective) lead to political action. Yet, if one reads terrorism-related literature, progress in counterterrorism appears to be related to both establishing a credible narrative and damaging "their" narrative. This present chapter further examines the nature of narratives by demonstrating that, contrary to what is overwhelmingly suggested, a narrative is not a simple "story" or "message." While narratives can be constructed, planned, and promoted by specific actors to achieve desired objectives, they are not messages that get "delivered." They do not "spread" like viruses either. Instead, they keep on existing through a collective reconstruction and retelling process. This chapter ultimately suggests that a greater understanding of the social construction of narratives can inform a better assessment of what is feasible in the "war of ideas" against violent extremism.

The analysis will develop in two parts. The first will briefly review the use of the concept of narrative within the broader domain of the social sciences and, in particular, in relation to extremism. The discussion sets the stage for critically questioning the way in which the term is currently employed. The second part of the chapter then examines the meaning of narrative as a relational product and explains its relevance in relation to a global communication environment that could be conceived as a "hall of mirrors" in which overlapping reflections represent multiple possible individual interpretations. This section will also highlight the problems in the way narratives are currently approached in terrorism research and counterterrorism, as well as the empirical challenges in conducting narrative analysis in relation to security issues. The chapter ends with some considerations about the practical implications of treating narratives as evolving collective constructions rather than messages.

5.1   The ubiquity of narratives

5.1.1   The rise of narrative

As part of what is referred to as the "narrative turn" (Smith and Sparkes 2008)[1] in the social sciences, an increasing number of scholars have been suggesting that our lives and societies are shaped by stories (Bruner 1986; Polkinghorne 1988; Sarbin 1986; Taylor 1989). Beyond academic research, it is not difficult to see how stories have always, throughout history, been central to the practice of politics, from the references to myths used in ancient Greece "to point out the expediency of a proposed course of action" (Hart 1992: 632), to US president Obama's compelling narrative of change. Narratives are "story lines which can explain events convincingly and from which inferences can be drawn" (Freedman 2006: 22). They provide a "concise statement of what [an actor] is doing, why, and how that links to a positive vision of the future with the individual actions of members of its own societies and members of other societies whom it wishes to influence" (Betz 2008: 522). Because they are "designed or nurtured with the intention of structuring the responses of others to developing events" (Freedman 2006: 22), narratives are often called "strategic."

Strategic narratives are central to the practice of international relations. States use narratives selectively and purposely to achieve desired objectives: defining their identities; explaining their role in the world; identifying allies and enemies; establishing the nature of the relationships among them; and contextualising historical events as well as policy decisions (Antoniades, Miskimmon and O'Loughlin 2009; Roselle 2010). Two key state activities – public diplomacy and country branding – are geared towards the strategic promotion of a national story: "image cultivation," and the "managing" of a country's reputation as "a source of national power" (Melissen 2007a: 3).

The context in which contemporary international relations take place is not, however, characterised by interaction among states only. Access to global communications has empowered a wide range of actors, as several authors have acknowledged over the last few decades (see, as early examples, Keohane and Nye 1981; Rosenau 1990). Apart from states, NGOs, corporate actors, transnational actors, and even private citizens have acquired a voice. Armed with communication technologies that facilitate the sharing of information and networking in real time – like mobile phones, the Internet, social media like Twitter and Facebook – non-state actors can effectively reshape international politics, as most forcefully demonstrated in the "Arab Awakening" of 2011 (Seib 2012). In fact, non-state actors might not have substantial financial, material, or military resources, yet through the persuasive power of ideas, they can mobilise audiences across national borders (Douglas 2007; Betz 2008).

Strategic narratives are particularly relevant in the post 9/11 context: they play a crucial role in the "war of ideas" between Western democracies and Al Qaeda. David Betz (2008: 510), on this point, writes:

> The contemporary operations environment ... in the "Global War on Terror" ... has two dimensions: the first is the actual tactical field of battle in which bullets fly, bombs explode and blood is shed; the second is the virtual, informational realm in which belligerents contend with words and images to manufacture strategic narratives which are more compelling than those of the other side and better at structuring the responses of others to the development of events.

Strategic narratives act as interpretative lenses, tying local to global events. Although they exist in a cognitive dimension, they have very real consequences. The military operations in Afghanistan can be seen either as an occupation of a Muslim land – yet another act of aggression by the West against Islam – or as part of an international effort to eradicate terrorism. From the former perspective, the sending of more troops to Afghanistan by President Obama in late 2009 could have been read as a renewed and more direct challenge against Islam. This interpretation could explain the shifts in the focus of global terrorist activities in that period: Pakistan and Afghanistan appeared to have replaced Iraq as the "preferred destination for prospective jihadists, including Europeans" (Jacobson 2009). In turn, the influx of fighters led to an increase in attacks in the broader region: in Pakistan, 890 attacks claimed 1,340 victims in 2007; in 2008 at least 1,839 attacks killed 2,293 people (Jacobson 2009). In 2010, 2,113 attacks caused 2,913 deaths (Pakistani Institute for Peace Studies 2010: 2).

The realisation that both terrorism and counterterrorism take place beyond the material and military dimension, in the realm of ideas, values, and perceptions has led to a strong interest in narratives within both terrorism research and counterterrorism practitioners' circles. The next section critically examines the arguments both in academia and within reports by governments and think tanks.

5.1.2 Narratives, counter-narratives and violent extremism

Research on radicalisation, including official documents, has recently started to refer to a "narrative" being developed by Al Qaeda (for example: Homeland Security Policy Institute [HSPI] and the University of Virginia Critical Incident Analysis Group [CIAG] 2007: 2; Neumann 2008a: 5; Roy 2008a, 2008b: 5; Bergin et al. 2009: 2; Levitt 2009: 3; Presidential Task Force 2009; Stevens and Neumann 2009: 12; Home Office 2011). The term narrative is used so often that it has truly become a buzzword. An American presidential document (White House 2011: 6) about preventing violent extremism, for example, states: "Radicalization that leads to violent extremism includes the diffusion of ideologies and narratives that feed on grievances, assign blame, and legitimize the use of violence against those deemed responsible." In 2010, the Dutch National Coordinator for Counterterrorism released a whole collection of contributions about "Countering Violent Extremist Narratives." The narrative of "oppression and victimhood" (Home Office 2009: 155) being suffered by Muslims around the world at the hands of Western aggressors that is promoted by the Al Qaeda terrorist organisation was regarded as the main fuel for the growth of extremism in the UK government's 2009 antiterrorism strategy (ibid.: 141). The more recent *Prevent* strategy (Home Office 2011: 29) still frequently mentions the terrorists' "narrative," the existence of which is now taken for granted: the highest priority in counterterrorism is constituted by "activity which challenges the terrorist ideology, for example speakers challenging terrorist narratives." The narrative is widely identified as the motivating factor for joining Al Qaeda and, in turn, as the source of a continuous supply of new recruits ready to fight for the cause of the terrorist group. As already alluded to in Chapter 3 and Chapter 4, the Internet is widely regarded to be the main vehicle for the diffusion of the terrorist narrative. As the presidential document (White House 2011: 6) further states: "we [the government of the United States] will continue to closely monitor the important role the Internet and social networking sites play in advancing violent extremist narratives."

In most of the literature, "narrative" is used as a self-explanatory term, often as a synonym for ideology.[2] Where it is defined, it is conceived as a story. As such, it is regarded as a device exploited by terrorists not only to maintain internal cohesion within a violent extremist group and give direction to cells that might be operating on their own, but also for publicising their political cause, recruiting new followers, and providing a rationale for their activities (Quiggin 2009: 23). The narrative-as-a-story is seen by some in very simple terms as a tale with a "beginning point, a middle part and an end" (ibid.). The first part, as Tom Quiggin (2009) explains, contains a "grievance or difficult situation." The middle part provides either a hero or a possible solution to the initial problem. The end either shows the solution or encourages the listeners to act and tackle the problem (ibid.). Steven Corman (2011), in a more sophisticated interpretation, formally distinguishes "narrative" from "story." A story, in his view, "is a sequence of events, involving actors and actions, grounded in desire (often stemming from a conflict) and leading to an actual or projected resolution of that desire" (ibid.: 36). As an example, he presents the popular American story of the "midnight ride of Paul Revere." Revere was a leading patriot who in 1775, on the eve of the war of independence (conflict), rode from Boston to Lexington to warn about a surprise incursion by British troops, who were seeking a patriot arms cache. As a result of Revere's famous ride, which was animated by the desire to protect fellow patriots, the British were attacked and forced to retreat (resolution) (ibid.: 36–37). A narrative, instead, is "a system of stories that share themes, forms, and archetypes." In other words, a narrative is made up of many stories whose combination is "greater than the sum of its parts" (ibid.: 37). Corman offers, as an illustration of this last instance, the narrative of the American Revolution, of which the "midnight ride" tale is a constituent story. He states that narratives that are consistently retold over time achieve the status of "master narratives." They grow from "local narratives" (ibid.: 40). They are characterised by the fact that they can be invoked with simple words or phrases. In a study about master narratives of Islamist extremism – by examining public statements, text and videos from a range of extremist groups – he and colleagues (Halverson, Goodall and Corman 2011) identify 13 master narratives. One of them is encapsulated in the notion of al-Nakbah – "the catastrophe." This contains the stories of the loss of Palestine to Israel (1948) but also extends to Jerusalem and Palestine as holy sites and burial places of prophets and patriarchs (Corman 2011: 38–39).

Progress in counterterrorism appears to be related in the literature to both establishing a credible narrative and damaging "their" narrative. William Casebeer and James Russell (2005), for instance, suggest that the most effective way to counter terrorism is by developing a "better story" to replace "their" narrative. For this purpose a special communication office, the Research, Information and Communications Unit (RICU) was set up in Whitehall in 2007. Its task was specifically to "use messaging to disrupt the Al Qa'ida narrative" (Home Office 2009: 153; see also 2011: 51–52). A US Presidential Task Force report (2009) also argues for "rewriting the narrative."

While several stress that countering the extremist narrative should not be limited to words but also to engagement with local communities and a consistency between words (rhetoric) and deeds (policy), there is a strong emphasis on "messaging" (Presidential Task Force 2009: 13–20; Cornish, Lindley-French and Yorke 2011: 33–35; Shanahan 2011: 1). Messaging can take the form of rebutting the ideology of terrorist organisations by emphasising the ideology's internal contradictions. This would involve, in the case of Al Qaeda, pointing out that the terrorist group does not offer a viable programme for the future, neither in economic nor political terms, and that most of the victims of its violence are in fact Muslims (Presidential Task Force 2009: 16). Cheryl Benard (2011), more specifically, suggests a strategy of "delegitimisation" (see also Larson 2011). Beyond undermining the legitimacy of the "message" – for example, by emphasising that the terrorists' beliefs are not consistent with Islam – Benard further recommends damaging the credibility of the leaders by raising questions such as: "Are they pocketing wealth from their followers to indulge in luxuries for themselves?" (Ibid: 106). "We" could damage the image of the followers of the terrorist message by expressing understanding for those "whose idealism or youthful credulity or personal problems are being exploited by the extremists" (ibid.: 107). We could question the terrorists' methods, particularly the use of vulnerable individuals such as widows, the disabled, and children as suicide bombers (ibid.: 108–109), as well as the outcomes: by pointing out, for instance: "What is Islam the answer to?" (Ibid: 109). Another suggestion, partially overlapping what has already been said, is magnifying the internal controversies or "fissures" (Presidential Task Force 2009: 16), particularly through the voices of former jihadists. In addition to this, while Anne Speckhard (2011: 173) argues for openly rebutting the Al Qaeda rhetoric through "intellectually and emotionally provocative materials," possibly through multimedia (see also Ashour 2010), the Presidential Task Force (2009: 16) recommends, instead, a "noncombative" rhetoric, especially refraining from the phrase "war on terror," which lends legitimacy to the terrorist group's claim that the West is at war with Islam. An alternative is the creation of "honey pots": "websites which resemble extremist sites could also be created to further the spread of disinformation" (HSPI/CIAG 2007: 16).

The focus on crafting the "right" message against violent extremism is accompanied by the belief that there are certain characteristics that make it more effective in relation to target audiences, as suggested by this excerpt of the *NETworked Radicalization* report: "*There can be no compelling counter-narrative until the extremist narrative itself is well understood* – including how the message is couched, what is emphasized and ignored, what references and allusions are made, what audiences are targeted, and how messages are adapted to reach new audiences and respond to new events" (HSPI/CIAG: 15, emphasis in original).

While all that has been mentioned sounds plausible, the reification of the narrative – particularly its being treated as a script – and attention to the delivery of the "right" message, are a contradiction to the deeply social nature of stories in our society. These assumptions are also an obstacle to understanding communication in the twenty-first century. The next section takes a step back to question the very nature of narrative and to suggest a different perspective on how information is *socially appropriated* rather than *transmitted*.

5.2 The narrative concept: valuable contributions and problems

5.2.1 Narratives and the communication age

We all intuitively understand the meaning of "narrative": it is a spoken or written account of a sequence of events that are tied together by a plot line. Technically, however, a narrative is something deeper and thicker. The concept, mainly developed in the social sciences, comes with specific assumptions about the way the social world works. These assumptions are the basis for understanding the process through which narratives are constructed. As Stephanie Lawler (2002: 242, her emphasis) states, narratives do not simply "carry ... a set of 'facts'": they are "*social products* produced by people within the context of specific social, historical and cultural locations." They are "interpretive devices through which people represent themselves, both to themselves and to others" (ibid.). In this sense, narratives are central to the construction of identity (Somers and Gibson 1994; Benwell and Stokoe 2006: 42).

Narratives are social products in two respects. First, a narrative does not exist independently from individual agency. Narrative is the means through which people "connect together past and present" (Lawler 2002: 242). This occurs through a process of "emplotment," through which apparently unrelated events become "episodes" of a coherent plot (ibid.: 245–246). For example, Hayden White (1973 in Czarniawska 2007: 383) suggested that historians *emplot* events into histories, rather than simply *find* them. The narrative resulting from the emplotment is not unproblematic for the researcher. The remembrance of the past, in fact, involves a continuous engagement, recall, retelling, and reinterpretation in light of an individual's understanding and knowledge at any given time (Lawler 2002: 248–249). As Charlotte Linde (2009), who analyses the practices through which institutional memories are constructed, explains, the stability of a narrative over time should not be seen as a given. Continuity is rather an accomplishment (ibid.: 9) that involves a group's working and reworking of the past, its invoking, retelling – often selective – for present purposes (ibid.: 3). Second, a narrative is a collective construction. As Linde, again, points out, even "an individual's life story is not the property of that individual alone, but also belongs to others who have shared the events narrated – or were placed to have opinions about them" (Linde 1993 in Linde 2009: 4) by having "some expertise or authority" (ibid.: 5). Dennis Mumby (1993: 5) underlines that the study of narrative is about understanding the struggle over the construction of social meaning – a struggle that is related to power, politics, and the ability of some actors to "fix" meaning (ibid.: 7).

This understanding of narrative helps making sense of the social and political impact of communication in the twenty-first century. Particularly, it both complements and improves explanations of the way individuals become involved in extremism, especially complementing those analyses that envisage a dynamic relationship between individual agency and social structural facilitating conditions (Neumann and Rogers 2007; Neumann 2008b) rather than reducing radicalisation mainly to exposure to radical ideas (see Bergin et al. 2009, for instance). As an example of the former literature, Peter Neumann and Brooke Rogers (2007) describe, through the lens of social movement theory, the process by which individuals come to join terrorist organisations. Terrorist organisations, according to the authors, are engaged in a mobilisation effort that involves the communication of messages ("frames") to audiences, but also a "frame alignment" (ibid.: 16). This is "the convergence between the movement narrative and the views of the recruits" (ibid.). Frame alignment, or the sharing of the same view of the world, however, is "rarely sufficient" in persuading people to engage in acts of extreme violence. A process of "socialization" should also take place in which the individual "alters the perceptions of self-interest and increases the values of group loyalties and personal ties" (ibid.). The authors suggest that there is a message (frame); that this message is embraced by individuals (frame alignment); and that the difference between sharing an extremist view of the world and translating it into action is made by intense interaction within a group. My argument, as illustrated in the previous chapters, is that the concept of narrative, relationally constructed and changeable over time, is more effective in explaining this process. The individual narrative is a social actor's account of: his/her identity as shaped by a constellation of relationships at any given time, resulting in a vision of the world and in corresponding action. In this perspective, joining an extremist group is not the result of an external narrative being received and internalised by the individual, as if the collective narrative of the group substituted the individual's narrative. Becoming part of an extremist group means, rather, having developed, as a result of shifting patterns of relationships, an individual narrative that is compatible with the collective narrative of the group. Individual and collective narratives coexist.

This explanation of radicalisation emphasises the active role of the individual. Although the position within the set of relationships that constitutes the social space defines who we are, what we know and the way we think, and how we act, this is not meant in deterministic terms. It is, in fact, the individual who ultimately manages the social ties. Additionally, any incoming information is not flowing straight into one's mind, but is always selected and read through the prism of the individual narrative.

The uniqueness of both the selection and interpretation of incoming information that take place as part of the development of the individual narrative, challenges the widespread rhetoric about strategic communication, particularly the idea that it is possible to target selected audiences with the right messages to achieve a predefined set of objectives. Instead, no firm assumptions can be made about the kind of information to which an individual or a target audience will be exposed. The fact that a few decades ago most countries would have had only a handful of radio stations and TV channels, could have led to the reasonable expectation that a substantial proportion of each respective nationwide audience had been exposed to the content of the same evening news bulletin. The interpretation of the information conveyed through that bulletin would have still been unique to each individual. So would have been the way each member of the audience could have discussed that information with family members, friends, and work colleagues. This would have further contributed to the evolution of the personal reading of the initial "message." So, no certain prediction could have legitimately been made about the effects of that information. The mainstream media sources of information, however, were fairly limited and at least identifiable. Today, instead, the availability of countless national and international sources of information through the Internet, cable TV, satellite dishes, mobile phones, and social media platforms, and the possibility to share text, images, videos, and links with a potentially far broader circle of individuals than would have been possible in the past, fatally undermines the planning that certain messages are going to be consumed by desired audiences.

Availability of information and connectivity are, of course, not limit-less. It is true that, even if hundreds of newspapers are available on the Internet, no one is going to consult them all. Even if citizen journalists around the world tell us what is happening in their respective neighbour-hoods, we simply do not have the time to read their accounts, and we are still referring to newspapers. That is why we still need journalists and editors, as well as foreign correspondents from abroad to tell us to what we should pay attention. Consumption is limited by the time we have at our disposal to sieve through the information tide, and the amount of attention we can devote to it. Professional communicators do, indeed, exploit the fact that information does not flow randomly. We are all familiar with the feeling of being spied upon when ads about products we have recently researched online start popping up in the corner of our computer screens ... . Nonetheless, the range of pieces of information an individual will be exposed to every day is increasingly unpredictable.

The simultaneous communication and construction of narratives by each individual social actor in a global (and potentially transparent) information environment could be compared, in its complexity, to the overlapping reflections in a hall of mirrors. Figure 5.1 visually represents the way narratives are socially constructed in a global communication environment. It is based on the communication model developed in Chapter 3. The elaboration of narratives takes place in a relationally constituted social space. The overlapping networks of relationships in which every social actor is enmeshed is purposely *not* represented in the figure in order to avoid thinking that narratives are being trans-mitted across the social links as if they were bits of data sent through fibre optic cables. Instead, the obligations, information, demands, and expectations that are attached to any relationship should be conceived as the pulling force of a gravitational field. Every actor (A, B, C, D ...) could be seen as a mirror, and the information each individual receives from the outside could be thought of as light. In a global and transpar-ent information environment, light comes virtually from all directions. The image each mirror (each individual) will reflect will depend on the individual's position within his/her constellation of relationships. As Lawler (2002: 253), talking about the relationship between narra-tives and the social context in which they are produced, expresses it: "[D]ifferent social positioning is reflected in the kinds of stories people tell." The position affects the "amount of light" reflected – in other words the selection of information made by the individual within the available data deluge.

In this communication environment, messages are not simply transmitted, but they are constantly reinterpreted. Continuing with the hall of mirrors metaphor, the position within the social field will affect the orientation of each individual's mirror: its surface (whether it will be smooth or rough), whether the mirror will be straight, concave or convex (emphasising a part of an image much more than the rest or leading to an upside down reflection – an opposite reading perhaps). The position also affects to where (to which people) the image is going to be further reflected. Some actors might plan to convey specific images/messages, but the image they will ultimately reflect is itself shaped by their own position in the set of relationships. The planned image/narrative an individual might intentionally convey is being reinterpreted at each stage of the communication process. The image is being reflected further and, again, the way it looks at every stage depends on the position of each mirror and on the nature of the mirror's shape and surface. There is no guarantee that the image will keep the same form. For example, the actor, A, in the figure might want to promote a specific narrative (represented by the triangle) in an attempt to mobilise other individuals around a political cause. Other actors, who are exposed to that "message," like B, C, D, F, might, however, read it in completely different terms. Only E might read it in similar terms. Not because E has somehow "absorbed" that narrative, but because E's relational setting facilitates a reading that closely matches E's narrative. J, while "listening" to what A is arguing, might entirely disagree and, contrary to what A is hoping for, develop an entirely oppositional reading (the inverted triangle).

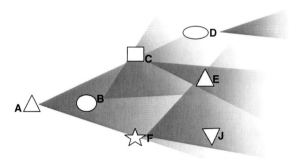

Figure 5.1 The global communication environment as a hall of mirrors: the simultaneous coexistence of multiple individual narratives

The concept of narrative helps understanding the way the terrorist "story" is constructed by the organisation's leaders, but the story manages to spread and keep on existing over time through the retelling by sympathisers, engaged supporters, and new recruits. The terrorists' narrative, as with any narrative, is the result of a collective construction. It is certainly promoted by specific actors, in the case of Al Qaeda by terrorist leaders, but there is evidence that it is being appropriated by individuals and local groups, most notably in what is mistakenly referred to as "self-radicalisation" (Jenkins 2007: 5–6). The retelling of these narratives is done by a range of different actors with varying agendas and very diverse intended audiences. Each individual potentially sees a different "story." As Betz (2008: 521) describes this process:

> Bin Laden and his associates do not appear endlessly on the British Broadcasting Corporation, or Cable News Network or even Al-Jazeera defending these talking points [basic elements of their strategic narrative]: this work is done (very effectively) by largely voluntary networks which have open access, share material, work collectively, and have a diversity of motives. Not everybody in the network needs to be a committed Jihadi, they may or may not like the idea of living under a restored Caliphate, they may indeed in some circumstances not be Muslim at all because the mindset of sullen resentment, which is what animates the movement, is shared by diverse groups from anti-globalists to anti-vivisectionists.

5.2.2 Conceptual problems in using "narrative"

The current use of the concept of narrative presents three main shortcomings. The first is the tendency to overlook the sociological depth of the narrative concept and, instead, take strategic narrative as a synonym for a "story". Literature on the role of the Internet in allegedly promoting the radicalisation of extremists, for example, identifies "an effective *tale* of an imaginary 'clash of civilizations' in which, supposedly, a monolithic West has been engaged in an aggressive struggle against a monolithic Islam for centuries, since the time of the Crusades" (HSPI/CIAG 2007: 2, my emphasis). The implication is a reification of the narrative, the belief that it has an objective existence outside the mind of audiences – a notion that clashes with the understanding of narrative as a social product only existing through its continuous retelling. Such understanding is arguably the legacy of outdated communication models related to the successful distribution of propaganda messages being applied to the current "war of ideas" between extremism and liberal democracy. This notion of the narrative particularly appears to resemble some aspects of the "Hypodermic Needle Model" of communication (Rogers 2003: 303). This was developed in the early twentieth century and postulated powerful, immediate, and direct effects of mass media on audiences (ibid.). It was based on the idea that audiences could be "inoculated" with a message, which would then trigger predictable and homogenous behavioural change.

A modification of this linear model of communication, to illustrate the difference with the previous and more complex process through which narratives are constructed (Figure 5.1), is represented in Figure 5.2. The idea is that a message (represented by the triangle), once crafted by an actor A, exists independently of individual agency and can be "sent" to other actors (actor B, for example). B can then either pass the message forward or not (C, for instance, does not pass the message on to E). An actor might pass on just part of the message (the smaller triangle passed from B on to C).

The fact that this model informs most works about extremism is supported by widespread statements in the literature about the power of the terrorist narrative to "spread" (Gupta 2011; Presidential Task Force 2009), by the use of terms like "infected" (Speckhard 2011: 172) or the very idea that the effectiveness of "our" counter-narratives can be assessed by measuring the reach of our message, such as by counting the visits, clicks and downloads on a media product (such as a video) that contains "our" message (Lemieux and Nill 2011; Speckhard 2011: 171–172). This linear model is, however, misleading: the narrative is not a "message" to be sent out to an audience in order to trigger certain expected (and predictable) behaviours. Communication is crucial,

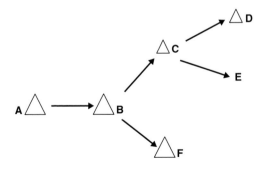

Figure 5.2 Old models of communication: the linear transmission of a message

but more emphasis is needed on the differentiated ways in which the narrative is appropriated, interpreted, and retold by individuals.

The understanding of the narrative as a message or a story leads to a second problem: a tendency to concentrate on the content of the narrative, particularly on how to craft the "right" message, and how it can best be delivered to a target audience. The emphasis is on achieving a successful transmission. Corman (2009b), in this respect, points out that US public diplomacy efforts, which should communicate American values and contribute to "winning hearts and minds" in the global "war of ideas," are based on oversimplified models of communication. According to him, the current way in which US officials attempt communicating with foreign publics to curb extremism is based on the notion that "messages" are transmitted by an "Information Source" through a "Transmitter" (via a "Signal") to a "Receiver," which will then convey the message to the desired "Destination." The implications are: that communication occurs only when messages are sent; that successful communication can be achieved by improving the skill of the communicator; by reducing the "noise" in the system; by carefully planning the content of the message and carefully transmitting it (ibid.). This is a model that was developed by David Berlo in the 1960s and was based on the study of telephone communication systems. Corman explains its current role in shaping official thinking through the fact that, having being taught across communication and public relations courses over decades, it has become part of the way public diplomacy practitioners in the United States read the reality of international communications (Corman 2010). Yet, this model of communication, as he puts it, was "cutting-edge at the time of Eisenhower" (2009b). Its continued existence is nonetheless confirmed by a whole range of statements contained in the recent "Report on Strategic Communications" issued by the US Department of Defense in 2009.[3] Indeed, the fact that the model appears in the "Information Operations Primer: Fundamentals of Information Operations" of the US Army War College (2011) shows that that it is still part of the training curriculum at the time of this writing.

Especially the last link between Berlo's model and "information operations" suggests the influence of "information warfare" doctrine on current approaches to counterterrorism. The doctrine of information operations developed out of the integration of "command and control" warfare and information warfare in the 1990s and is based on the acknowledgement that information is "an element of power across the spectrum of peace, conflict, and war" (ibid.: 3). The purpose of information operations is "to influence the *behavior* of target audiences by changing their ability to make decisions, while simultaneously defending the friendly capability to make proper decisions. This is no different from the exercise of the other forms of national power. In this instance the means is information, but the resulting outcome is the same" (ibid.). The notion that information can replace bullets to fight war underpins the whole discourse of strategic communication and messaging.

The messaging model, however, does not fit the complexity of current global communications. There is no longer the possibility, as when propaganda studies actually developed at the time of the diffusion of radio and TV, that a message could be targeted at a specific audience (as, in its crudest form, by physically dropping leaflets behind enemy lines, for instance). The feature of the current information environment that makes it radically different from the past is its transparency. It is true that information does not flow randomly, and that there are blind spots represented by areas where communication infrastructures are either underdeveloped (issues of access in African countries, for example) or controlled (as in China). Nonetheless, information is far less constrained by national state borders, and through its digital format can travel almost seamlessly across communication platforms like the Internet, TV, and mobile phones (de Waal 2007). As Corman (2009a) writes elsewhere:

> Communication is not a process of transmission of messages but of dialogue with an audience. Modern media systems make exclusively targeting narrow audiences difficult or impossible. Communication systems are so complex that planning is of limited use. You can't straightforwardly assess results and tweak your tactics, as if you were a strategic communication version of a forward artillery spotter.

The third shortcoming of current approaches in counterterrorism is empirical, and related to the methodologies to study the narrative. The weakness appears to derive from the fact that the concept of narrative has only recently entered the field of security studies. Narrative comes originally from literature, but has been applied "from philosophy, education, theology and psychology to economics, medicine, biology and environmental science" (Webster and Mertova 2007: 1). Having been developed by foreign disciplines, this concept still lacks a methodological set of techniques to deal with the issues at hand: mobilisation, specifically by terrorist organisations, and fighting extremism.

The situation is made worse by the fact that since the purposes of studying narratives have varied from investigating issues as diverse as personal narratives related to women's health (Kohler Riessman 1993), teachers' culture (Cortazzi 1993), and the extent to which stories contribute to problem solving in organisations (Mitroff and Kilmann 1975), there is no set way of conducting narrative analysis. This might involve discourse analysis, interviews, content analysis, and ethnographic methods (Clandinin 2007). Indeed, as David Boje (1991: 107) points out in a study of storytelling as a management tool in a commercial organisation, even what might look like the absence of a narrative might be relevant: the "audible story" is just a fraction of what is not said and yet is shared.

This does mean that narratives cannot be studied in relation to security. However, it is problematic to "import" methodologies, as they might well be able to deal with a narrative (its structure, content, characteristics ...), but not with the purposes for which the analysis of that narrative is being conducted. Casebeer and Russell (2005: 11), to illustrate this point, argue that the elaboration of an "effective counter-strategy [against terrorism] will require understanding the components and content of the story being told so we can predict how they will influence the action of a target audience." Besides assuming that the narrative is a story, and that the story can be communicated to a target audience and trigger an expected behaviour (an example of the older communication models at work), they suggest using the Aristotelian model of rhetoric to assess the effectiveness of the narrative. The rhetoric analysis would consist in focusing on: *ethos* or the credibility of the speaker who articulates the narrative; *pathos*, the appeal to the audience's emotions; and *logos*, the content or the support provided by facts. These are certainly worthwhile aspects to investigate. They are actually crucial in shaping a narrative's *potential* resonance with an audience. However, they are clearly insufficient in the above-stated objective of predicting "how they will influence the action of a target audience." Analysing a narrative to inform our understanding of the way terrorist achieve their strategic goal of mobilisation has to include consideration of the way the narrative contributes to creating a sense of identity; in other words how the narrative is being *appropriated by* – rather than merely *delivered to* – audiences.

5.3   Conclusions: what is feasible in the "war of ideas" against terrorism?

Understanding the collectively constructed nature of strategic narratives affects the assessment of what can and cannot be achieved in the war of ideas against Al Qaeda: while it is not possible to "stop" Al Qaeda's narrative from being communicated, and it is not feasible to rewrite "their" narrative, the best way forward is for one's own narrative to be consistent. These points will now be illustrated in turn.

The narrative is not just a story. It is a story that is being continuously retold. The idea that the spreading of the Al Qaeda narrative can be stopped by interfering with the group's communication channels is based on the idea that the story is being told through a one-way process: the "message" is being sent by Al Qaeda members to audiences. While Al Qaeda members have an interest in promoting that narrative, this is a reductive understanding of not only communication processes, but also of the way they take place in the twenty-first century media-saturated environment. There are too many channels to stop the narrative from being communicated. Beyond the Internet, the "old technologies" are still there: Carl Björkman (2010: 242–243), for instance, in talking about jihadi–Salafi terrorism in Italy, writes that military manuals and jihadi documents from prominent thinkers have, over the last decade, "spread ... on CD-ROMs, videos and audio-cassettes." In countries with poor literacy levels, as in Afghanistan, face-to-face interaction is still the most widely used form of communication between radicals and the wider population (Johnson 2007). Besides, disrupting communications, for example by taking down websites, leads to a loss in terms of sources of information (International Crisis Group 2006: 2). In addition to this, the narrative is only in part actively promoted by the Al Qaeda leadership. The reason why the narrative keeps on existing is that it is constantly retold and re-evoked by wider audiences. They do not just involve terrorist sympathisers. Al Qaeda's narrative might be contained in a journalistic report about the Al Qaeda leadership's latest message, in a critique of the terrorist organisation, or in an academic study about it.

Replacing "their" narrative with a "better story" as Casebeer and Russell (2005: 9) suggest, especially in relation to Al Qaeda's founding myth, is unrealistic, at least for Western governments. The myth is part of the group's identity and is constantly constructed and reconstructed by the members of the group. The myth is itself a narrative that can be changed, through collective reconstruction over time. Any contribution that appears to be coming from the West, however, lacks credibility. As Betz (2008: 511) points out, the debate about the correct interpretation and implementation of the meaning of jihad is an intra-Muslim debate, "not one which we as outsiders can contribute to in a sophisticated and convincing way." A better way to go about it would be encouraging public debate in the Muslim world.

In this perspective, attempting to target radicalised individuals with the "right" message is a waste of time. The influence of ideas based in information warfare doctrine leads to the belief that sound bites can replace bullets. The logic is that, instead of physically killing opponents, we can affect their behaviour by changing their minds through the appropriate message. This is, again, completely unrealistic. For a start, terrorists are already listening to what Western governments, think thanks, and media are saying, as is demonstrated by the fact that the Al-Fajr Centre, the media hub that coordinates the distribution of online communiqués, videos and statements by Al Qaeda and other jihadi groups (Iraqi insurgency groups, Palestinian, Somali, and Saudi jihadi groups ...) also has an "intelligence brigade" (Katz in Committee on Homeland Security 2007: 18) in charge of monitoring the websites and output of organisations like the White House, the US Army, the RAND corporation, the Jamestown Foundation, and *Time* magazine (see also Geltzer 2010: 22–23). Additionally, most of those involved in terrorist plots live in Western societies, where they are constantly exposed to potential counter-narratives. Both public discourse and media coverage are overwhelmingly filled with the notion that terrorism and violence are deplorable, as is Al Qaeda. The reason why "our" narrative is not having any effect on the extremist mindset is that "our message" is filtered through a very different personal narrative, grounded in a specific constellation of relationships. In this perspective, communication is, counter-intuitively, most effective when not directed at the terrorists or violent extremists, but *around* them.

While Western democracies cannot stop the continuous reconstruction of the narrative, they can stop fuelling the terrorists' narrative by being consistent with what they claim to represent and what they actually do. Ultimately, competing with the mobilising power of an opponent's narrative involves increasing one's own appeal. A better understanding of Al Qaeda's strategic narrative (especially of how it portrays Western democracies, as well as of the way it is appropriated by audiences) can certainly aid in avoiding words and deeds that might help in confirming that identity perception in the Muslim world. The use of torture and extraordinary rendition are at odds with the respect for human rights that should be at the core of Western democracies' identity. They serve to reinforce the idea promoted in the Al Qaeda strategic narrative that the West is morally corrupt and engaged in a crusade against Islam. The way forward lies, therefore, in consistency between rhetoric and deeds – what Betz (2008: 530) calls "narrative alignment" – and in being consistent with one's own values.

Branding is a concept which matches the social depth of the narrative. It additionally fits with the strategic context of security studies. It is about the establishment of a distinct identity, and also comes with an already established set of analytical tools to measure the extent of audience appropriation of that identity. I am now turning to explaining how branding could assist in the empirical study of strategic narratives.

6
The Al Qaeda Narrative as a Brand

The previous chapter developed the argument that a narrative is more than a story. The concept of narrative contributes to understanding the processes through which, in a global and porous information environment, some interpretations of the world are purposely promoted by social actors – such as governments, political parties or terrorist organisations – to achieve specific objectives. The continued existence of these interpretations, however, depends on wider members of the audience appropriating them and, collectively, continuously retelling them. This chapter takes further the notion that narratives are socially constructed and that they contribute to shaping the identities of both those who have built them and those who appropriate them. More specifically, it will examine and measure the strength of the Al Qaeda identity by applying an analytical tool from the world of marketing: the concept of branding. The purpose of the analysis is to show that there is scope for translating the communication approach to terrorism that has been developed throughout the book into useful empirical research. Not only can some of it be far more adventurous than counting fatalities on the enemy's side, but as will be illustrated, it can also contribute to alternative and more effective measurements of progress in counterterrorism.

The argument will develop in three stages. The first will offer an overview of what a brand is and how it can be applied to Al Qaeda. As a second step the analysis will offer an example of that application to strategic narratives of a brand-related concept, Kapferer's "identity prism" (Kapferer 2004: 107–111). The identity prism was originally designed to identify the unique characteristics that constitute a brand's identity. Here the prism framework will be adapted and expanded in order to apply it to the study of governments, organisations, and publics involved in terrorism and counterterrorism. This section will provide examples of how the prism framework can assist in measuring the narrative of Al Qaeda, that of Western democracies, and their respective appropriation by audiences. The third part of the chapter outlines the contributions that the application of branding can make to measuring progress in counterterrorism, particularly in relation to the definition of what "success" means for "us" and for "them." The conclusions highlight the challenges, for Western governments involved in counterterrorism, in establishing and managing a "democratic brand."

6.1 What is a brand? And is Al Qaeda, technically, a brand?

Al Qaeda has often been referred to as a "brand" in a variety of contexts by officials, journalists, and academics. The term appears to be used inconsistently. The reasons why Al Qaeda is labelled a "brand" are, in fact, various. Sometimes the terrorist group is called a "brand" because its activities, in the mind of the person or the organisation applying the term, appear vaguely related to the operations of a global company. Former MI5 chief Jonathan Evans, for instance, in a speech delivered in Manchester on 5 November 2007, referring to the creation of the new "Al Qaeda in the Lands of the Islamic Maghreb" said: "This sort of extension of the Al Qaeda *brand* to new parts of the Middle East and beyond poses a further threat to us in this country because it provides Al Qaeda with access to new centres of support which it can motivate and exploit, including in its campaign against the UK" (Evans 2007; see also Roy 2004). *The Economist* (Thomas 2008) both echoes and takes further this idea of Al Qaeda as a multinational corporation by writing that, "To explain the [Al Qaeda] movement, many experts draw parallels with globalisation. Some describe it as a venture capital firm that invests in promising terrorist projects. Others speak of it as a global 'brand' maintained by its leaders through their propaganda, with its growing number of 'franchises' carrying out attacks." In other cases the "brand" tends to coincide with a "narrative" relentlessly promoted by the terrorist group through the full spectrum of global communications. According to the leaked Home Office report, "Challenging Violent Extremist Ideology Through Communications," Whitehall's Research, Information and Communications Unit (RICU) was set up in 2007 specifically to "taint the Al Qaeda brand" (Travis 2008b). In practice, the activity of RICU consisted in undermining the groups' "narrative of grievance" in which Muslims are portrayed as victims of Western injustice (Travis 2008a). Alternatively, a "brand" is simply a synonym for a "label" or an instantly recognisable "logo." Daniel Kimmage (2008a: 1), in his analysis of Al Qaeda-related videos and websites, observes for example that all jihadist media products that appear on the Internet are "systematically branded." He refers to the fact that they all underline their "official" status through the graphic logos of the media production and distribution outlets associated to Al Qaeda, which make their material immediately recognisable when they are posted online (ibid.: 3).

A full review of the literature on branding and its different branches exceeds the scope of this chapter. For the present purposes suffice it to say that branding is not necessarily related to selling and making a profit. Specialised strands of literature exist on how the concept can be applied to entities as complex and as symbolically laden as nations and countries (nation branding: Olins 1999; Van Ham 2001; Anholt 2002; Gilmore 2002; Olins 2002; Anholt 2007); places (Harrison 2002; Kotler and Gertner 2002; Morgan, Pritchard and Piggott 2002; Hankinson 2004; Anholt 2005; Csaba 2005: 141–147); services (Taylor 1992; de Chernatony and Dall'Olmo Riley 1999); and nonprofit organisations (Hankinson 2002, 2004; Ewing and Napoli 2003; Csaba 2005: 131–140).

Branding is, essentially, about differentiation. The term branding originates from the ancient practice of fire marking ownership on cattle (Blackett 2003: 14–15). Branding should not be confused with marketing. The focus of marketing is on advertising through the mass media (Godin 2002, chapter 1). Although aspects of marketing, such as logos, trademarks, advertisement, and publicity campaigns all contribute to making the brand distinctive and memorable, contrary to popular beliefs, branding is not just a "cosmetic exercise" (Clifton 2003: 6).[1] Branding is about establishing – positioning – an identity in the market (Kapferer 2004, chapter 5).

The identity is defined by the brand *platform*, constituted by a vision, a mission, and values. They are, as Bahr Thompson (2003: 86) phrases it, the "central building blocks for the brand." The vision is the brand's reason to exist, a compelling idea. It answers the question "what are we here for?" (Davidson 2005: 16), "what is the purpose of our organisation?" This might be "giving the customer the best value deal" for Virgin – which aspires to provide "value for money, quality, innovation, fun and a sense of competitive challenge" (Virgin.com n.d.) – but can extend to establishing a Caliphate based on Sharia law in the case of Al Qaeda (Lia 2009: 13), or "giving Earth a voice" (Greenpeace.org n.d.) for an NGO like Greenpeace.

The mission sets the short-term objectives that an organisation needs to achieve in order to realise the long-term vision. It answers the questions: Where are we going? What are our goals? (Davidson 2005: 16). These objectives might change depending on external circumstances. In corporate terms, for example, Hewlett Packard has moved, after 50 years of producing the instrumentation it was originally known for, to mini-computers, calculators, touch-screen personal computers, workstations, printers, medical equipment, and digital imaging (Brenkel 1997: 137). In the case of Al Qaeda, Edwin Bakker and Leen Boer (2007) identify three distinct phases in the evolution of the organisation. While the mission was always the same – establishing a Caliphate – the organisation changed as a result of evolving local and international conditions: in the period of the late 1980s to 1996, Al Qaeda transformed from a "vanguard" planning terrorist operations, first from Afghanistan, then Saudi Arabia, Sudan, and then again Afghanistan (ibid.: 11), into a "base" supporting terrorist groups throughout the world through providing training (ibid.: 11–12); then to a "maxim," "a methodology rather than an organisational structure," after most of its training facilities and operative cadres had been destroyed in the aftermath of 9/11 (ibid.: 12). It is also possible to identify a shift in priorities. Brynjar Lia (2009: 15), in assessing the consistency of the statements released by Osama bin Laden and Ayman Al-Zawahiri, points out that, while striking at economic enemy targets has been a consistent call after 9/11, oil facilities in Iraq and the Gulf have more recently emerged as priorities: "The war of economic attrition-theme has become even more prominent in bin Laden's discourse after the US financial crisis erupted with full force in late 2008."

The brand values, instead, capture the "morals and ethics" of an organisation and guide its members' behaviour as well as their relationship to the external world (Bahr Thompson 2003: 86–87; Davidson 2005: 16). The values of Hewlett Packard are, for example, "reliability and quality, being somewhat conservative, no matter where it is in the world or what business it is in" (Brenkel 1997: 134). Al Qaeda's values could be summed up in "jihad only" (Lia 2009: 3): the belief at the core of Al Qaeda's ideology that the struggle in which the organisation and its followers are engaged is only to "please God" and make "God's word supreme," not for worldly gain. While a brand's mission can change over time to assure that the brand stays relevant and meets possible challenges in the short term, the overall vision and values should remain constant. Indeed, the main reason brands are successful is their ability to stick to their vision and their core values while adapting to changing circumstances (Brymer 2003: 69–71).

The "brand identity" emerging from the elements of the brand platform might be created by a company, an institution, or a social movement, but as Lynn Upshaw (1995) points out, it "lives entirely in the mind of the beholder." In his words: "An identity is not what a marketer creates, but *what consumers perceive has been created*. That, in turn, hinges on who consumers are as individuals, the environment in which they live, and the signals sent from the brand itself" (ibid.: 12–13, my emphasis).

A brand thus exists when it occupies a portion of our "mental territory," which does not involve only those audiences who directly engage with the brand. Nicola-Maria Riley (1995), for example, investigates the application of branding to industrial relations. She conducts a study of the image of four teachers' unions in Britain (NUT, NASUWT, ATL, and PAT).[2] By interviewing members of the different unions as well as non-members she concludes that the four unions do not differ from one another in terms of their "objectively identifiable functions," which are essentially the same, but by virtue of "their distinct image in the mind of the individual teacher" (ibid.: 9). In addition to this, the features of the most successful brands (NUT and ATL) were confidently known even by non-union members. Both members and non-members of NUT, for example, saw the union as an organisation with "strong convictions and a sense of mission" (ibid.: 11). The only difference between the members and non-members was that the former felt that the image reflected their own values, while the latter saw the same aspects in a negative light. Because they saw them as "dominant and destructive" (ibid.) they also found NUT unappealing. Most of the interviewees had clear perceptions of where each of the unions stood in relation to the others (ibid.).

As such, the brand appears to be related to a broader set of "relationships in the market place" (ibid.: 3). These involve: a relationship between the brand and the individual, between the individual and other individuals they perceive will be buying (not literally) into the brand and those who will not; and between the brand and alternative brands. Communication is key to establishing these relationships, not only in terms of shaping the knowledge of each individual about a brand and its alternative competitors, but also in terms of affecting the individual's awareness of the position of all other actors (other individuals and brands) in the broader social environment.

A brand, once it has taken a place in our mental territory, serves a heuristic function for the information we receive. It contributes to the way in which each individual will make sense of the features of products, services, or policies offered by the brand. For example, the same feature of a car, an ABS, can be seen as a means to increase the security of the vehicle (Volvo) or as a device that allows a more sporty driving (BMW) (ibid.: 5). Applying this to the branding of teachers' unions: membership is interpreted by ATL members as a "purchase of a professional insurance," while NUT members see joining the union as an expression of "the will of the collective to fight for an individual member in a time of need" (ibid.). Extending the concept further to terrorism and antiterrorism, it is possible to understand (in terms of brands) the relevance of "narratives" in shaping the understanding of global events: on the one hand, Al Qaeda, portraying Muslims as the victims of Western oppression and aggression; on the other hand, democracies engaged in the struggle to protect individual freedoms and human rights. These narratives are nothing else than the result of the individual appropriations of the Al Qaeda and the "democracy" brands, respectively, by followers of the Al Qaeda ideology and citizens in Western countries.

These parallels between narratives and brands exist because, ultimately, brands *are* narratives. This supports the use of branding as an analytical tool to assist in the study of strategic narratives. Having said that, it is important to remember that narratives and brands are not the same thing. Beyond the obvious realisation that Al Qaeda is not a can of beans, strategic narratives in the context of terrorism and counterterrorism are much more complex than commercial brands. I have previously explained the way in which narratives promoted by governments and terrorist organisations are actively interpreted by individuals through the prism of their own individual narratives. Both individual narratives and narratives promoted for the purposes of political mobilisation develop on already existing layers of meaning (which we might call "culture" or "tradition"). This is somehow already suggested by some in the literature. Although I do not entirely agree with the points that will be made in the following examples, they support the argument that narratives that are promoted by either terrorist organisations or democratic governments are not developed in a vacuum. According to Richard Barrett (2008: 13) narratives are rooted in the culture and history of a society and, at the same time, resonate with individual experiences. David Betz (2008: 519) argues that the "quality of credibility and persuasiveness" of strategic narratives depends on their "vertical coherence" or capacity to appear "natural." By drawing on Ann Swidler he explains how narratives are able to link "ideology" with "tradition" and "common sense." Gilles Kepel and Jean-Pierre Milelli (2008: 6) point out that the content of electronic material published by Al Qaeda is rooted in a "telescoping of time between Middle Ages and today": "in this literature, history is simply the infinite repetition of a single narrative: the arrival of the Prophet, the rise of Islam, the struggles to extend its dominion, and its expansion throughout the world."

Another distinction between the brands of a terrorist organisation or a Western government and commercial brands is that for a manager of a commercial brand it is possible to plan the brand platform and tightly control its delivery. Even if the brand has to be "lived" by all employees (de Chernatony and Dall'Olmo Riley 1999), compliance with the brand platform can be enforced through the corporate organisation. Managing strategic narratives in the real world, instead, is far more problematic. For Western democracies the thorny issue is how to balance the brand consistency with democracy and free speech. Besides, who should decide what the core values of Western societies are? Nonetheless the concept of brand is useful in bringing together both the physical and the virtual aspects of terrorism and counterterrorism.

The concept of brand appears far more complex than the single dimensions the loose use of the term describes when commonly applied to Al Qaeda. The next section explains that, if used more rigorously, the concept of brand can lead to useful insights about the threat presented by the terrorist organisation.

6.2 Measuring the narrative by applying branding's analytical tools: the "identity prism"

Understanding Al Qaeda's narrative is important because it constitutes a heuristic framework that offers guidance to local extremist groups in relation to the objectives to be achieved, which motivates them by covering the values of the organisation and explaining the reasons why the fight against the West is being waged. The narrative, in other words, firmly establishes the group's background and identity. Johnson (2007: 319), for example, explains the importance of narratives as a historically important tool of mobilisation in Afghan society: for instance against the Soviet occupiers. Narratives are told and retold orally and, especially in rural areas, through poems and songs (ibid.: 319–320).

The branding literature is, in this respect, useful in providing templates for measuring the strength of a brand on the basis of its capacity to differentiate itself from other brands – its identity. Here, through examples, I am going to illustrate the application of the concept of "identity prism" (Kapferer 2004: 107) to the mapping of "our" narrative and Al Qaeda's. I will explain to what the different facets of the prism refer by providing examples of how they could assist in coding information about the two narratives. I will then move on to show how the concept can further be adapted to highlight the extent of similarities and differences among the narratives (especially the way they construct identities) of different terrorist groups, governments (or government departments), and over time. The prism could also be used, through a comparison between the "official" narrative and the narrative perceived by different segments of the audience, to assess the "effectiveness" of the projected narrative. In this perspective "effectiveness" does not consist so much in how an actor tells a story, that is, on the ability of a country's government or the leadership of Al Qaeda to be consistent or "on message." Although the communication of the narrative and its delivery are certainly essential, what matters here is the extent to which the retelling of the narrative – what the audience actually perceives the narrative to be – corresponds to the original "story."

6.2.1 The identity prism

For Jean-Noël Kapferer (2004) identity is essential to the positioning of the brand, to establishing its uniqueness. Identity does not coincide with the aesthetic image of a brand. It is about what makes a brand distinguishable and recognisable, while at the same time constituting the common thread (ibid.: 96) among many possible products, services, or policies that a company, an organisation, or a government might provide. Brand identity involves six facets. They can be placed, as can be seen in Figure 6.1, along two axes. The vertical dimension contrasts the "picture" built by the sender to the "picture" built by the receiver. The horizontal dimension, instead, contrasts the internal aspects of the brand to the way they are interpreted and lived externally. Although related, each aspect addresses a dimension of the brand's uniqueness (ibid.: 112).

A first adaptation of the prism to the issues of terrorism and counter-terrorism consists in applying the whole prism to each context in which a narrative might exist. The prism is about the internal and external dimensions of a brand, the "picture of sender" being about the image the promoter of the brand constructs about him/her/itself and the "picture of receiver" being the constructed image of the audience. They do not refer to two different dimensions (brand promoter versus audience). They are contained within each narrative: the narrative promoted by the terrorist leaders, for example, or the narrative perceived by public opinion in the Middle East. To further explain: the US administration in the aftermath of 9/11 placed the terrorist attacks against the Twin Towers and the Pentagon in a narrative that defined not only the role of the administration and its new interpretation of the world (the constructed sender)

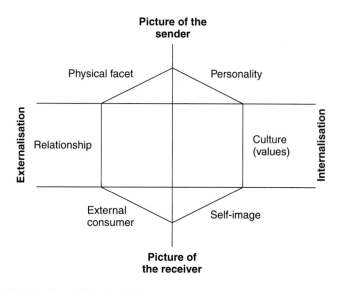

Figure 6.1   Kapferer's Identity Prism
Source: Kapferer 2004.

but also extended to constructing the public reaction (it defined the very identity of the receiver). For example, President Bush said that America was a "resilient society," that had been "tested before" and that it would be able to recover from the post-9/11 "time of trial." He described what the administration would do in order to respond to the attacks (internal dimension), but also how citizens in American society should act on the basis of the American way of life and its values (external dimension): The nation was "peaceful, but fierce when stirred to anger" (Bush 2001a) American society was compared to a sleeping "mighty giant" (Bush 2001c), who had been awoken by evil terrorists, and who would persevere in its determination to bring the perpetrators to justice, no matter what it took or how long. President Bush also described who the terrorists were and their motives. He said, for example, that terrorism was a global threat, a "scourge," a "crime against all civilization and humanity," which was not motivated by ideology or rational thought, but was the expression of "flat evil" (Bush 2001b).

This aspect is related to a second adaptation of the prism. Each prism is about establishing an identity (the self), but is also about differentiating that identity from "the other." Each of the prisms could therefore extend to covering, for each facet (where available), the corresponding features of "the enemy."

The facets of the prism, according to Kapferer (2004) are physique, personality, culture, relationship, reflected consumer, and self -image. I am going to explain each of these aspects, showing how they can be more appropriately renamed for the study of organisations rather than products, and applied to "our" narrative and Al Qaeda's (compare Figure 6.1 with Figures 6.2 and 6.3). I will present some examples taken from the Al Qaeda and the UK government's strategic narratives. Figures 6.2 and 6.3, while containing just few examples of content, offer an illustration of how the prism framework could be used to map the two narratives. I will refer to a translation of Al-Zawahiri's *Knights under the Prophet's Banner* (Mansfield 2006) and the *United Kingdom's Strategy for Countering International Terrorism* (Home Office 2009), also known as Contest 2.

Physique. This facet covers the salient objective features of a brand, what a brand is normally associated with. As Riley puts it: if the brand was a flower, the physique would be the stem (Riley 1995: 6). It refers to the "functional qualities" (ibid.), those features without which the brand would not be recognisable. Rather than what it looks like, in the case of an institution like a country, the physique could be interpreted as: What does it do? What are the features without which it would not exist as such? What is it that makes it distinctive, its reason for existing? This aspect could be regarded as covering the defining *goals* of the organisation – in the case of the countries involved in counterterrorism, the institution of democracy. As Contest 2 puts it: "our response [to terrorism] has included changes to our laws to reflect the threat we face, but has at all times upheld the principles and values of the UK as a liberal democracy" (Home Office 2009: 18). As for the Al Qaeda narrative, at the very beginning of *Knights under the Prophet's Banner*, Al-Zawahiri explains that the purpose of the mujahideen is "serving the cause of Islam in its ferocious war against the tyrants of the new Crusade" (Al-Zawahiri in Mansfield 2006: 19).

Personality. "The way in which it [the brand] speaks of its product or services shows what kind of person it would be if it were human" (Kapferer 2004: 108). This feature is not to be confused with the portrayal of the ideal receiver. It answers the question: what are the features of the brand if it were a person? In the case of terrorist organisations and Western democracies, these features are actually embodied in the characteristics of their most visible members – their *leaders*. The characteristics of the mujahedeen personalities, Western leaders, and citizens could be gathered under this label.

Again in relation to the Al Qaeda narrative, Al-Zawahiri writes that those who fight for Islam "possess a quality their enemies cannot hope to acquire. They are the people who most eloquently bear witness to their God's power, Who has given them a strength drawn from His Own Strength" (Al-Zawahiri in Mansfield 2006: 21). The Afghan mujahideen have "true hearts" (ibid.: 42). A "pioneer of jihad in Egypt" in the 1960s, Yahia Hashim, is described as follows:

> God endowed him with a proud spirit and high morale. Which prompted him to sacrifice everything, disregarding the vanities of this world. He had another good quality – his enthusiasm for what he believed in. He had – may God have mercy on him – a pure soul that sympathized with his brother Muslims.
>
> Yahya Hashim was acting prosecutor – a post desired by many young men. But he did not care about this post. He was always ready to sacrifice this post for the sake of God, disregarding the ephemeral things of his world. (Ibid.: 64)

The narrative Al-Zawahiri contributes to construct also extends to establishing the identity of Western opponents: they are "enemies" who "pursue the mujahideen" with "viciousness" and "ferocity" (ibid.: 24, emphasis added).

The UK government, instead, is described by former prime minister, Gordon Brown (Home Office 2009: 6), as being engaged in "a comprehensive approach to international terrorism" in which "the first priority ... is to ensure the security and safety of the nation and all members of the public." Authorities are "fully prepared" and will make "whatever changes are necessary" to face the "evolving" threat. They "have learned the lessons of recent experience" to make sure they develop "the strongest possible response."

Culture (values). This is constituted by the "set of values feeding the brand's inspirational power" (Kapferer 2004: 108), "it indicates the ethos whose values are embodied in the products and services of the brand" (ibid.: 109). For example, Mercedes embodies German values, especially order (ibid.). Ralph Laurent is "WASP [White Anglo Saxon Protestant]." "Culture is also the basis for most bank brands: choosing a bank means choosing the kind of relationship with money one wishes to have" (ibid.). For analysing the identity of an organisation, this facet answers the question: What are the values the organisation stands for? The "core values" that characterise the UK government and British society are: "human rights, the rule of law, legitimate and accountable government, justice, freedom" (Home Office 2009: 56). In Al-Zawahiri's words, the supreme value for the mujahideen is "God's Shari'ah" (Mansfield 2006: 103).

Relationship. A brand is essentially based on relationships: between the brand, other brands, and the consumers. This aspect of the brand is about "the mode of conduct that most identifies the brand" (Kapferer 2004: 110). This is not a description of the relationship between the brand and the consumer. It is a description of the consumer's external relationships as a result of embracing the brand. This aspect is important for non-corporate organisations and institutions. Nicola-Maria Riley (1995: 7), in applying this aspect of the prism to teachers' unions, writes that relationship is "of particular significance ... as a union is a community of employees whose intra-group relations may play an important role in the mind of the potential member."

The relationships among citizens and between them and political institutions in Western societies can be summed up in "tolerance and opportunity for all" (Home Office 2009: 56). In the Al Qaeda narrative, the relationship among mujahedeen is described as "comradeship-at-arms against the enemies of Islam" (Al-Zawahiri in Mansfield 2006: 38).

Reflected Consumer. This is how the customer "wishes to be seen as a result of using a brand" (Kapferer 2004: 110). It is not necessarily the market segment targeted by the marketer. This aspect does not describe who the consumers are, but what they wish to be as a result of purchasing a brand. For example, the description of the Reflected Consumer of the Ralph Lauren brand is: "they are comfortable, young men of good standing, nice, rich: ideal son-in-law" (ibid.: 112). Applying this to the context of terrorism and counterterrorism it does not refer to how the public looks, but how it is expected to behave on the basis of society's values. It is therefore labelled, as it can be seen in Figure 6.3, as "Expected Action."

According to the Al Qaeda narrative, the public is expected to engage in individual jihad (Al-Zawahiri 2001 in Mansfield 2006). As for Western societies, Home Secretary Jacqui Smith, in an interview following the release of the 2009 counterterrorism strategy, referred to the need for the public to actively engage in defending society's values (Smith in Chrichton 2009). The counterterrorism strategy (Home Office 2009: 87) describes it as follows:

> The duty on all of us – Government, citizens and communities – is to challenge those who, for whatever reason or cause, reject the rights to which we are committed, scorn the institutions and values of our parliamentary democracy, dismiss the rule of law and promote intolerance and discrimination on the basis of race, faith, ethnicity, gender or sexuality.

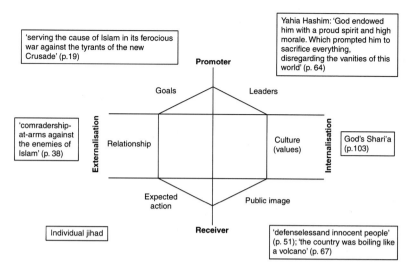

Figure 6.2 Application of the identity prism to mapping the Al Qaeda narrative

Source: Home Office 2009.

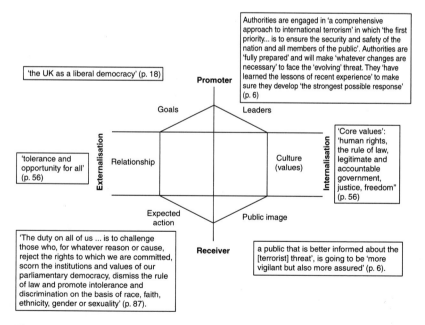

Figure 6.3 Application of the identity prism to mapping the UK government narrative

Source: Mansfield 2006.

Self-image. This is the way the consumer sees him/herself as a result of buying into the brand. Self-image is different from the reflected consumer because it is not how others see a user of the brand, it is the way the user sees him/herself. To show this difference by referring again to the previous example, the self-image of Ralph Lauren would be: "I am discreetly elegant, I am always correct although casual" (Kapferer 2004: 112). Applied to organisations, this aspect covers the *public image*, the way the public should see itself. For example Al-Zawahiri, in constructing the Al Qaeda narrative, several times describes the public in Egypt: masses are portrayed first as "defenceless and innocent people" (ibid.: 51); after they have joined the mujahideen struggle through their support, they are filled with anger at Egyptian authorities: "the country was boiling like a volcano" (ibid.: 67). UK former prime minister, Gordon Brown, instead, in the foreword to the 2009 UK *Strategy against International Terrorism* describes a public that, by being "better informed about the [terrorist] threat." is going to be "more vigilant but also more assured" (Brown in Home Office 2009: 6).

6.2.2 What could the identity prism do?

The utility of the prism is not the detection of the contents of the narrative per se, although the relationship among the different facets does capture the distinctiveness of the identity being constructed through the narrative. In terms of content detection the prism has actually an important limitation: it provides *a snapshot of a narrative constructed by one actor at a specific time* – for example in a policy document, a video or, depending on the timeframe in which the analysis is conducted, in a series of texts, speeches, or policy initiatives. The narrative, however, is constantly evolving and is the result of the activity of a range of actors – terrorist leaders, authorities, terrorist sympathisers, journalists, and members of the public, each of them with different motives – who keep on retelling the story. The key is, therefore, combining the contents of the narratives in different contexts to get a more accurate reconstruction of the dynamic nature of the resulting collective narrative – something similar to assembling a series of snapshots taken from different angles to obtain a 3D image.

The identity prism could be applied to both Western democracies' narrative/s and Al Qaeda's narrative/s. Different prisms could be identified, for example, within different departments of Western governments, or in relation to different figures of the Al Qaeda leadership. More prisms could be constructed to map how different audiences' segments perceive these strategic narratives: for example, in European countries, in Asia, the United States, or specific countries in the Middle East. Further to the perception of the Al Qaeda narrative among audiences, there could be a prism about the Al Qaeda identity in relation to supposedly self-radicalised individuals (who have, for example, become engaged in organising a terrorist plot); another one about perceptions by sympathisers (supporting Al Qaeda's objectives while not actually getting involved in any violent action). There could be a prism about perceptions of the UK government's narrative by British audiences, another one by audiences in the Middle East.

The contents of the facets could be filled by data generated through different methods: content analysis of governmental statements and the Al Qaeda leadership's messages; interviews and focus groups with members of the public and former extremists; content analysis of media coverage.

One of the problems related to the empirical investigation of narratives is the arbitrariness in identifying the very aspects that constitute them. As Kohler Riessman (1993: 2) puts it: "Nature and the world do not tell stories, individuals do. Interpretation is inevitable because narratives are representations." It might be argued that also what the researcher decides to fit into the identity prism is the result of interpretation (Kohler Riessman 2008: 154). This is certainly true and, to an extent, there is no escape from a certain level of subjectivity. The analysis has to be carried out by a human being. The framework offered by the prism, however, minimises the level of arbitrariness by offering a consistent benchmark for systematic comparisons at different levels.

The prism could be used to check the consistency of the brands involved in the struggle against terrorism over time. Lia (2009) for example, points at some inconsistencies between the contents of Al Qaeda leaders' statements across the years. There is not a clear identification of who the enemies of Al Qaeda are: "Americans? Crusaders? Zionists? Jews? Forces of Global Unbelief? The New World Order?" (Ibid.: 4–9). It is difficult, however, to establish the seriousness of the inconsistencies when one does not have a clear picture of what the overall narrative consists. The identity prism structure could help in quantifying the extent of the changes over time.

The prism could contribute to the detection of differences among affiliated groups to assess to what extent it is really possible to talk about a global narrative promoted by Al Qaeda. Hanna Rogan (2009) shows an inconsistency between the statements of Al Qaeda central and Al Qaeda in the Maghreb, but the extent to which they could actually damage the global Al Qaeda brand is unclear because there is no independent measure of whether they constitute a significant part of the terrorists' narrative.

The framework offered by the prism could also be the basis for developing a measure of the effectiveness of Western democracies' narrative/s against Al Qaeda's based on the extent to which the audience is aware of the two different narratives. According to Kapferer, the identity prism can test the relative strength of a brand: strong brands, as also demonstrated by Riley (1995), possess all six facets of the identity prism, while weaker brands possess just some of them (Kapferer 1991 in Riley 1995: 6). It is true that this is not a measure of the extent to which audiences *support* one side or the other. Their awareness of both, however, could be at least the basis for a more balanced independent interpretation of local and world events.

Knowing which aspects of our "story" are known could also provide an indication of which facets of the brand could be more effectively promoted. Although better promotion does not necessarily mean a change in the understanding by the audience. For example, a survey of public opinion in the Islamic world has investigated public attitudes towards Al Qaeda terrorism and US policies (Kull et al. 2009). Large majorities appear to know Al Qaeda's narrative, particularly its goals and the terrorist organisation's version of US foreign policy drivers. Matching the view of the world promoted by Al Qaeda leaders, large portions of the public in several Muslim countries state that Al Qaeda's goals are: establishing sharia law – 65 per cent in Egypt, 49 per cent in Indonesia, 76 per cent in Morocco, 76 per cent in Pakistan (ibid.: 22); getting the United States to withdraw from Muslim countries – 87 per cent in Egypt, 65 per cent in Indonesia, 72 per cent in Morocco, 60 per cent in Pakistan (ibid.: 20); keeping Western values out of Muslim countries – 88 per cent in Egypt, 76 per cent in Indonesia, 64 per cent in Morocco, 60 per cent in Pakistan (ibid.: 22).

They appear to believe the US goals are as described within the narrative promoted by Al Qaeda: spreading Christianity – Egypt: n.a., Indonesia: 55 per cent, Pakistan: 71 per cent, Morocco: 67 per cent (ibid.: 12), weaken and divide Islam – Egypt: 87 per cent, Indonesia: 62 per cent, Morocco: 78 per cent, Pakistan: 74 per cent (ibid.: 11), maintaining control over oil – Egypt: 88 per cent, Indonesia: 67 per cent, Morocco: 82 per cent, Pakistan: 62 per cent (ibid.: 12). By contrast, just small minorities think that the United States, as in the narrative actually promoted by the American administration, favours democracy in Muslim countries[3] – eight per cent in Egypt, 13 per cent in Indonesia, ten per cent in Pakistan (ibid.: 13). These figures are lower than the levels of support for the idea that the United States opposes democracy in Muslim countries – 37 per cent in Egypt, 17 per cent in Indonesia, 25 per cent in Pakistan (ibid.). Only minorities, again, think that the United States respects international law – 20 per cent in Egypt, 12 per cent in Indonesia, 20 per cent in Pakistan (ibid.: 16); against the notion that it does not – 67 per cent in Egypt, 55 per cent in Indonesia, 78 per cent in Pakistan (ibid.).

The purpose is not only to verify whether the narrative has been understood "correctly" by audiences – which could point to a problem in communicating the "message" – but also to measure the level of appropriation of the narrative by audiences. The exercise would also shed light on what the brands actually mean to audiences – the narrative in the audiences' minds might well be different – and what motivates the appropriation of a narrative rather than an alternative.

The extent to which a terrorist group's narrative is constituted by justifications about their activities could be an indirect measure of the expected appropriation of their story by the audience. For example, insurgent factions in Iraq in 2006, after a phase of dissent that led to public lengthy justifications and attention towards legitimising attacks (2004–05), started issuing very succinct communiqués (from mid-2005). An explanation for this change is that the audience had become sufficiently aware of the insurgents' narrative, which had been established and almost institutionalised through a "well established corpus of authoritative texts and documents" (International Crisis Group 2006: 13).

6.3   Branding and new indicators of counterterrorism

The application of the concept of brand leads to four main contributions to counterterrorism, which will now be illustrated in turn.

6.3.1   Focusing on the intangibles of the fight against terrorism

The branding approach focuses on the intangible aspects of the fight against terrorism, particularly on its communication dimension.

There is an increasing awareness that the fight against terrorism is being played out in the realms of perceptions and communications as much as, if not more than, through financial, legal, and military measures. Alex Schmid (2005: 143) says, for example, that "if terrorism is a form of psychological warfare, we should be focusing as much if not more on countering propaganda as we focus on preventing and controlling terrorist violence."

Perceptions are so important that both the former Brown government in the United Kingdom and the US administration since the election of President Obama have stopped using the expression "Global War on Terror" to address the current counterterrorism efforts (Kamen 2009). According to former foreign secretary David Miliband the phrase had not only fuelled the terrorist narrative of an organised attack on Islam, it had also played directly into Al Qaeda's hands by unifying very different groups under its umbrella (Miliband 2009).

The essential role of communications was underlined by Contest 2, the 2009 UK government's strategy to counter international terrorism: "Communications to the public, stakeholders and affected communities are a vital part of our counterterrorism work. Good communications enable us to convey the reality of the threats we face, the principles which govern our response, the choices we make and the successes we achieve" (Home Office 2009: 152). Yet, despite their "vital" role, the topic of communications took barely four pages out of a 175-page document. The new *Prevent* strategy (2011), despite often mentioning the role of narratives and counter-narratives confines the explicit discussion of communication to the equivalent of a single page of text (48–49) and almost exclusively in relation to the activity of the Research, Information, and Communications Unit (RICU).

The branding approach would not only raise the profile of communications in the current fight against terrorism; it would also support a more systematic effort in their planning, development, and study of effects as a key tool of counterterrorism.

6.3.2   Emphasising Al Qaeda's weaknesses rather than its strengths

The widespread loose (if not sloppy) application of the term *brand* is not helpful, as it is skewed towards emphasising the strengths of Al Qaeda. A brand is certainly an asset when it is appropriately managed. As Matt Haig (2003: 5) points out, however, "brands fail every single day." Perceptions are, in fact, fragile. The bond between an individual and a brand can easily break down. This can occur, for example, in the case of a brand extension in which the brand either becomes "watered down" by losing its original distinctiveness, or simply ends up delivering services, products, or policies that are inconsistent with its mission and values. High visibility also means higher exposure: it can lead "to intense scrutiny and make the brand vulnerable to criticism" (Csaba 2005: 137).

In this respect, the Algerian Salafist Group for Preaching and Combat (GSPC) joining Al Qaeda in January 2007 and changing its name to

Al Qaeda Organisation in the Islamic Maghreb, was widely presented as a "merge" that would extend Al Qaeda's reach and pool of resources. The Algerian group had actually pledged "nothing but obedience" (Abu Musab Abdul Wadud, emir of the group, in Katz and Deven 2007) to Osama bin Laden in September 2006, but the official change of name was announced four months later, after the then terrorist leader had approved it. The waiting for Al Qaeda's blessing was seen as an attempt by the terrorist organisation to "protect" its brand name, particularly its reputation, credibility and core ideology, in the global jihadist movement.

Having said that, not only approved groups join Al Qaeda. Many of their supporters, including individuals who are actually engaged in violent actions, are not under the control of the Al Qaeda leadership. The key feature of the fluidity, decentralisation, and grassroots proliferation of the movement is emphasised by Marc Sageman in his *Leaderless Jihad*. Lee Hamilton and others (2006), in this respect, identify at least five layers within the terrorist "multidimensional network": Al Qaeda headquarters and operatives; the affiliated terrorist groups with loose links to Al Qaeda, such as Lashkar-e-Taibe in Kashmir and Jemaah Islamiyah in Indonesia; "al-Qaeda-seeded groups," including members who had contacts with the Al Qaeda leadership in the shape of training, planning or participating to a previous jihadi operation, including the perpetrators of the 7/7 London bombings and the Madrid attacks; the "self-starter cells" (also referred to elsewhere as "self-radicalised" individuals) who are inspired by Al Qaeda ideology without having actual connections with the terrorist group; the wider "pool" of sympathisers who support the objectives of radical Islam even if disapproving of its extremist methods (ibid.: 4).

It is not clear to what extent and to what degree of effectiveness individuals inspired by Al Qaeda ideology can manage plots on their own. In summer 2008 an academic row erupted between the Hoffman and the Sageman camps (Sciolino and Schmitt 2008): for Bruce Hoffman, Al Qaeda had largely reconstituted in Pakistan and the source of the threat was the Al Qaeda leadership; for Sageman the threat actually came from the bottom up. Will McCants (2008), commenting on the debate, remarked then that the threat actually sprang from a combination of grassroots activism and a powerful Al Qaeda central. It has also been pointed out that a closer look at the "homegrown" terrorist threat reveals contacts with the actual Al Qaeda organisation. For instance, a researcher from the anti-extremism think tank Quilliam Foundation, shows that police and investigation evidence indicate that "each of the major terrorist plots affecting the United Kingdom since the 9/11 attacks in the United States have had ties back to al-Qaʾida's central organisation in Afghanistan and Pakistan" (Brandon 2009: 10).

The point is that, regardless of whether they are actually connected with Al Qaeda, groups acting *in the name of Al Qaeda* could potentially damage its brand by developing inconsistencies with the organisation's ideology and methods. This has already occurred in Iraq. The horror inspired by filmed beheadings of hostages ordered by Al-Zarkawi before his death in 2006 largely alienated local support in Iraq. Al-Zawahiri criticised such brutality in a letter: "I say to you: that we are in a battle, and that more than half of this battle is taking place in the battlefield of the media ... . The Muslim populace who love and support you will never find palatable ... the scenes of slaughtering the hostages" (in Ensor 2005). Richard Barrett (2008: 8) also mentions another tactical degeneration: the increasing "coercion and criminality as a way of self-financing" of local cells, as in the case of the Islamic State of Iraq, a group founded in October 2006.

Al Qaeda's extension in the Maghreb, to go back to the earlier example, is regarded as evidence of Al Qaeda's ability to become a "terrorism multinational." Not only is this debatable, but it might not necessarily be a positive outcome, either. As for the first point, Al Qaeda in the Maghreb (AQIM) does not really appear to have "gone global." In 2009 the group was still managed from Algeria by mostly Algerian elements, and ideological and strategic developments had occurred largely because of internal dynamics and individual power struggles (Rogan 2009). Barrett (2008: 8) also pointed out that "if the Algerian group had hoped to present itself as a part of a global movement, it in fact remains fixed on local objectives. Its attacks have killed many more local people than foreigners." The idea that the adoption of the brand name Al Qaeda could have been important for symbolic purposes, possibly opening up new pools of potential recruits, does not appear so far to have materialised (Thornberry and Levy 2011).

In relation to the second point, being a "global brand" could well be a liability considering that, while Al Qaeda's narrative offers "its supporters a sense of belonging and importance by taking personal or local grievances and setting them in a global context" (Barrett 2008: 13), the terrorist organisation's objectives are also seen as "vague": beyond the general notion of establishing an Islamic state governed by sharia law, there is a lack of political priorities and policies (ibid.: 5). This has become particularly evident through the lack of a role for Islamic extremism in the recent popular uprisings (one of them supported by military intervention) that led to the overthrow of the Tunisian, Egyptian, and Libyan regimes (Ashour 2011). In addition to this, several internal rifts have already emerged within Al Qaeda. An example of a former Al Qaeda member who openly rejected the organisation's ideology is Sayyid Imamal-Sharif, more widely known as Dr. Fadl. A former leader of the Egyptian terrorist group al-Jihad and author of two of the most influential books in modern Islamist thought, he announced in 2007 a new book rejecting Al Qaeda's violence (Wright 2008). Also, in 2007 Shaik Salman al-Awdah, a well-known preacher in radical circles, appeared on a widely watched Middle Eastern channel to criticise Al Qaeda's attacks on Muslim women and children (Presidential Task Force 2009: 3; Barrett 2008: 6).

The reliance on the full spectrum of communication technologies is also another source of risk to the Al Qaeda brand. Indeed, as Kimmage (2008b) pointed out, as late as March 2008, most of Al Qaeda communications appeared to be "stuck in Web 1.0": jihadist media products, even if available online and presented in the most appealing form possible, are nothing but traditional propaganda, that is, unidirectional messages (Kimmage 2008a). Al Qaeda tried to embrace interactivity, at least as a façade, with a Q&A session with Ayman Al-Zawahiri (Al-Zawahiri 2008; NEFA Foundation 2008a, b). The inability of Al Qaeda to deal with potential dissent is proven by the defensive way in which the session was handled. Users were free to post their questions. Indeed some of them were critical – "Do you consider the killing of women and children to be Jihad?" (Al-Zawahiri 2008: 2). Al-Zawahiri did tackle the challenging questions, but replies were posted with a delay of at least a couple of months. A more recent analysis of terrorist websites (Seib and Janbek 2011: 52) shows an effort at connecting with users: multimedia files offer an "entertaining alternative to simple text." Beyond being able to access and download pictures, videos, and audios, users can send "Islamic e-cards," submit material to poster competitions, and send feedback to organisations. As the authors conclude, however: "While there are a range of Web 2.0 features on many of these sites, and while users are able to voice their opinions, censorship and forum rules continue to restrict what can be written" (ibid.: 54). Perhaps it is just a matter of time until Al Qaeda implodes under the weight of user-generated content that challenges its brand's narrative. As Barrett (2008: 13) puts it: "A free debate, whether on the Internet or elsewhere, is likely to weaken Al Qaeda, particularly as its skill lies more in spreading propaganda in set pieces films, videos or audio tapes, rather than in the interactive, consumer led form that has come to dominate the web."

As Jonathan Feiser (2004) further expresses it, Al Qaeda "must rely on the illusive power of its manufactured symbolism." The problem here is that the wider the audiences reached by Al Qaeda's messages, the greater the possibility, in the absence of a rigid hierarchical structure, that its symbolism gets out of control.

6.3.3 Developing more systematic and reliable indicators of progress in the fight against terrorism

Ten years after both 9/11 and the start of the war in Afghanistan it is unclear whether efforts against global terrorism are being successful. US defence secretary, Donald Rumsfeld, famously wrote in October 2003: "Are we winning or losing the Global War on Terror? Are we capturing, killing or deterring and dissuading more terrorists every day than the madrassas and the radical clerics are recruiting, training and deploying against us?" (Rumsfeld 2003). His words raised the issue of how to make sense of both material indicators and the effects of perceptions. There is widespread recognition that there is a problem with material indicators (Walker 2005; Stohl 2006; Perl 2007; van Dongen 2009; De Graaf 2011; van Um and Pisoiu 2011). For example, Perl (2007: 10) points out that

> policy makers often tend to define success by the absence of attacks ... . Yet terrorists sometimes define success in terms of making governments expend limited resources trying to defend an enormous number of potential targets [ibid.]. While we attribute importance to "body counts" and figures, terrorists might measure success in terms of "honour" or "revenge."

In this context, the branding approach can offer two positive contributions. First, the brand platform – mission, vision, and values – could constitute a dynamic definition of what "success" means. Terrorism and counterterrorism would be approached as processes in which relative gains should be assessed in relation to "our objectives" and "their objectives," what it means to "win" for "us" and for "them" (see Figure 6.4).

In turn, these multifaceted definitions of "success," as a second contribution, offer a framework to assess whether not only material indicators but also perceptions and broader policies contribute to progress in the fight against terrorism. At the moment, in fact, aspects of a completely different nature are taken as isolated evidence that we are either "winning" or "losing": sometimes it is the number of attacks or fatalities, at other times the volume of statements or videos released, and at others the number of plots foiled. Even an increase in the number of vegetables

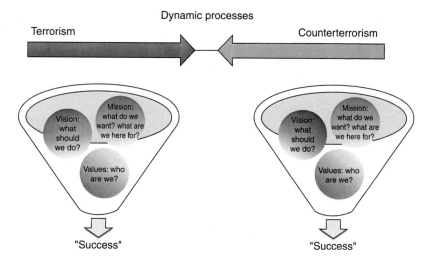

Figure 6.4   The brand platform as a definition of "success" in terrorism and counterterrorism

on sale at the local market in Afghanistan can be taken as evidence that poppy harvesting, a source of finance for the terrorists, is decreasing.[4] The problem is, however, that no measurement can contribute to drawing any firm conclusion about "how well we are doing" unless it can be fitted into a broader picture establishing exactly what "our" and "their" objectives are, in both the long and short term. As Daniel Benjamin (2008) wrote: "Numbers tell you about plots that succeeded, but to gauge the threat, we also need a sense of the jihadists' ambition."

The main criteria for establishing whether objectives are being achieved would then be the consistency with which the brand platform elements are being implemented and perceived. This would be the basis for establishing the credibility of the brand. In this respect, the branding approach would place a strong emphasis on the consistency of counterterrorism measures with the mission and values of the brand – for example, emphasis on whether Western democracies, through counterterrorism measures limiting civil liberties, are actually undermining their own brand's credibility rather than contributing to progress in the fight against terrorism (Anonymous blogger 2009). Further to this point, Jack Yan (2003: 452–455) suggests that US foreign policy, in order to manage its reputation, should be consistent with the UN Charter.

Attention towards the consistency of the brand as key to its success can guide practical choices about how to implement policies against terrorism. Compare the following two policies: on the one hand the idea that the US government should support non-democratic local governments in developing countries (as in Somalia) because they have expressed opposition to Al Qaeda (Maslikowski and Justus 2009). On the other hand the stand taken by the British government in distancing itself from any Muslim organisation which, even if not directly advocating violence, shows signs of intolerance towards British values, such as respect for the rule of law or individuals' race, faith, ethnicity, and sexual orientation (Home Office 2009: 87). Both are certainly controversial issues – not least the question of who should define what "British values" actually are. The second approach, nonetheless, has the potential of raising the credibility of the British government, while the first further damages the US reputation for applying "double standards." From a branding perspective, either of the examples would not be seen as a choice between pragmatic measures and aesthetic concerns about image. Reputation and perceptions related to credibility are crucial to the effectiveness of practical measures.

6.3.4 Countering the terrorist threat by focusing on the power of social bonds

The branding approach places the focus on the relationship of audiences with the brand, particularly on their engagement with the brand values, rather than, as in the aftermath of 9/11, on the communication of the "message" – what Mark Leonard (2002) refers to as the "hard sell." This relationship-focused approach appears to be better suited to developing resilience by strengthening social bonds. As Bill Durodié (2005: 17–18) argues:

> Real resilience, at a deeper social level, depends upon identifying what we are for, not just what we are against. This will not be resolved by training ourselves to respond to disasters, but by a much broader level of debate and engagement in society, not just relating to terrorism and other crises, but to far broader social issues.

The social engagement that comes from mobilisation around the brand, particularly in "living the brand," also fits with what former U.K. home secretary, Smith, called "civil challenge": "Where people may not have broken the law but nevertheless act in a way that undermines our belief in this country, in democracy, in human rights, in tolerance, and free speech, there should be a challenge made to them, not through the law but through a civil challenge" (Smith in Chrichton 2009). This requires a greater awareness of the values at the basis of the brand identity and an effort to uphold them.

6.4   Conclusion: managing the democratic brand

This chapter has explored the analytical merit of the brand concept. While the idea comes from marketing and can at first sight appear a theoretical overstretch, branding does provide a powerful framework for making sense of the communication strategy against terrorism, particularly of the essential importance of credibility that results from operating consistently with one's values. A brand platform also offers clear guidance on practical strategies, such as how to implement anti-terrorism policies while being more aware of their effects both on practical grounds and in the intangible (but not unmeasurable) realm of perceptions.

In order to gain the full benefits of the brand – recognition and credibility – democratic governments face two challenges. The first is the very definition of their brand platform. While "our" identity and values need to be clearly identified, they cannot just be imposed from above. The second challenge arises when the platform is in place: how to manage the brand? The issue here is finding the right balance between, on the one hand the need to act and communicate consistently with the brand, on the other hand allowing the brand platform to change in order to stay relevant. Both these aspects need to be openly discussed. Although it is reasonable to expect a high degree of controversy, it is worth bearing in mind that vigorous debate, even disagreement, is perfectly consistent with the democratic brand and cannot but add substance to its platform.

7
The Way Forward

The previous chapters have torn up much of the existing approach to terrorism, reassembled the pieces into a new model, suggested an alternative reading of the phenomenon of terrorism, and outlined practical implications for counterterrorism. This chapter wraps up the arguments by looking at the future of both terrorism research and of the countering of extremism.

7.1 Terrorism Studies: where do we go from here?

The reality of world politics is changing at a quicker pace than either academic paradigms' or policymakers' abilities to interpret it. This particularly applies to events, whose roots (before they take place) and consequences (after they have occurred) stretch well beyond traditional state borders. Terrorism – with its international connections and repercussions – is one such evolving puzzle. Worse, the thinking currently used to make sense of it, in a globalised world, is outdated.

The most dangerous threat, in this context, is not radicalism or the plotting of the next "spectacular," but the very inability of those who should be protecting "our" security, to question what they (think they) know. Most of what constitutes Terrorism Studies has gone unchallenged for decades due to the closed nature of the system in which that knowledge has been produced. Despite the much-touted need to think differently in light of an (alleged) existential threat to our societies, there is very little evidence that this has so far taken place. Indeed, as Thomas Hegghammer (2008) wrote in an article for *The Times* about the state of jihadi studies: "From a historical perspective, [the] ignorance about the enemy makes the war on terror unique. Rarely have so many resources been deployed on the basis of such vague understanding about the enemy and how it functions." As he further explains in a later interview in occasion of the 9/11 ten year anniversary (in Abu Muqawama 2011), there are structural reasons for this: the way in which, in academia, certain lines of enquiry fit within career patterns and promotion opportunities. More specifically, according to him, the obstacle to specialising in the study of jihadi groups is the "incentive structure in the universities":

> Studying Al Qaeda usually involves qualitative methods and requires high-level skills in Arabic or some other oriental language. Graduate students with an interest in jihadism thus work against two strong biases: the quantitative methods hegemony in the social sciences and the skepticism in American Middle East Studies toward the study of hard security issues. These biases affect hiring decisions and have some striking aggregate effects: for example, there are virtually no tenured faculty specialising in terrorism (let alone jihadism) in any Ivy League school or in any Middle East Studies department in America. Rational graduate students with academic ambitions see this and wisely stay clear of the topic. (Ibid.)

Beyond jihadi studies and the presence of gaps in what we know about terrorism, as the analysis in the previous chapters has pointed out, the structure of the field conjures up to produce groupthink of epic proportions. This is not necessarily the researchers' fault, but the outcome of the circulation of ideas within broader but *closed* networks. Edna Reid (1993), in relation to this point, conducted a study of the diffusion of ideas about terrorism by analysing the patterns of publications (journal articles, books, reports, anthology chapters, and papers presented at conferences), their contents, and impacts on policy between 1960 and 1990. She finds that the US government "had a major impact in stimulating scientific growth in terrorism research by providing resources[,] ... dissemination of ideas, and retrieval of information" (n.p.).[1] The small number of researchers, combined with reliance on government documents and media coverage as major – but, in themselves, limited sources of data – led to reliance on each others' publication. As Reid explains: "The research process and the flow of terrorism information such as researchers' publications, government documents and media reports seem to constitute a closed system in which information is created, processed, published, and disseminated." This is a "static environment" in which "the same hypotheses, definitions, and theories" continue "to be analyzed, assimilated, published, cited, and eventually retrieved."

Such a situation had, in turn, further negative consequences: the closed system provided an avenue for rapid publication of "non-refereed material" (a trend supported by the tendency to publish terrorism studies as reports and in specialised anthologies); established authors were given redundant publications ("Alexander's article on terrorists' manipulation of the media was published five times!"); ideas were "marketed" "so that they [would] spark talk and further writings," (possibly making the arguments more extreme than they needed to be?).

It would be difficult to deny that the same tendencies are not thriving today: as emphasised throughout this book, there are claims about the role of the media in terrorism research that would not stand the shadow of a chance of publication if reviewed by communication and media scholars; the competition to attract the significant amount of funding made available after 9/11 has led to an artificial inflation of the severity of the terrorist threat (Mueller 2005, 2012); the circulation of the same ideas has reached the surreal point in which one can find repetition even of the complaints about the shortcomings of the field and the very fact that it relies on recycled material (Silke 2004a: 2; Silke 2004c: 59; Schmid and Jongman 2005: 137).

Add the fact that international relations have radically changed as a result of the advances of communication technologies. This has led policymakers to struggle in responding to events being reported in real time, as was recently demonstrated by the "Arab Awakening" (Seib 2012). Also, terrorism scholars have been forced to sail in unchartered waters. Magnus Ranstorp (2007a: 3), for instance, comments about the shift of Terrorism Studies, from being a small academic community – "a handful of political scientists, sociologists and military strategic experts" – into the limelight of worldwide concern after 9/11:

> Retrained academic cold warriors and war correspondents competed to translate anything on Al Qaeda into a commercial success often without regard for quality, sources, or other sound academic praxis. Within the United States, journalists entered the academic world without formal qualifications and good academics left for government vacancies ... . More traditionally oriented academics struggled to readjust to the explanatory power of international relations theory to the dominance and challenge of sub-state actors. Some like John Gray, Keohane and Richmond, partially succeeded while many other theory specialists are still lost in the wilderness of a hostile, alien and new intellectual non-state-centric environment. (Ibid.)

Scholars at the core of an academic field are those who find it most difficult to cope with new paradigms. The reason why they are at the core of an academic discipline is precisely the fact that their work reflects the most established and widely accepted lines of enquiry within that field. While working within the boundaries of those tracks might well be a good thing for scientific accumulation, it also has a hidden downside. It reduces the likelihood of disagreement, deviation from the accepted paradigms – in other words *innovation*. Since the greatest scientific breakthroughs in the history of humanity were brought about by people who refused to accept "things as they were" (Braben 2004: 1), there is an argument that stresses how peer review, whether in funding bids or journal publication, might tragically become a "pathway to mediocrity" (Braben 2011). As Donald Braben (2004: 5), who has investigated the nature of scientific innovation, writes, peer review often acts as a "systematic stifling of dissent." Peer review, in fact, tends to encourage the pursue of research that sits well within the boundaries of an established academic paradigm. This is, in a bureaucratic perspective, very effective at minimising risk: it is "safer" to fund a project whose results can already be envisaged rather than an exploratory investigation of new and so far unknown research areas – but is de facto also "strangling scientific creativity" (ibid.: 8). As Robert Crotty (1999: 3) further explains, research knowledge cannot be detached by the research community that has generated it. The status of community comes precisely from the sharing of common assumptions, expectations, and methods (ibid.) – what Kuhn (1962) calls a "paradigm." As Crotty (1999: 3) phrases it: "scientists look at the world and puzzle over it with a collective pair of spectacles." Scientists strive for recognition, which in the academic field is awarded by way of publication, "but this recognition is granted only to those contributions which conform to the current cognitive and technical norms" (ibid.: 5). In this sense "editors, referees and editorial advisers represent the 'authority' who protect the discipline area and the legitimate academics" (ibid.: 6). In other words, "legitimate academics are considered to be those who have learned the paradigm and now support it" (ibid.).

Terrorism Studies is not immune from these wider structural features of the academic field that work against innovation. As such, they are affected by a vicious circle, which has added negative effects due to its connection to government: scholars at the core of a field are those in the position to circulate their ideas most widely, as well as to affect policy most deeply (Reid 1993). The most widely circulated ideas are also the most unchallenged. As in other aspects of life, also in terrorism studies, something that gets repeated enough times – as the notion that the Internet fuels radicalisation – starts acquiring a life of its own (and when it becomes the basis for a policy it practically becomes set in stone). But because the established scholars are too often the least equipped to deal with a fast-changing reality, the ideas they produce are also the least useful.

The situation is made worse by the fact that policymakers demand quick and simple solutions to be able to act decisively – or at least to be seen as doing so (Cilluffo 2008; Githens-Mazer 2010: 47). Unfortunately, reality is complicated, and simplifying it too much for policy purposes often means ending up dealing with a different problem than that one originally wanted to tackle – a problem that might not exist at all. It is easy to think that media messages can have a predictable effect on publics and trigger certain corresponding behaviours – for example the notion that exposure to extremist ideas can lead to terrorism, which underpins much of radicalisation literature. This can support a fairly clear policy course of action: censoring online extremist content, for instance. As the previous chapters have made clear, however, the starting assumption on which this measure is based is totally wrong.

The worrying final result is that policy measures often are based on the simplest (but not necessarily most accurate) assumptions, and on flimsy research and generalised conclusions that should not be applied to all situations regardless of context.

Where is innovation going to come from in these circumstances? First, a greater realisation of the relationship between the constellation of networks researchers belong to and how they can limit the understanding of the world (or the range of conceptual tools one uses to analyse it) can be a starting point for breaking free (or *freer*, since we cannot exist outside social networks) of such constraints. This book wanted to be a reflection on the construction of scientific knowledge about violent extremism, particularly on its bias.

A second direction from where innovation is to come is all-out multi-disciplinarity. In this I totally disagree with the assessment of Avishag Gordon (2001). In writing about the "scholarly communication system" of Terrorism Studies, he argues that, in order to mature as a field, Terrorism Studies needed to close down "to sources outside the academic circle" (ibid.: 123). In Gordon's assessment, the fact that terrorism scholars have relied on secondary information sources, such as government documents and media reports, made the field "open," and this was a problem because "information that flows from outside sources does not follow the rules of the academic system and is not refereed, checked or verified" (ibid.). His argument is that only a field that "constantly feeds itself" is "able to create its own theories and paradigms" (ibid.).

This reasoning is flawed in three respects. First, it tends to conflate the impact on Terrorism Studies of the contributions by non-academics (people) with the effects of the use of non-academically produced data (sources). These are two completely different issues, neither of which, by itself, is an obstacle to the advance of academic enquiry. Second, the phenomenon of violent extremism – especially in the case of one wanting to understand both its social roots and impacts beyond the mere planning and execution of terrorist attacks – involves virtually anything we can think of in terms of subjects for investigation: Politics, Sociology, Psychology, Economy, Journalism, History, Urban Architecture, Chemistry, Informatics, Philosophy, Transport Studies … . The list could go on and on. Terrorism Studies needs the contributions of myriad disciplines. The third reason is related to the mechanisms of the diffusion of innovation: researchers at the periphery of a field are in the best position to bring new and original insights. As Mark Granovetter (1973) initially pointed out in a landmark study of social mobility (how people find jobs), individuals at the periphery of social cliques have a crucial role in conveying new information. In Granovetter's analysis, 83 per cent of his respondents (282 people living in the Boston suburb of Newton) had found a job during the previous year through individuals who, counter-intuitively, were not close friends. These individuals were, in network analysis terms, "weak ties" because they were "only marginally included in the … network of contacts, such an old college friend or a former workmate or employer, with whom sporadic contact had been maintained" (ibid.: 1371). Yet, their "strength" (the title of Granovetter's article is "The Strength of the Weak Ties") lay precisely in this distance from the core of an individual's network. Because close friends (like academic colleagues) form a closely knit clique, and information tends to be shared inwardly (as by referencing each other's work and reading the same specialised publications), there is not much information close friends possess that an individual in the clique would not already know. Beyond employment issues, it is not difficult to see how the same argument could apply to the circulation of ideas within an entire academic field of study.[2] By combining the approaches of Communication and Media Studies, Political Communication and Marketing with Terrorism Studies, I hope this book has demonstrated how multidisciplinarity can contribute to alternative readings of violent extremism, particularly through new analytical tools, comparative perspectives, and methodologies.

7.2 Countering extremism: a not-so-unpredictable "age of uncertainty"

In the literature about terrorism, a common complaint is that, on the one hand, those whose job it is to think (academics) are not directly involved in counterterrorism and intelligence. They are often forced to speculate due to the fact that empirical data is off-limits, locked behind a door of secrecy erected in the name of "national security." On the other hand, the intelligence and counterterrorism communities, which have access to real data, are too busy dealing with the devastating prospect of a new terrorist attack to pause and think. Githens-Mazer (2010: 15) describes the outcome of these juxtaposing trends as "theory-less policy and policy-less theory." The existence of these two distinct communities is reflected in the notion that thinking about terrorism is one thing, dealing with it is a wholly different matter.

Challenging this view, this book has made the point that, regardless of the data we have access to, the way we conceptualise violent extremism has deep implications for the way we, in practical terms, tackle it.

More specifically, my argument has been that terrorism is what we make of it. Some scholars have made terrorism a conundrum by isolating it from its social context. And, indeed, if taken out of context, terrorism becomes really incomprehensible. The "failure" in predicting future terrorist attacks, in this perspective, is not related to any fault in the methodology used or the difficulty of the subject (let alone the so much lamented inability to define the phenomenon!), but in two related misconceptions.

The first misconception is assuming that reality can be explained through linear models of representation. As Andrew Abbott (1988: 170) writes, they are based on the assumption that the social world consists of "fixed entities (the units of analysis)" that have "attributes (the variables)." The variables have only one "causal meaning (one pattern of effects) in a given study" (ibid.), without consideration of the fact that the causal meaning can vary in relation to other variables, is affected by their sequence, and is also influenced by the context of other units of analysis (ibid.: 181) – in other words, that causes of social phenomena are affected by time and context.[3]

As illustrated in the analysis of radicalisation and the social construction of narratives, the notion that the combination of a given set of general causal factors linearly leads to terrorism can be compared to the simplistic belief that just by adding up a range of ingredients one is going to obtain a Michelin-star dish. Baking a mixture of water, butter, and flour is not necessarily going to generate pastry. As any expert chef knows, the basic ingredients – we could think of a perceived sense of grievance as an essential component of the terrorism "dish" – are only part of what good cooking requires. What makes the difference between fragrant pastry and an inedible gluey goo is the timing and order in which ingredients are added up, the temperature of the water, the folding of the dough, the resting between the foldings, the coolness of the kitchen board, the temperature of the oven ... . An ever-so-slight difference in any of these aspects will produce a different result. Similarly, different kinds of (violent) extremism arise out of the unique combination of time- and space-specific circumstances.

The second misconception in current research that has made terrorism look like an intractable problem is related to the previous point and consists in attributing to scientific research predictive powers that it does not have. I have argued that it is not possible to foresee with mathematical certainty where and when violent extremism will arise, and that it is not only the material resources radicals rely on (which can be seen) and the people they exchange information with (who can be tracked, counted, whose conversations can be overheard) that are relevant to understanding terrorism, but also a whole non-material world: the imagined relationships with people an extremist has never had direct contact with, and related ideas and symbols.

This might make terrorism look more elusive and shadowy than it already is. That assessment is, however, wrong. The realm in which extremism develops might be non-material, but even perceptions, identities, and narratives, as shown in Chapter 6, can be identified, measured, and analysed. In addition to this, the fact that they are always the result of processes of *collective* construction makes them, if anything, easier to detect. In this respect, the communication approach (based on social relationships) which I have developed, underlines the connections, rather than the divide, between "us" and "them." These connections are twofold. They can, first, consist in providing the ideological fertile ground where more than extremist ideas can flourish. As unpalatable as it might sound, this ground is often located within the boundaries of democratic debate. In the aftermath of the killings that took place in Norway in July 2011, it became apparent that Anders Breivik had been following American anti-Muslim blogs, which were extensively quoted in his manifesto (Breivik 2011). The bloggers distanced themselves from the brutality of the events by pointing out they had never advocated violence in their postings. As Sageman has argued, however, if Salafi Islam is the ideological terrain from which Al Qaeda emerged, then anti-Muslim bloggers "are the infrastructure from which Breivik emerged" (Sageman in Shane 2011). In other words, as Sageman powerfully sums it up: "This [non-violent, but still radical] rhetoric is not cost-free." The second way in which there is a link between "us" and "them" is in the form of relationships of opposition: to what extent have "we" consolidated Al Qaeda's identity every time we have proclaimed "our" opposition to it? To which degree are counterterrorism policies, counterterrorism organisations, and relative budgets contributing to the continued existence of terrorist groups?

In terms of detecting terrorism, although again we cannot tell the day and time when a terrorist attack will take place, violent extremism is far from a random phenomenon. In this respect, studying terrorism can be compared to assessing the likelihood of earthquakes. Earthquakes are famously unpredictable. As recently observed (Lewis Mernit 2011), however, this is true only if we define "earthquake" as the "big bang" – the strongest and most devastating tremor. In this view there is a big tremor (the earthquake), followed by aftershocks. Aftershocks are regarded to be more manageable in analytical terms because they tend to manifest themselves in fairly predictable patterns. But, what if we expanded our definition of what is an earthquake to include the smaller tremors that happen over time before the strongest one? What if, more specifically, the "big bang" was itself an aftershock of a previous rupture? We would then start to realise that the big tremor is not the beginning of seismic activity. Irrespective of its magnitude, we would be able to fit it within a more predictable pattern. Just like earthquakes, the detonations of terrorists' bombs cannot be anticipated. However, we can detect smaller tremors: even if narratives and networks keep on changing, they do so as the result of collective processes that can be broadly observed over time.

This argument underlines that it is how we establish the boundary of the phenomenon we intend to study that affects what we are able to see. Bringing this argument to its logical conclusion, we could even come to the realisation that terrorism does not really exist. As Michael Smith (2009: 322) points out in reviewing Terrorism Studies:

> I write from the standpoint of a strategic theorist: that is, someone who studies correlations between ends and means, and who discerns the use, or threat of use, of armed force as a conscious choice of political actors who are intent on rationally pursuing their objectives. For strategic theorists, therefore, terrorism exists only as one possible means to an end that can be employed by any social agent

in any context to attain specific goals. Accordingly, there can be no truly meaningful study of terrorism, as it is neither a material nor observable phenomenon. It is merely a method, a tactic.

In this book I have suggested that extremism should be approached as social movement whose repertoire is violence.

7.3   A positive last note

Saying that democracies, in countering terrorism, have to fight "with a hand tied behind their backs" has become a favourite cliché to express the frustration with the perceivedly restrained measures by which Western democracies are forced to deal with terrorism. These involve several aspects of counterterrorism, from the lack of engagement of international allies (Clark 2002), to the government's reluctance in restricting civil freedoms to the point where counterterrorism could be most effective (*Daily News* 2010, for one example).

Perceptions of restraint in tackling terrorism also refer to countering the messages of our opponents – fighting the "propaganda war." As Donald Rumsfeld, then US defence secretary, wrote in 2006:

> Terrorists have skilfully adapted to fighting wars in today's media age, but, for the most part, America and the governments of the other democracies have not. Consider that the violent extremists have their own "media relations committees" aimed at manipulating elite opinion. They plan and design headline-grabbing attacks using every means of communications to intimidate and break the collective will of free people.
>
> They know that communications transcend borders, and that a single news story, handled skilfully, can be as damaging to our cause – and as helpful to theirs – as any military attack. And they are able to act quickly with relatively few people, and with modest resources compared with the vast, expensive bureaucracies of democratic governments.

The argument – which he maintains by offering the example of "false allegations of the desecration of Koran" in the previous year – is that terrorists can lie and fabricate stories to attack "our" reputation, while "we," as democracies, cannot use the same means. Terrorists are not bound by moral obligations, while Western governments have a duty to present accurate and truthful information to their citizens.

The alleged outcome is that terrorists are effectively exploiting the media and advancing their objectives, while "we" have to sit and watch, in what appears like an unfair confrontation.

The arguments presented in this book are intended to squarely challenge these perceptions in two respects. First, by demonstrating that the effects of communication cannot be inferred from the message. The notion that an information war consists in a battle in which words simply replace bullets is a gross underestimation, particularly of the mental functions of both terrorists and worldwide publics. Radicals are not going to change their behaviour because they are "hit" with the "right" message. Indeed, the message might never even reach them. Not only because the text/image/video in which the "right" message is contained are not among the sources of information consumed by the target, but also because it will be read through the lens of an individual's interpretation of the world, in turn shaped by his/her interaction with the respective social milieu. Our "right" message, in fact, could well end up confirming radical views.

Second, a greater attention to the communication aspects of the fight against violent extremism, particularly to the narrative that our governments attempt to project, would make us realise the crucial importance of consistency between words and deeds. Upholding human rights by respecting civil freedoms and rejecting torture, for instance, is not a nicety but a statement about "our" very identity as democracies. If we truly embraced this perspective, rather than mentioning it as a rhetorical exercise, then we would understand that Western democracies do not have a hand tied behind their backs at all.

This book, despite its criticism towards existing paradigms, ultimately offers a positive message for the future. The perceived limitations in countering terrorism, both in the understanding of the phenomenon and in the practice of counterterrorism, are of our own making. As such, we can choose to overcome them. For ten years it has been said that we need to think out of the box. Perhaps it is really time to start doing it.

Notes

Introduction: A Different Perspective on Terrorism

1. Critical Terrorism Studies, in the aims of the journal *Critical Studies on Terrorism*, seeks to take a more distinct self-reflective approach to terrorism than does "Orthodox Terrorism Studies." According, among others, to Anthony Burke Critical Terrorism Studies marks the end of "traditionally state-focused and directed 'problem-solving' terrorism studies." For Richard Jackson (2009: 3) it translates into "a critical orientation, a sceptical attitude, and a willingness to challenge received wisdom and knowledge about terrorism." This book shares with Critical Terrorism Studies the critique toward existing approaches to terrorism, particularly the acknowledgement that the phenomenon is socially constructed. As Jackson (2009: 4) puts it: "[Terrorism's] nature is not inherent to the violent act itself, but is dependent upon context, circumstance, intention, and crucially, social, cultural, legal, and political processes of interpretation, categorisation and labelling." Overall, however, the arguments presented in this book transcend the division between "Critical Terrorism Studies" and "Orthodox Terrorism Studies." The root problem, as the following chapters will show, is not the political agenda behind the research or the method, but the very conceptualisation of social reality – an issue that can apply to both academic camps. On the case for Critical Terrorism Studies, see: Gunning (2007); Breen Smyth, Gunning, Jackson, and Kassimeris (2008a,b); and Jackson (2009); on the case against it see Horgan and Boyle (2008).
2. For a chronology of the events see *Spiegel Online* (2011).

1 The Problems with Terrorism Research

1. According to an FBI chronology (n.d.: 288) the desk clerk who checked Hamza Aghamdi out of the Hotel Days at 5.52am of 11 September 2001 noticed he was "wearing cologne."
2. Crenshaw's articles have inspired further work about the end of Al Qaeda by Cronin (2006; 2009).
3. A consultation of the syllabi collected on the website "Teaching Terror" (http://www.teachingterror.net/syllabi.htm) shows that Hoffman's text appears in virtually every terrorism course's reading list.
4. "Transition Network," http://www.transitionnetwork.org/
5. British National Party website, http://www.bnp.org.uk/policies/immigration
6. Global Terrorism Database (GTD) website: http://www.start.umd.edu/gtd/
7. For Bennett and George theory testing should involve, besides controlled comparison, also another method of causal inference such as process-tracing (Bennett and George 1997: 2). Process-tracing is a method to

"generate and analyze data on the causal mechanisms, or processes, events actions, expectations, and other intervening variables, that link putative causes to observed effects" (ibid.: 5.)

8. It could be argued that also this law has conditions of validity, as water always boils at 100°C at sea level.

2 Terrorism, Communication, and the Media

1. It could be argued that the hostage taking was not at all an act of terrorism and should not have been used by Schmid to illustrate his argument.
2. For more information about this event see *BBC News* (2007).
3. Adam Dolnik, in an interview with the author, stresses the greater operational capability of recruits who have received training against the 'self-starters': "we have seen a definite difference in the capabilities of the home-grown groups that had contact and training with groups in Pakistan or Afghanistan and the groups that try to do it all on their own. There is a huge capability difference" (Dolnik 2011b).
4. On this point see also Stevens (2009).
5. For a range of critical views on the extent to which communication technologies sustain different kinds of online communities, from diasporic groups to migrants, less-abled people, and transnational movements, see Silverstone (2005). For more on online activism and advocacy, see: Hick and McNutt (2002); McCaughey and Ayers (2003).
6. An example of the belief that online communities of Muslim extremists uncontroversially exist is offered by Gendron (2006). Drawing on Sageman (2004) she writes that: "Internet connections create a bond between individuals and a 'virtual' Muslim community which is an approximation of an ideal Islamic society: one that is all that is just, egalitarian, and universal in its simplicity and purity" (Gendron 2006: 16).
7. Kohlmann is not alone in believing that images are more powerful than text: see also HSPI/CIAG (2007: 18).
8. The very distinction between agents and structures that characterises all Sociology, according to Margaret Somers and Gloria Gibson (1994: 12), is part of the constructed "metanarrative of modernity." This point will be further developed in Chapter 3.
9. I will more fully develop this metaphor in the conclusions (Chapter 7).

3 A Communication Approach

1. According to Charles Lave and James March (1993: 3) a model is "a simplified picture of a part of the real world. It has some characteristics of the real world, but not all of them. It is a set of interrelated guesses about the world." Because these "guesses" reflect the researcher's interpretation of a set of causal mechanisms that explain reality, I use the term "model" interchangeably with "theoretical framework."
2. Harrison White is notoriously obscure in his writing. The reader might want to become familiar with his thought through Azarian's (2005) analysis of the author's work.

3. There are further ways in which objects participate in social action (Latour 1999: 183-190). They fall beyond the focus of the analysis here.
4. For Tilly (2002: 88) a social movement is "a kind of campaign ... [that] demands righting of a wrong, more often a wrong suffered by a well-specified population. The population in question can range from a single individual to all humans."
5. Tilly (2002: 118) describes repertoire as the "limited number of previously created performances within which the people involved [in political contention] can make claims."
6. Snow at al. (1986: 476-478) acknowledge, themselves, the limitations of their "frame alignment" approach.
7. See Seib (2012, forthcoming) for an excellent discussion of the role of social media in the uprising in North Africa and the Middle East in 2011.
8. Emirbayer and Mische (1998: 971) point out that, in Relational Sociology, it is possible to identify three constitutive aspects of agency: iteration or "the selective reactivation by actors of past patterns of thought and action, as routinely incorporated in practical activity"; "projectivity," that is the imagination of "possible future trajectories of action"; and "evaluation," or the ability of actors to assess situations and responding to "demands, dilemmas, and ambiguities" of developing circumstances. I agree with the authors in recognising the existence of these interrelated components, and also share with them the understanding of agency as "temporally embedded process of social engagement." I prefer, however, to talk about "individual narrative" rather than "agency" to emphasise the fact that, although there is a relationship between consciousness (our interpretation of reality) and action (what we actually do), they do not coincide.
9. Anderson (1983: 15) used this term to explain the rise of nationalism: "nations are imagined because the members of even the smallest nation will never know most of their fellow-members, meet them, or even hear of them, yet in the minds of each lives the image of their communion."
10. This argument fits with the relationship between consciousness and action advocated by symbolic interactionism: social action is not shaped by "quasi-objectively existing forces," but by the *meaning* that is attributed to them by actors (Joas and Knöbl 2009: 132). The meaning changes depending on the context. Hans Joas and Wolfgang Knöbl (ibid.) present the example of a tree which, they explain, is never only a material object: it can be the subject of scientific research for a biologist, but can also have a romantic significance for somebody who, for instance, had a first rendezvous by an oak at the edge of the woods. Meaning can also change over time and across situations: I might look at my computer as a simple typewriter until a technical problem occurs. At that point, by being forced to deal with the malfunction, I start learning how it works and begin to see it in a different light.
11. "ABC News 1972 Munich massacre coverage," 6 September, http://www.youtube.com/watch?v=lTqZPKZ4_wk
12. "Che cosa è 'Settembre Nero'? [What is 'Black September?]," and "La dichiarazione dei terroristi [The terrorists' declaration]," *L'Unità*, 6 September, p. 6; "Settembre Nero [Black September]," *La Stampa*, 6 September, p. 3 (Ascari 2009b).

13. "E così lo sport è finito in trincea [How sport ended up in the trench]," *Gazzetta dello Sport*, 6 September, p. 1 and 13 (Ascari 2009a).
14. "Il dramma e il mito [The drama and the myth]," *L'Unità*, 6 September, p. 10; "Violata l'ultima isola di pace [Violated the last island of peace]," *Corriere della Sera*, 6 September, p. 3 (Ascari 2009a).
15. The US Department of Defence (2002: 1) stated that, as of May 2002, there were "68 nations supporting the global war on terrorism ... 20 nations have deployed more than 16,000 troops to the U.S. Central Command's region of responsibility."
16. I am not arguing that individuals should be criminalised only for what they say or think rather than for what they do. In fact, radical statements could well be made for merely rhetorical or attention-seeking purposes. They could be empty declarations that never get translated into deeds, let alone violence. The point here is that mapping what people say/think – imagined relationships and broader vision of the world – through their personal and/or group narrative over time can provide support and early warning signals to understanding their *actions*. Narrative analysis should be conducted in *addition* to (not in substitution of) existing methods used by practitioners in counterterrorism, such as surveillance and police investigation.

4 Explaining Radicalisation

1. Reviewing the extensive volume of work about radicalisation in its entirety goes beyond the scope of this chapter. See Al-Lami (2009) for a review of the literature. For a comprehensive annotated bibliography, see Homeland Security Institute (2006). For a more recent review of definitions of radicalisation, see Kühle and Lindekilde (2010: 22-27).
2. For other definitions see: Homeland Security Policy Institute (HSPI) and the University of Virginia Critical Incident Analysis Group (CIAG) (2007: 3).
3. All quotes from this study are my translation.
4. For more information about the events in Valle Giulia see Bennett and Graebner (2009).
5. Della Porta and Bosi (2010: 44) find similar attitudes among Italian young Muslims.
6. As Beski-Chafiq et al. (2010b: 13) point out, in France ethnic or religious censuses are not allowed. It is therefore not possible to establish how many Muslims live in Lille. The authors write that a plausible number for the whole Nord-Pas-de-Calais region is between 150,000 and 180,000 (Beski-Chafiq et al. 2010a: 25).
7. The individual "appropriation" of the narrative does not cover only the personal *interpretation* of extremist contents, but also the way in which they are "lived" through social action.

5 The Role of Narratives

1. Somers (1994: 613) goes as far as to suggest that the attention towards narratives is leading a "revolution...in our contemporary knowledge culture."

2. Although the meaning of the term has changed through the nineteenth and twentieth centuries, Knight (2006: 625) observes that it has consistently been used to refer to "coherent and relatively stable set of beliefs or values."

3. One of these statements is that the "strategic communication" which supports public diplomacy is "an adaptive, decentralized process of trying to understand selected audiences thoroughly, hypothesizing physical or informational signals that will have the desired cognitive effect on those audiences, testing those hypotheses through action, monitoring the actual result through feedback, and disseminating the best solutions quickly" (US Department of Defense 2009: 3).

6 The Al Qaeda Narrative as a Brand

1. Jack Yan (2003: 449) talks about a general "misunderstanding of branding."

2. NUT (National Union of Teachers), NASUWT (National Association of Schoolmasters and Union of Women teachers), ATL (Association of Teachers and Lecturers), PAT (Professional Association of Teachers) (Riley 1995: 9).

3. Among the following figures, data about Morocco was not available.

4. In Afghanistan in 2009 a unit began "to catalogue the variety of vegetables on sale in the local markets as evidence that farmers were growing more than poppy" (Abu Muqawama 2009).

7 The Way Forward

1. Although Reid does not specify that her study is about the US, her article appears to assume that all research is produced there. This is most probably a result of her focus on English language publications within her timeframe of analysis (1960-1990).

2. See more about the role of networks in the diffusion of innovation in Rogers (2003, chapter 8).

3. Abbott (1988), among several examples, presents the case of the relationship between a "wife's outside employment" and "marital instability." The relationship between the two variables, in a linear representation of reality, could follow the lines of the following causal mechanism: "marital interaction may be decreased by wife's employment. Household tasks that used to be handled by the wife while the husband was at work may cut into time previously allotted to joint activities" (Booth et al. 1984 in ibid: 174). This causal explanation contains five "steps": wife working hours; wife income; spousal interaction; marital disagreement; marital problems and instability. As Abbott points out: "The model assumes that these various attributes of marriages fluctuate [change] over equivalent time periods, or that attributes earlier in the list fluctuate [change] more slowly than those later. Yet in fact there is no conceptual reason to think that employment rates ["wife income"] fluctuate [changes] more slowly than do, for example, marital problems" (ibid).

Bibliography

Abbott, A. (1988) "Transcending General Linear Reality," *Sociological Theory* 6 (2): 169–186.

Abu Muqawama (2009) "On Metrics in Afghanistan," Abu Muquawama: Post, 28 March, http://www.cnas.org/blogs/abumuqawama/2009/03/metrics-afghanistan.html

Abu Muqawama (2011) "Special Tenth Anniversary of 9/11 Q&A with Thomas Hegghammer," Center for a New American Security, 11 September, http://www.cnas.org/blogs/abumuqawama/2011/09/special-tenth-anniversary-911-qa-thomas-hegghammer.html

Alali, A. O. and K. K. Eke (eds) (1991) *Media Coverage of Terrorism: Methods of Diffusion* (London: Sage).

Alexander, D. (2010) "Offline and Online Radicalization and Recruitment of Extremists and Terrorists," *Journal of Homeland Security*, September, http://www.homelandsecurity.org/journal/Default.aspx?t=350&AspxAutoDetectCookieSupport=1

Alexander, Y. (1978) "Terrorism, the Media, and the Police," *Journal of International Affairs* 32 (1): 101–113.

Al-Lami, M. (2009) Studies of Radicalisation: State of the Field Report (London: Royal Holloway).

al-Zawahiri, A. (2008) "The Open Meeting with Shaykh Ayman al_Zawahiri," NEFA Foundation, http://www.nefafoundation.org/miscellaneous/FeaturedDocs/nefazawahiri0408.pdf

Ambinder, M. (2010) "Al Qaeda's First English Language Magazine is Here," *The Atlantic*, 30 June, http://www.theatlantic.com/international/archive/2010/06/al-qaedas-first-english-language-magazine-is-here/59006/

"Amm Sam" (2010) "Preventing, Er, Countering Violent Extremism Comes to America: Part Two – It's All Relative," *Free Radicals Blog*, 7 January 2010, http://www.icsr.info/blog/Preventing-er-Countering-Violent-Extremism-comes-to-America-Part-Two—Its-all-relative

Anderson, B. (1983) *Imagined Communities: Reflections on the Origin and Spread of Nationalism* (London: New Left Books).

Andrews, M., C. Squire and M. Tambouku (eds) (2008) *Doing Narrative Research* (London: Sage).

Anholt, S. (2002) "Foreword," *Journal of Brand Management* 9 (4/5): 229–239.

Anholt, S. (2005) *Brand New Justice: How Branding Places and Products Can Help the Developing World* (London: Elsevier).

Anholt, S. (2007) *Competitive Identity: The New Brand Management for Nations, Cities and Regions* (Basingstoke: Palgrave).

Anonymous blogger (2009) "Ferrying Away Our Freedom," HeresyCorner, 29 March, http://heresycorner.blogspot.com/2009/03/ferrying-away-our-freedom.html

Antonello, P. and **A. O'Leary** (eds) (2009) *Imagining Terrorism: The Rhetoric and Representation of Political Violence in Italy 1969–2009* (Oxford: Modern Humanities Research Association and Maney Publishing).

Antoniades, A., A. Miskimmon and **B. O'Loughlin** (2009) "Great Powers and Strategic Narratives: The State of the Field," paper presented at the workshop "Great Powers after the Bush Presidency: Interests, Strategies, and Narratives," International Studies Association annual convention, New York, 14 February.

Archetti, C. (2010) *Explaining News: National Politics and Journalistic Cultures in Global Context* (New York: Palgrave).

Archetti, C. and **P. Taylor** (2005) "Managing Terrorism after 9/11: The War on Terror, the Media, and the Imagined Threat," final report for ESRC project "Domestic Management of Terrorist Attacks" (L147251003).

Ascari, A. (2009a) "I giochi olimpici – 'Materiale dai giornali," http://www.ada. ascari.name/studio/storia/protagonisti.html#olimpiade

Ascari, A. (2009b) "Settembere Nero – Materiale dai giornali," http://www.ada. ascari.name/studio/storia/protagonisti.html#settembre

Ashour, O. (2010) "Online De-radicalization? Countering Violent Extremist Narratives: Message, Messenger and Media Strategy," *Perspectives on Terrorism: A Journal of the Terrorism Research Institute* 4 (6): 15–19, http://www. terrorismanalysts.com/pt/index.php/pot/article/view/67/138

Ashour, O. (2011) "The Arab Spring is Al-Qaeda's Winter," *The Daily Star*, 9 September, http://www.dailystar.com.lb/Opinion/Commentary/2011/ Sep-09/148318-the-arab-spring-is-al-qaedas-winter.ashx#axzz1jibnAF7T

Awan, A. (2007a) "Radicalization on the Internet?" *The RUSI Journal* 152(3): 76–81.

Awan, A. (2007b) "Virtual Jihadist Media: Function, Legitimacy and Radicalizing Efficacy," *European Journal of Cultural Studies* 10 (3): 389–408.

Awan, A., A. Hoskins and **B. O'Loughlin** (2011) *Radicalisation and Media: Connectivity and Terrorism in the New Media Ecology* (Milton Park: Routledge).

Azarian, G. R. (2005) *The General Sociology of Harrison G. White: Chaos and Order in Networks* (Basingstoke: Palgrave).

Bahr Thompson, A. (2003) "Brand Positioning and Brand Creation," in R. Clifton and J. Simmons (eds) *Brands and Branding* (London: The Economist and Profile Books), pp. 79–95.

Bakker, E. (2006) *Jihadi Terrorists in Europe: Their Characteristics and the Circumstances in Which They Joined the Jihad: An Exploratory Study* (The Hague: Netherlands Institute of International Relations).

Bakker, E. and **L. Boer** (2007) *The Evolution of Al-Qaedaism: Ideology, Terrorists, and Appeal* (The Hague: Netherlands Institute of International Relations).

Ball, J. and **S. Brown** (2011) "Why BlackBerry Messenger Was Rioters' Communication Method of Choice," *The Guardian*, 7 December, http:// www.guardian.co.uk/uk/2011/dec/07/bbm-rioters-communication- method-choice?newsfeed=true

Ball, J. and **P. Lewis** (2011) "Twitter and the Riots: How the News Spread," *The Guardian*, 8 December, http://www.guardian.co.uk/uk/2011/dec/07/ twitter-riots-how-news-spread?newsfeed=true

Barnhurst, K. G. (1991) "The Literature of Terrorism: Implications for Visual Communications," in A. O. Alali and K. K. Eke (eds) *Media Coverage of Terrorism: Methods of Diffusion* (London: Sage), pp. 112–137.

Barrett, R. (2008) *Seven Years after 9/11: Al-Qaida's Strengths and Vulnerabilities* (London: International Centre for the Study of Radicalisation and Political Violence).

Barth, F. (1970) *Ethnic Groups and Boundaries* (London: G.Allen and Unwin).

Bassiouni, M. C. (1981) "Terrorism, Law Enforcement, and the Mass Media: Perspectives, Problems, Proposals'," *Journal of Criminal Law and Criminology* 72 (1): 1–51.

BBC Editorial Guidelines (n.d.) "Language When Reporting Terrorism," http://www.bbc.co.uk/editorialguidelines/page/guidance-reporting-terrorism-full

BBC News (2003) "Al-Qaeda Suspect Tells of Bomb Plot," 27 May, http://news.bbc.co.uk/1/hi/world/europe/2941702.stm

BBC News (2005a) "London Bomber: Text in Full," 1 September, http://news.bbc.co.uk/1/hi/uk/4206800.stm

BBC News (2005b) "The Bombers," no date, http://news.bbc.co.uk/1/shared/spl/hi/uk/05/london_blasts/investigation/html/bombers.stm (accessed November 2011).

BBC News (2007) "Timeline: Failed Car Bomb Attacks," 6 July, http://news.bbc.co.uk/1/hi/uk/6260626.stm

Bearman, P. S. and **K. Stovel** (2000) "Becoming a Nazi: A Model for Narrative Networks," *Poetics* 27: 69–90.

Belaala, S. (2008) *Les facteurs de création ou de modification des processus de radicalisation violente, chez les jeunes en particulier* (Paris : Compagnie Européenne d'Intelligence Stratégique).

Bell, J. B. (1978) "Terrorist Scripts and Live-Action Spectaculars," *Columbia Journalism Review* 17 (May/June): 47–50.

Bell, M. (2007) "The Frenzy of News," *The Guardian*, 3 July, http://www.guardian.co.uk/commentisfree/2007/jul/03/thefrenzyofnews

Benard, C. (2011) "The Mechanics of De-Legitimization," in L. Fenstermacher and T. Leventhal (eds) *Countering Violent Extremism: Scientific Methods and Strategies* (Wright-Patterson AFB, OH: AF Research Laboratory), pp. 106–110.

Benjamin, D. (2008) "What Statistics Don't Tell Us," *Slate*, 30 May, http://www.slate.com/articles/news_and_politics/foreigners/2008/05/what_statistics_dont_tell_us.html

Bennett, A. and **A. L. George** (1997) "Process Tracing in Case Study Research," paper presented at the MacArthur Foundation Workshop on Case Study Methods, Belfer Center for Science and International Affairs, Harvard University, http://www.georgetown.edu/faculty/bennetta/PROTCG.htm

Bennett, D. and **W. Graebner** (2009) "Rome: The Second Time," http://romethesecondtime.blogspot.com/2009/11/battle-of-valle-giulia.html

Benwell, B. and **E. Stokoe** (2006) *Discourse and Identity* (Edinburgh: Edinburgh University Press).

Bergin, A., S. B. Osman, C. Ungerer and **N. A. M. Yasin** (2009) "Countering Internet Radicalization in Southeast Asia," Issue 22, http://www.rsis.edu.sg/short%20reports/Countering_internet_radicalisation.pdf

Beski-Chafiq, C., J. Birmant, H. Benmerzoug, A. Taibi and **A. Goignard** (2010a) *Jeunes et radicalization islamiste: Lille, France* (Aarhus: Centre for Studies in Islamism and Radicalisation), http://cir.au.dk/fileadmin/site_files/filer_statskundskab/subsites/cir/Rapport5_Frankrig2.pdf

Beski-Chafiq, C., J. Birmant, H. Benmerzoug, A. Taibi and **A. Goignard** (2010b) *Youth and Islamist Radicalisation: Lille, France. English Summary*

(Aarhus: Centre for Studies in Islamism and Radicalisation), http://ps.au.dk/fileadmin/site_files/filer_statskundskab/subsites/cir/SummaryFINAL_Eng_rapport5_.pdf

Betz, D. (2008) "The Virtual Dimension of Contemporary Insurgency and Counterinsurgency," *Small Wars & Insurgencies* 19 (4): 510–540.

Björkman, C. (2010) "Salafi-Jihadi Terrorism in Italy," in M. Ranstorp (ed.) *Understanding Violent Radicalisation: Terrorist and Jihadist Movements in Europe* (Oxon: Routledge), pp. 231–255.

Bjørgo, T. (2005a) "Conclusions," in T. Bjørgo (ed.) *The Root Causes of Terrorism: Myths, Reality, and Ways Forward* (London: Routledge), pp. 256–264.

Bjørgo, T. (ed.) (2005b) *The Root Causes of Terrorism: Myths, Reality, and Ways Forward* (London: Routledge).

Bjørgo, T. and J. Horgan (2009) *Leaving Terrorism Behind: Individual and Collective Disengagement* (London: Routledge)

Blackett, T. (2003) "What is a Brand?" In R. Clifton and J. Simmons (eds) *Brands and Branding* (London: The Economist and Profile Books), pp. 13–25.

Blumler, J. G. and E. Katz (1974) *The Uses of Mass Communication* (Newbury Park, CA: Sage).

Boje, D. M. (1991) "The Storytelling Organization: A Study of Story Performance in an Office-Supply Firm," *Administrative Science Quarterly* 36 (1): 106–126.

Bonanate, L. (1979) "Some Unanticipated Consequences of Terrorism," *Journal of Peace Research* 16 (3): 197–211.

Bourdieu, P. and J. S. Coleman (eds) (1991) *Social Theory for a Changing Society* (Oxford: Westview Press).

Braben, D. W. (2004) *Pioneering Research: A Risk Worth Taking* (Hoboken, NJ: John Wiley & Sons).

Braben, D. W. (2011) "Pioneers Need Not Apply," *The Times Higher Education*, 8 September, http://www.timeshighereducation.co.uk/story.asp?storycode=417376

Braiker, B. (2011) "Branding Bin Laden: How Osama's Death Will Affect the Al-Qaeda Name," *AdWeek*, 3 May, http://www.adweek.com/news/advertising-branding/branding-bin-laden-131292

Brandon, J. (2009) "Al-Qa'ida's Involvement in Britain's 'Homegrown' Terrorist Plots," *CTC Sentinel* 2 (3): 10–12, http://www.farhanaqazi.com/uploads/6/8/4/5/6845221/ctcsentinel-vol2iss3.pdf

Breen-Smyth, M., J. Gunning, R. Jackson, G. Kassimeris, and P. Robinson (2008a) "Critical Terrorism Studies: An Introduction," *Critical Studies on Terrorism* 1 (1): 1–4.

Breen-Smyth, M., J. Gunning, R. Jackson, G. Kassimeris, and P. Robinson (2008b) "Editors' Introduction: Negotiating Stormy Waters," *Critical Studies on Terrorism* 1 (2): 145–149.

Breivik, A. (2011) *"2083: A European Declaration of Independence,"* http://www.slideshare.net/darkandgreen/2083-a-european-declaration-of-independence-by-andrew-berwick

Brenkel, J. (1997) "Hewlett-Packard: Keeping the Brand Vision Alive," in F. Gilmore (ed.) *Brand Warriors: Corporate Leaders Share Their Winning Strategies* (London: Harper Collins Business), pp. 133–144.

Brooker, W. and D. Jermyn (2003) *The Audience Studies Reader* (London: Routledge).

Bruner, J. (1986) *Actual Minds, Possible Worlds* (Cambridge, MA: Harvard University).

Brymer, C. (2003) "What Makes Brands Great," in R. Clifton and J. Simmons (eds) *Brands and Branding* (London: The Economist and Profile Books), pp. 65–76.

Burke, A. (2008) "The End of Terrorism Studies," *Critical Studies on Terrorism* 1 (1): 37–49.

Burke, J. (2004) "Theatre of Terror," *The Observer*, 21 November, http://www.guardian.co.uk/theobserver/2004/nov/21/features.review7

Bush, G. W. (2001a) "President's Remarks at Day of National Prayer and Remembrance," White House Archive, 14 September, http://georgewbush-whitehouse.archives.gov/news/releases/2001/09/20010914–2.html

Bush, G. W. (2001b) "President: FBI Needs Tools to Track Down Terrorists," White House Archive, 25 September, http://georgewbush-whitehouse.archives.gov/news/releases/2001/09/20010925–5.html

Bush, G. W. (2001c) "Governor Ridge Sworn-In to Lead Homeland Security," White House Archive, 8 October, http://georgewbush-whitehouse.archives.gov/news/releases/2001/10/20011008–3.html

Calhoun, C. (1991a) "Indirect Relationships and Imagined Communities: Large Scale Social Integration and the Transformation of Everyday Life," in P. Bourdieu and J. S. Coleman (eds) *Social Theory for a Changing Society* (Oxford: Westview Press), pp. 95–121.

Calhoun, C. (1991b) "The Problem of Identity in Collective Action," in J. Huber (ed.) *Macro-Micro Linkages in Sociology* (London: Sage), pp. 51–75.

Calhoun, C. (ed.) (1994) *Social Theory and the Politics of Identity* (Oxford: Blackwell).

Carafano, J.J. and **J. Zuckerman** (2011) "40 Terror Plots Foiled Since 9/11: Combating Complacency in the Long War on Terror," The Heritage Foundation, Backgrounder #2604, 7 September, http://www.heritage.org/research/reports/2011/09/40-terror-plots-foiled-since-9–11-combating-complacency-in-the-long-war-on-terror

Casebeer, W. D. and **J. A. Russell** (2005) "Storytelling and Terrorism: Towards a Comprehensive 'Counter-Narrative Strategy'," *Strategic Insights* 4 (3), http://0-www.ciaonet.org.wam.leeds.ac.uk/olj/si/si_4_3/si_4_3_caw01.pdf

Castells, M. (1996) *The Rise of the Network Society* (vol. I) (Oxford: Blackwell).

Cento Bull, A. (2009) "Political Violence, *stragismo* and 'Civil War': An Analysis of the Self-Narratives of Three Neofascist Protagonists," in P. Antonello and A. O'Leary (eds) (2009) *Imagining Terrorism: The Rhetoric and Representation of Political Violence in Italy 1969–2009* (Oxford: Modern Humanities Research Association and Maney Publishing), pp. 183–199.

Chadwick, A. (2006) *Internet Politics: States, Citizens, and New Communication Technologies* (New York: Oxford University Press).

Change Institute (2008) *Studies into Violent Radicalisation: Lot 2: The Beliefs Ideologies and Narratives* (London: Change Institute).

Chermak, S. (1997) "The Presentation of Drugs in the News Media: The News Sources Involved in the Construction of Social Problems," *Justice Quarterly* 14 (4): 687–718.

Chibnall, S. (1977) *Law and Order News: An Analysis of Crime Reporting in the British Press* (London: Tavistock Publications).

Choudhury, T. (2007) *The Role of Muslim Identity Politics in Radicalisation* (London: Department for Communities and Local Government).

Chrichton, T. (2009) "UK Citizens Encouraged to Confront Terror Threat," *The Herald*, 25 March, http://www.heraldscotland.com/uk-citizens-encouraged-to-confront-terror-threat-1.905910

Cilluffo, F. (2008) Interview with author, Washington, DC, Homeland Security and Policy Institute, 4 March.

Clandinin, D. J. (ed.) (2007) *Handbook of Narrative Enquiry: Mapping a Methodology* (London: Sage).

Clark, W. (2002) "An Army of One?" *Washington Monthly*, September, http://www.washingtonmonthly.com/features/2001/0209.clark.html

Clifton, R. (2003) "Introduction," in R. Clifton and J. Simmons (eds) *Brands and Branding* (London: The Economist and Profile Books), pp. 1–9.

Clifton, R. and J. Simmons (2003) (eds) *Brands and Branding* (London: The Economist and Profile Books).

Cohen-Almagor, R. (2005) "Media Coverage of Acts of Terrorism: Troubling Episodes and Suggested Guidelines," *Canadian Journal of Communication* 30 (3): 383–409.

Coleman, S. and J. G. Blumler (2009) *The Internet and Democratic Citizenship: Theory, Practice and Policy* (Cambridge: Cambridge University Press).

Coll, S. and S. B. Glasser (2005) "Terrorists Turn to the Web as Base of Operations," *Washington Post*, 7 August, A01.

Collins, R. (1988) *Theoretical Sociology* (London: Harcourt Brace Jovanovich).

Commission of the European Communities (2005) "Terrorist Recruitment: Addressing the Factors Contributing to Violent Radicalization," Communication from the Commission to the European Parliament and the Council, Brussels, 21 September, http://www.libertysecurity.org/IMG/pdf/COM_2005_313_final.pdf

Committee on Homeland Security (2007) "Using the Web as a Weapon: The Internet as a Tool for Violent Radicalization and Homegrown Terrorism," hearing before the Subcommittee of Intelligence, Information Sharing, and Terrorism Risk Assessment of the Committee on Homeland Security House of Representatives, 6 November, Serial No. 110–83, http://www.fas.org/irp/congress/2007_hr/web.pdf

Conway, M. (2006) "Terrorism and the Internet: New Media—New Threat?" *Parliamentary Affairs* 59 (2): 283–298.

Conway, M. and L. McInerney (2008) "*Jihadi Video and Auto-Radicalisation: Evidence From an Exploratory YouTube Study,*" paper presented at EuroISI 2008, First European Conference on Intelligence and Security Informatics, 3–5 December, Esbjerg, Denmark.

Corman, S. R. (2009a) "Same Old Song from GAO on Strategic Communication," *The COMOPS Journal*, 3 June 2009, http://comops.org/journal/2009/06/03/same-old-song-from-gao-on-strategic-communication/

Corman, S. R. (2009b) "What Power Needs to be Smart," paper presented at the Digital Media and Security Workshop, University of Warwick, 21 May 2009.

Corman, S. R. (2010) "Public Diplomacy as Narrative," paper presented at the International Studies Association annual convention, New Orleans, 20 February 2010.

Corman, S. R. (2011) "Understanding the Role of Narratives in Extremist Strategic Communications," in L. Fenstermacher and T. Leventhal (eds) *Countering Violent Extremism: Scientific Methods and Strategies* (Wright-Patterson AFB, OH: AF Research Laboratory), pp. 36–43.

Cornish, P., J. Lindley-French and **C. Yorke** (2011) *Strategic Communication and National Strategy: A Chatham House Report* (London: Royal Institute of International Affairs).

Cortazzi, M. (1993) *Narrative Analysis* (London: Falmer Press).

Council of the European Union (2007) "Conclusions on Cooperation to Combat Terrorist Use of the Internet ('Check the Web')", 2807th Justice and Home Affairs Council Meeting, Luxembourg, 12–13 June.

Council on Foreign Relations (n.d.), "November 17, Revolutionary People's Struggle, Revolutionary Struggle," http://www.cfr.org/greece/november-17-revolutionary-peoples-struggle-revolutionary-struggle-greece-leftists/p9275

COT (2007) *Lone-Wolf Terrorism* (The Hague: Instituut voor Veiligheids- en Crisismanagement).

Craig, R. T. and **H. L. Muller** (eds) (2007) *Theorizing Communication: Readings across Traditions* (London: Sage).

Crelinsten, R. D. (1987) "Power and Meaning: Terrorism as a Struggle over Access to the Communication Structure," in P. Wilkinson and A. M. Stewart (eds) *Contemporary Research on Terrorism* (Aberdeen: Aberdeen University Press).

Crenshaw, M. (1981) "The Causes of Terrorism," *Comparative Politics* 13 (4): 379–399.

Crenshaw, M. (1991) "How Terrorism Declines," *Terrorism and Political Violence* 3 (1): 69–87.

Cronin, A. K. (2006) "How al-Qaida Ends: The Decline and Demise of Terrorist Groups," *International Security* 31 (1): 7–48.

Cronin, A. K. (2009) *How Terrorism Ends: Understanding the Decline and Demise of Terrorist Campaigns* (Princeton: Princeton University Press).

Crotty, R. (1999) "Towards a Sociology of Academic Publishing," paper presented at the Australian Association for Research in Education annual conference, Melbourne.

Csaba, F. F. (2005) "The Limits of Corporate Branding: The Application of Branding to Non-Profit Organizations and Places," in M. Schultz, Y. M. Antorini, and F. F. Csaba (eds) *Corporate Branding: Purpose/People/Process* (Copenhagen: Copenhagen Business School Press), pp. 127–149.

Curran, J. and **M. Gurevitch** (eds) (2005) *Mass Media and Society* (London: Hodder Arnold).

Curtis, A. (2004) *The Power of Nightmares: The Rise of the Politics of Fear,* video documentary broadcast on BBC2 20 October-3 November, 180 min. (3 parts).

Czarniawska, B. (2007) "Narrative Inquiry in and about Organizations," in D. J. Clandinin (ed.) *Handbook of Narrative Enquiry: Mapping a Methodology* (London: Sage).

Dalgaard-Nielsen, A. (2008) *Studying Violent Radicalization in Europe I: The Potential Contribution of Social Movement Theory,* Working Paper no 2008/2 (Copenhagen: Danish Institute for International Studies).

Daily News (2010) "Our Own Worst Enemy: Fighting Terror War with One Hand Tied behind Our Back," *Daily News,* 6 May, http://articles.nydailynews.com/2010–05–06/news/29438016_1_faisal-shahzad-terror-gap-lists

Davidson, H. (2005) *The Committed Enterprise: Making Vision, Values and Branding Work* (London: Elsevier).

Day, M. (2011) "Anders Behring Breivik: 'I Am the Commander of Norway's Resistance Movement'," *The Telegraph*, 14 November, http://www.telegraph. co.uk/news/worldnews/europe/norway/8889182/Anders-Behring-Breivik-I-am-the-commander-of-Norways-resistance-movement.html

Dayan, D. and **E. Katz** (1992) *Media Events: The Live Broadcasting of History* (Cambridge: Harvard University Press).

de Chernatony, L. and **F. Dall' Olmo Riley** (1999) "Experts' Views About Defining Services Brands and the Principles of Services Branding," *Journal of Business Research* 46: 181–192.

De Graaf, B. (2011) *Evaluating Counterterrorism Performance: A Comparative Study* (London: Routledge).

Della Porta, D. (1995) *Social Movements, Political Violence, and the State* (New York: Cambridge University Press).

Della Porta, D. and **L. Bosi** (2010) *Young Muslims in Italy: Parma and Verona* (Aarhus: Centre for Studies in Islamism and Radicalisation).

De Vaus, D. (2001) *Research Design in Social Research* (London: Sage).

De Waal, M. (2007) "From Media Landscape to Media Ecology: The Cultural Implications of Web 2.0," *Open* 13: 20–33, http://www.skor.nl/article-3429-nl.html?lang=en

Dodd, V. (2007) "Three Extremists Used Internet to Urge Muslims to Follow Bin Laden and Join Holy War, Court Told," *The Guardian*, 24 April, http://www.guardian.co.uk/uk/2007/apr/24/terrorism.topstories

Dodd, V. (2010) "Roshonara Choudhry: I Wanted to Die ... I Wanted to Be a Martyr," *The Guardian*, 4 November, http://www.guardian.co.uk/uk/2010/nov/04/stephen-timms-attack-roshonara-choudhry?INTCMP=ILCNETTXT3487

Dolnik, A. (2011a) "Conducting Field Research on Terrorism: A Brief Primer," *Perspectives on Terrorism* 5 (2): 3–35.

Dolnik, A. (2011b) Interview with author, Marshall Centre for Security Studies, Garmisch-Partenkirchen, 29 June.

Douglas, F. S. (2007) "Waging the Inchoate War: Defining, Fighting, and Second-Guessing the 'Long War'," *Journal of Strategic Studies* 30 (3): 391–420.

Dowling, R. E. (1986) "Terrorism and the Media: A Rhetorical Genre," *Journal of Communication* 36 (1): 12–24.

Durodié, B. (2005) "The Limitations of Risk Management: Dealing with Disasters and Building Social Resilience," *Politik* 8 (1): 14–21.

Duyvesteyn, I. (2007) "The Role of History and Continuity in Terrorism Research," in M. Ranstorp (ed.) *Mapping Terrorism Research: State of the Art, Gaps and Future Direction* (London: Routledge), pp. 51–75.

Eatwell, R. and **M. J. Goodwin** (2010a) "Introduction: The 'New' Extremism in Twenty-First Century Britain," in R. Eatwell and M. J. Goodwin (eds) *The New Extremism in 21st Century Britain* (London: Routledge), pp. 1–20.

Eatwell, R. and **M. J. Goodwin** (eds) (2010b) *The New Extremism in 21st Century Britain* (London: Routledge).

Eke, K. K. and **A. O. Alali** (1991) "Introduction: Critical Issues in Media Coverage of Terrorism," in A. O. Alali and K. K. Eke (eds) *Media Coverage of Terrorism: Methods of Diffusion* (London: Sage), pp. 3–11.

Emirbayer, M. (1997) "Manifesto for a Relational Sociology," *The American Journal of Sociology* 103 (2): 281–317.

Emirbayer, M. and **A. Mische** (1998) "What is Agency?" *The American Journal of Sociology* 103 (4): 962–1023.

English, R. (2004) *Armed Struggle: The History of the IRA* (London: Macmillan).

Ensor, D. (2005) "Al Qaeda Letter Called 'Chilling'," CNN website, 12 October, http://edition.cnn.com/2005/WORLD/meast/10/11/alqaeda.letter/

Ericson, R. V., P. M. Baranek and **J. B. L. Chan** (1989) *Negotiating Control: A Study of News Sources* (Toronto: University of Toronto Press).

Esser, F. and **B. Pfetsch** (eds) (2004) *Comparing Political Communication: Theories, Cases, and Challenges* (Cambridge: Cambridge University Press).

Eubank, W. L. and **L. Weinberg** (1994) "Does Democracy Encourage Terrorism?" *Terrorism and Political Violence* 6 (4): 417–435.

Evans, J. (2007) "MI5 Chief's Warning – Full Text," *The Guardian*, 5 November. http://www.guardian.co.uk/uk/2007/nov/05/terrorism.world

Ewing, M. T. and **J. Napoli** (2003) "Developing and Validating a Multidimensional Nonprofit Brand Orientation Scale," *Journal of Business Research* 58: 841–853.

Eyerman, J. (1998) "Terrorism and Democratic States: Soft Targets or Accessible Systems," *International Interactions* 24 (2): 151–170.

Federal Bureau of Investigation (FBI) (n.d.) "Working Draft Chronology of Events for Hijackers and Associates (Part 2)," "The Vault," http://vault.fbi. gov/9–11%20Commission%20Report/9–11-chronology-part-02-of-02/view

Feiser, J. (2004) "Evolution of the al-Qaeda Brand Name," *Asia Times Online*, 13 August, http://www.atimes.com/atimes/Middle_East/FH13Ak05.html

Fenstermacher, L. (2011) "Executive Summary," in L. Fenstermacher and T. Leventhal (eds) *Countering Violent Extremism: Scientific Methods and Strategies* (Wright-Patterson AFB, OH: AF Research Laboratory), pp. 4–23.

Fenstermacher, L. and **T. Leventhal** (eds) (2011) *Countering Violent Extremism: Scientific Methods and Strategies* (Wright-Patterson AFB, OH: AF Research Laboratory), http://www.nsiteam.com/pubs/U_Counter%20Violent%20 Extremism%20Final_Approved%20for%20Public%20Release_28Oct11v3.pdf

Ferguson, M. (ed.) *Public Communication: The New imperatives: Future Directions for Media Research* (London: Sage).

Fink, N. C. (2011) "The Death of Bin Laden: Whither Al-Qaida?" International Peace Institute, 3 May, http://www.ipacademy.org/news/comment-a-analysis/234-the-death-of-bin-laden-whither-al-qaida.html

Franks, J. (2009) "Rethinking the Roots of Terrorism: Beyond Orthodox Terrorism Theory – A Critical Research Agenda," *Global Society* 23 (2): 153–176.

Freedman, L. (2006) *The Transformation of Strategic Affairs*, Adelphi Paper 379 (London: International Institute for Strategic Studies).

Gartenstein-Ross, D. and **L. Grossman** (2009) *Homegrown Terrorists in the U.S. and the U.K.: An Empirical Examination of the Radicalization Process* (Washington, DC: Foundation for the Defense of Democracy's Center for Terrorism Research).

Geltzer, J. A. (2010) *US Counter-Terrorism Strategy and Al-Qaeda: Signalling and the Terrorist World-View* (Milton Park: Routledge).

Gendron, A. (2006) *Militant Jihadism: Radicalization, Conversion, Recruitment* (Ottawa: Canadian Centre for Intelligence and Security Studies).

George, A. L. (1997) "The Role of the Congruence Method for Case Study Research," paper presented at the International Studies Association annual convention, Toronto, 18–22 March.

George, A. L. and **A. Bennett** (2005) *Case Studies and Theory Development in the Social Sciences* (London: BCSIA Studies in International Security).

Gerrits, R. P. J. M. (1992) "Terrorists' Perspectives: Memoirs," in D. L. Paletz and A. Schmid (eds) *Terrorism and the Media: How Researchers, Terrorists, Government, Press, Public, Victims View and Use the Media* (London: Sage), pp. 29–61.

Gilmore, F. (2002) "A Country: Can It Be Repositioned? Spain – The Success Story," *Journal of Brand Management* 9 (4/5): 281–294.

Githens-Mazer, J. (2010) "Mobilization, Recruitment, Violence and the Street: Radical Violent Takfiri Islamism in Early Twenty-First-Century Britain," in R. Eatwell and M. J. Goodwin (eds) *The New Extremism in 21st Century Britain* (London: Routledge), pp. 47–66.

Githens-Mazer, J., R. Lambert, A-H. Baker, S. Cohen-Baker and **Z. Pieri** (2010) *Muslim Communities Perspectives on Radicalisation in Leicester, UK* (Aarhus: Centre for Studies in Islamism and Radicalisation).

Godin, S. (2002) *Permission Marketing: Turning Strangers into Friends and Friends into Customers* (London: Free).

Goodman, M. (2011) "Killer Apps: The Revolution in Network Terrorism," *Jane's Intelligence Review* 23 (7): 14–19.

Gordon, A. (2001) "Terrorism and the Scholarly Communication System," *Terrorism and Political Violence* 13 (4): 116–124.

Gordon, A. (2004) "Terrorism and Knowledge Growth: A Database and Internet Analysis," in A. Silke (ed.) *Research on Terrorism: Trends, Achievements and Failures* (London: Frank Cass), pp. 104–118.

Gordon, A. (2005) "The Peripheral Terrorism Literature: Bringing it Closer to the Core," *Scientometrics* 62 (3): 403–414.

Gordon, A. (2007) "Transient and Continuant Authors in a Research Field: The Case of Terrorism," *Scientometrics* 72 (2): 213–224.

Granovetter, M. G. (1973) "The Strength of the Weak Ties," *American Journal of Sociology* 78 (6): 1360–1380.

Gray, J. (2005) "A Violent Episode in the Virtual World," *New Statesman*, 18 July 2005, 16–17, http://www.newstatesman.com/200507180006

Greenpeace.org (no date) "About Greenpeace," http://www.greenpeace.org/international/about

Gunning, J. (2007) "A Case for Critical Terrorism Studies?" *Government and Opposition* 42 (3): 363–393.

Gupta, D. (2011) "Tracking the Spread of Violent Extremism" in L. Fenstermacher and T. Leventhal (eds) *Countering Violent Extremism: Scientific Methods and Strategies* (Wright-Patterson AFB, OH: AF Research Laboratory), pp. 44–55.

Haig, M. (2003) *Brand Failures: The Truth About the 100 Biggest Branding Mistakes of All Time* (London: MPG Books).

Hall, S., C. Critcher, T. Jefferson, J. Clarke, and **B. Roberts** (1978) *Policing the Crisis: Mugging, the State, and Law and Order* (Hong Kong: Macmillan Education).

Halliday, J. (2011) "London Riots: How BlackBerry Messenger Played a Key Role," *The Guardian*, 8 August, http://www.guardian.co.uk/media/2011/aug/08/london-riots-facebook-twitter-blackberry

Hallin, D. C. and **P. Mancini** (2005) "Comparing Media Systems," in J. Curran and M. Gurevitch (eds) *Mass Media and Society* (London: Hodder Arnold), pp. 215–233.

Halverson, J. R., H. L. Goodall and S. Corman (2011) *Master Narratives of Islamist Extremism* (New York: Palgrave).

Hamilton, L., B. Hoffman, B. Jenkins, P. Pillar, X. Raufer, W. Reich, F. Reinares (2006) *State of the Struggle* (Washington: Council on Global Terrorism).

Hankinson, G. (2004) "Relational Network Brands: Towards a Conceptual Model of Place Brands," *Journal of Vacation Marketing* 10: 109–121.

Hankinson, P. (2002) "The Impact of Brand Orientation on Managerial Practice: A Quantitative Study of the UK's Top 500 Fundraising Managers," *International Journal of Nonprofit and Voluntary Sector Marketing* 7 (1): 30–44.

Hankinson, P. (2004) "The Internal Brand in Leading UK Charities," *Journal of Product and Brand Management* 13 (2): 84–93.

Harrison, S. (2002) "Culture, Tourism and Local Community: The Heritage Identity of the Isle of Man," *Journal of Brand Management* 9(4/5): 355–371.

Hart, J. (1992) "Cracking the Code: Narrative and Political Mobilization in the Greek Resistance," *Social Science History* 16 (4): 631–668.

Hay, C. (2002) *Political Analysis: A Critical Introduction* (Basingstoke: Palgrave).

Hegghammer, T. (2005) *Al-Qaida Statements 2003–2004: A Compilation of Translated Texts by Usama Bin Laden and Ayman Al-Zawahiri* (Kjeller: Norwegian Defence Research Establishment).

Hegghammer, T. (2008) "Jihadi Studies," *The Times* Literary Supplement, 2 April, pp. 15–17.

Hesmondhalgh, D. and J. Toynbee (eds) (2008) *The Media and Social Theory* (Milton Park: Routledge).

Hick, S. and J. G. McNutt (eds) (2002) *Advocacy, Activism, and the Internet: Community Organization and Social Policy* (Chicago: Lyceum).

Hoffman, B. (2006) *Inside Terrorism*, rev. and exp. edn (New York: Columbia University Press).

Home Office (2009) *The United Kingdom's Strategy for Countering International Terrorism* (London: The Cabinet Office).

Home Office (2011) *Prevent Strategy* (London: The Cabinet Office).

Home Office OSCT (2011) "Implementation of Authority-to-Carry Scheme under Section 124 of Nationality, Immigration and Asylum Act 2002" (London: Home Office), http://www.homeoffice.gov.uk/publications/about-us/consulta-tions/authority-to-carry/impact-assessment?view=Binary

Homeland Security Institute (2006) *Radicalization: An Overview and Annotated Bibliography of Open Source Literature* (Arlington, VA: Department of Homeland Security).

Homeland Security Institute (2009) *The Internet as a Terrorist Tool for Recruitment and Radicalization of Youth* (Arlington, VA: U.S. Department of Homeland Security).

Homeland Security Policy Institute (HSPI) and the University of Virginia Critical Incident Analysis Group (CIAG) (2007) *NETworked Radicalization: A Counter-Strategy*, http://www.gwumc.edu/hspi/policy/NETworkedRadicalization.pdf

Horgan, J. (2007) "Understanding Terrorist Motivation: A Socio-Psychological Perspective," in M. Ranstorp (ed.) *Mapping Terrorism Research: State of the Art, Gaps and Future Direction* (London: Routledge).

Horgan, J. (2009) *Walking Away from Terrorism: Accounts of Disengagement from Radical and Extremist Movements* (London: Routledge).

Horgan, J. and **M. J. Boyle** (2008) "A Case against 'Critical Terrorism Studies'," *Critical Studies on Terrorism* 1 (1): 51–64.

Hoskins, A. and **B.** O'Loughlin (2009) "Media and the Myth of Radicalization," *Media, War & Conflict* 2 (2): 107–110.

Hoskins, A. et al. (2009) "Legitimising the Discourses of Radicalisation: Political Violence in the New Media Ecology: Full Research Report," ESRC end of award report, RES-181–25–0041 (Swindon: ESRC).

Huber, J. (ed.) (1991) *Macro-Micro Linkages in Sociology* (London: Sage).

Hughes, M. and **G. Rayner** (2011) "Norway Killer Anders Behring Breivik Had Extensive Links to English Defence League," *The Telegraph*, 25 July, http://www.telegraph.co.uk/news/worldnews/europe/norway/8661139/Norway-killer-Anders-Behring-Breivik-had-extensive-links-to-English-Defence-League.html

Husain, E. (2007) *The Islamist* (London: Penguin Books).

ICSR (International Centre for the Study of Radicalisation and Political Violence) (ed.) (2008) *Perspectives on Radicalisation and Political Violence: Papers from the First International Conference on Radicalisation and Political Violence* (London: ICSR).

Inkster, N. (2011) "9/11/11: A Decade of Intelligence," *Survival* 53 (6): 5–13.

International Crisis Group (2006) *In Their Own Words: Reading the Iraqi Insurgency*, Middle East report N. 50, http://www.c4ads.org/files/ICG_report_021506_iraqi_insurgency.pdf

Jackson, R. (2009) "Critical Terrorism Studies: An Explanation, a Defence and a Way Forward," paper presented at the British International Studies Association, Leicester, 14–26 December.

Jacobson, M. (2009) "Assessing Progress against the Global Jihadist Threat," *Policy Watch* 1514, 11 May 2009, http://www.washingtoninstitute.org/templateC05.php?CID=3051

Jamieson, A. (2007) "Identity and Morality in the Italian Red Brigades," *Terrorism and Political Violence* 2 (4): 508–520.

Jenkins, B. M. (2007) *Building and Army of Believers: Jihadist Radicalization and Recruitment*, testimony presented before the House Homeland Security Committee, Subcommittee on Intelligence, Information Sharing and Terrorism Risk Assessment on 5 April 2007, Rand Corporation, http://www.rand.org/pubs/testimonies/2007/RAND_CT278–1.pdf

Joas, H. and **W. Knöbl** (2009) *Social Theory: Twenty Introductory Lectures*, 3rd edn (Cambridge: Cambridge University Press).

Johnson, T. H. (2007) "The Taliban Insurgency and an Analysis of *Shabnamah* (Night Letters)," *Small Wars & Insurgencies* 18 (3): 317–344.

Joscelyn, T. (2011a) "Latest Issue of *Inspire* Highlights Al Qaeda's Succession," *The Long War Journal*, 19 July, http://www.longwarjournal.org/archives/2011/07/latest_issue_of_insp.php

Joscelyn, T. (2011b) "AQAP Releases 7th Edition of *Inspire*," *The Long War Journal*, 27 September, http://www.longwarjournal.org/archives/2011/09/aqap_releases_sevent.php

Kamen, A. (2009) "The End of the Global War on Terror," *The Washington Post*, 24 March, http://voices.washingtonpost.com/44/2009/03/23/the_end_of_the_global_war_on_t.html?hpid=news-col-blog

Kapferer, J-N (2004) *The New Strategic Brand Management: Creating and Sustaining Brand Equity Long Term* (London: Kogan Page).

Karpf, D. (2010) "Online Political Mobilization from the Advocacy Group's Perspective: Looking Beyond Clicktivism," *Policy & Internet* 2 (4), article 2 (n.p.).

Katz, R. and **J. Deven** (2007) "Franchising Al Qaeda," *The Boston Globe*, 22 June, http://www.boston.com/news/globe/editorial_opinion/oped/articles/2007/06/22/franchising_al_qaeda/

Keating, J. E. (2010) "What Do You Learn at Terrorist Training Camp?" *Foreign Policy*, 10 May, http://www.foreignpolicy.com/articles/2010/05/10/what_do_you_learn_at_terrorist_training_camp

Keohane, R. O. and **J. Nye** (eds) (1981) *Transnational Relations and World Politics*, 5th edn (Cambridge, MA: Harvard University Press).

Kepel, G. and **J-P Milelli** (2008) *Al-Qaeda in Its Own Words* (London: The Belknap Press of Harvard University Press).

Khosrokhavar, F. (2005) *Suicide Bombers: Allah's New Martyrs* (London: Pluto Press).

Kimmage, Daniel (2008) *The Al-Qaeda Media Nexus: The Virtual Network behind the Global Message* (Washington, DC: Radio Free Europe/Radio Liberty).

Kimmage, Daniel (2008a) The Al-Qaeda Media Nexus, workshop organized by the George Washington University Homeland Security Policy Institute, Washington DC, 4 April.

King, G., R. O. Keohane, and **S. Verba** (1994) *Designing Social Enquiry: Scientific Inference in Qualitative Research* (Princeton, NJ: Princeton University Press).

Knight, K. (2006) "Transformations of the Concept of Ideology in the Twentieth Century," *American Political Science Review* 100 (4): 619–626.

Kohler Riessman, C. (1993) *Narrative Analysis* (London: Sage).

Kohler Riessman, C. (2008) "Concluding Comments," in M. Andrews, C. Squire and M. Tambouku (eds) *Doing Narrative Research* (London: Sage).

Kohlmann, E. (2009) "A Web of Lone Wolves," *Foreign Policy*, 13 November, http://www.foreignpolicy.com/articles/2009/11/13/a_web_of_lone_wolves

König, T. (n.d.) "Frame Analysis: A Primer," http://www.restore.ac.uk/lboro/resources/links/frames_primer.php

Kotler, P. and **D. Gertner** (2002) "Country as Brand, Product, and Beyond: A Place Marketing and Brand Management Perspective," *Journal of Brand Management* 9(4/5): 249–261.

Kühle, L. and **L. Lindekilde** (2010) *Radicalization among Young Muslims in Aarhus* (Aarhus: Centre for the Studies in Islamism and Radicalisation).

Kuhn, T. S. (1962) *The Structure of Scientific Revolutions*, 2nd enlarged edn (London: The University of Chicago).

Kull, S., C. Ramsay, S. Weber, E. Lewis, E. Mohseni (2009) *Public Opinion in the Islamic World on Terrorism, Al Qaeda, and US Policies*, http://www.worldpublicopinion.org/pipa/pdf/feb09/STARTII_Feb09_rpt.pdf

Lambert, R. (2011) "Police and Muslims in Partnership," paper presented at the "Radicalisation and Extremism: A Symposium for Researcher and Practitioners," Lancashire Constabulary, Hutton, 1 December.

Laqueur, W. (1976) "The Futility of Terrorism," *Harper's Magazine*, March, 99–105.

Larson, E. (2011) "Exploiting Al-Qa'ida's Vulnerabilities for Delegitimation," in L. Fenstermacher and T. Leventhal (eds) *Countering Violent Extremism: Scientific Methods and Strategies* (Wright-Patterson AFB, OH: AF Research Laboratory), pp. 111–124.

Latour, B. (1991) "Technology is Society Made Durable," in J. Law (ed.) *A Sociology of Monsters: Essays on Power, Technology and Domination* (London: Routledge), pp. 103–131.

Latour, B. (1993) *We Have Never Been Modern* (Cambridge, MA: Harvard University Press).

Latour, B. (1999) *Pandora's Hope: Essays on the Reality of Science Studies* (London: Harvard University Press).

Latour, B. (2005) *Reassembling the Social: An Introduction to Actor-Network-Theory* (Oxford: Oxford University Press).

Latour, B. and S. Woolgar (1979) *Laboratory Life: The Construction of Scientific Facts* (Chichester: Princeton University Press).

Lave, C. and J. March (1993) *An Introduction to Models in the Social Sciences* (Lanham, MD: University Press of America).

Law, J. (ed.) (1991a) *A Sociology of Monsters: Essays on Power, Technology and Domination* (London: Routledge).

Law, J. (1991b) "Introduction: Monsters, Machines and Sociotechnical Relations," in J. Law (ed.) *A Sociology of Monsters: Essays on Power, Technology and Domination* (London: Routledge), pp. 1–23.

Law, J. (1999) "After ANT: Complexity, Naming and Topology," in J. Law and J. Hassard (eds) *Actor Network Theory and After* (Oxford: Blackwell), pp. 1–14.

Law, J. and J. Hassard (eds) (1999) *Actor Network Theory and After* (Oxford: Blackwell).

Lawler, S. (2002) "Narrative in Social Research," in T. May (ed.) *Qualitative Research in Action* (London: Sage), pp. 242–258.

Lazarsfeld, P.F., B. Berelson and H. Gaudet (1944) *The People's Choice: How the Voter Makes Up His Mind in a Presidential Campaign* (New York: Columbia University Press).

Lemieux, A. and R. Nill (2011) "The Role and Impact of Music in Promoting (and Countering) Violent Extremism," in L. Fenstermacher and T. Leventhal (eds) *Countering Violent Extremism: Scientific Methods and Strategies* (Wright-Patterson AFB, OH: AF Research Laboratory), pp. 143–152.

Leonard, M. (2002) "Diplomacy by Other Means," *Foreign Policy*, October, pp. 48–56.

Levitt, M. (2009) "Radicalization: Made in the USA?" HSPI Commentary Series #3, http://www.gwumc.edu/hspi/HSPI_Commentary03_RadicalizationInThe USA.pdf

Lewis Mernit, J. (2011) "Is San Francisco Next?" *The Atlantic*, June, pp. 17–18.

Lia, B. (2009) "Does Al-Qaida Articulate a Consistent Strategy? A Study of Al-Qaida Leadership Statements 2001–2009," paper presented at the International Studies Association annual convention, New York, 15–18 February.

Linde, C. (2009) *Working the Past: Narrative and Institutional Memory* (Oxford: Oxford University Press).

Luhmann, N. (2007) "What is Communication?" In R. T. Craig and H. L. Muller (eds) *Theorizing Communication: Readings across Traditions* (London: Sage), pp. 301–307.

Mackenzie, I. (2011) "Is Technology to Blame for the London Riots?" *BBC News Technology*, 8 August, http://www.bbc.co.uk/news/technology-14442203

Maguire, M., R. Morgan, and R. Reiner (eds) *The Oxford Handbook of Criminology*, 4th edn (Oxford: Oxford University Press).

Mahoney, J. (2003) "Tentative Answers to Questions About Causal Mechanisms," paper presented at American Political Science Association annual meeting, Philadephia, PA, 28 August.

Mansfield, L. (2006) *His Own Words: A Translation of the Writings of Dr. Ayman al Zawahiri* (Thief River Falls, MN: TLG Publications).

Martin, L. J. (1985) "The Media's Role in International Terrorism," *Terrorism: An International Journal* 8 (2): 127–146.

Maslikowski, M. and Z. S. Justus (2009) "Nationalism is from Venus, al-Qa'ida is from Mars," *COMOPS Journal*, 30 March, http://comops.org/journal/2009/03/30/nationalism-is-from-venus-al-qaida-is-from-mars/

May, T. (ed.) (2002) *Qualitative Research in Action* (London: Sage).

McAdam, D., S. Tarrow and C. Tilly (2001) *Dynamics of Contention* (Cambridge: Cambridge University Press).

McCants, W. (2008) "Smackdown! Sageman vs. Hoffman," *Jihadica*, 8 June, http://www.jihadica.com/smackdown-sageman-vs-hoffman/

McCaughney, M. and M. D. Ayers (eds) (2003) *Cyberactivism: Online Activism in Theory and Practice* (New York: Routledge).

McInerney, L. (2009) "The Iraq War 'YouTube Style': Mobilising en Masse?" paper presented at the International Studies Association annual convention, New York, 15–18 February.

McLuhan, M. (1994[1964]) *Understanding Media: The Extension of Man* (Cambridge, MA: MIT Press).

Melissen, J. (2007a) "The New Public Diplomacy: Between Theory and Practice," in J. Melissen (ed.) *The New Public Diplomacy: Soft Power in International Relations* (Basingstoke: Palgrave Macmillan), pp. 3–27.

Melissen, J. (ed.) (2007b) *The New Public Diplomacy: Soft Power in International Relations* (Basingstoke: Palgrave Macmillan).

Miliband, D. (2009) "War on Terror Was Wrong," *The Guardian*, 15 January, http://www.guardian.co.uk/commentisfree/2009/jan/15/david-miliband-war-terror

Miller, D. (1993) "Official Sources and 'Primary Definition': The Case of Northern Ireland," *Media, Culture and Society* 15 (3): 385–406.

Miller, T. (2008) "'Step Away from the Croissant': Media Studies 3.0," in D. Hesmondhalgh and J. Toynbee (eds) *The Media and Social Theory* (Milton Park: Routledge), pp. 213–230.

Mische, A. (2010) "Relational Sociology, Culture, and Agency," paper presented at the American Sociological Association annual meeting, Atlanta, GA, 14 August, http://rci.rutgers.edu/~mische/Mische_relational_sociology.pdf

Mitroff, I. I. and R. H. Kilmann (1975) "Stories Managers Tell: A New Tool for Organizational Problem Solving," *Management Review* 64 (7): 18–28.

Morgan, N., A. Pritchard, and R. Piggott (2002) "New Zealand, 100% Pure: The Creation of a Powerful Niche Destination Brand," *Journal of Brand Management* 9 (4/5): 335–354.

Morris, A. D. and C. McClurg Mueller (eds) (1992) *Frontiers in Social Movement Theory* (New Haven: Yale University Press).

Mueller, J. (2005) "Simplicity and Spook: Terrorism and the Dynamics of Threat Exaggeration," *International Studies Perspectives* 6: 208–234.

Mueller, J. (2012) "New Year Brings Good News on Terrorism: Experts Wrong Again," *The National Interest*, 3 January, http://nationalinterest.org/blog/the-skeptics/experts-predictions-wrong-6334

Muir, J. (2011) "Bin Laden Death: Effect on Al-Qaeda in Middle East?" BBC News, 2 May, http://www.bbc.co.uk/news/world-middle-east-13260545

Mumby, D. K. (1993) *Narrative and Social Control: Critical Perspectives* (London: Sage).

Municipality of Amsterdam (2007) "Amsterdam against Radicalization," http://www.eenveiligamsterdam.nl/publish/pages/164993/amsterdam_against_radicalisation.pdf

Musharbash, Y. (2011) "The Monster Lives On," *SpiegelOnline*, 2 May, http://www.spiegel.de/international/world/0,1518,760195,00.html

Nacos, B. L. (1994) *Terrorism and the Media: From the Iran Hostage Crisis to the Oklahoma City Bombing* (New York: Columbia University Press).

Nacos, B. L. (2002a) *Mass-Mediated Terrorism: The Central Role of the Media in Terrorism and Counterterrorism* (Oxford: Rowman and Littlefield).

Nacos, B. L. (2002b) "Terrorism, the Mass Media, and the Events of 9–11," *Phi Kappa Phi Forum* 82 (2): 13–19.

Nacos, B. L. (2003) "The Terrorist Calculus behind 9–11: A Model for Future Terrorism?" *Studies in Conflict & Terrorism* 26 (1): 1–16.

National Commission on Terrorist Attacks upon the United States (2004) *9/11 Commission Report* (Washington, DC: U.S. Government Printing Office).

National Coordinator for Counterterrorism (ed.) (2010) *Countering Violent Extremist Narratives* (The Hague: National Coordinator for Counterterrorism).

National Counterterrorism Center (n.d.) "Radicalization and Mobilization Dynamics Framework," http://www.nctc.gov/site/technical/radicalization.html

NEFA Foundation (2008a) "Selected Questions and Answers from Dr. Ayman al-Zawahiri – Part 1," 17 April, http://www.nefafoundation.org/miscellaneous/FeaturedDocs/nefazawahiri0508–2.pdf

NEFA Foundation (2008b) "Selected Questions and Answers from Dr. Ayman al-Zawahiri – Part 2," 17 April, http://www.nefafoundation.org/miscellaneous/FeaturedDocs/nefazawahiri0508–2.pdf

Neumann, P. R. (2008a) "Introduction," in ICSR (ed.) *Perspectives on Radicalisation and Political Violence* (London: ICSR), pp. 3–7.

Neumann, P. R. (2008b) *Joining Al-Qaeda: Jihadist Recruitment in Europe*, Adelphi Paper 399 (London: International Institute for Strategic Studies).

Neumann, P. R. and B. Rogers (2007) *Recruitment and Mobilisation for the Islamist Militant Movement in Europe* (London: ICSR).

Nossek, H. (2004) "Our News and Their News: The Role of National Identity in the Coverage of Foreign News," *Journalism* 5 (3): 343–368.

Olins, W. (1999) *Trading Identities: Why Countries and Companies are Taking on Each Others' Roles* (London: The Foreign Policy Centre).

Olins, W. (2002) "Branding the Nation: The Historical Context," *Journal of Brand Management* 9 (4/5): 241–248.

Pakistani Institute for Peace Studies (2010) "Pakistan Security Report 2010" (Islamabad: PIPS).

Paletz, D. L. and J. Boiney (1992) "Researchers' Perspectives," in D. L. Paletz and A. Schmid (eds) *Terrorism and the Media: How Researchers, Terrorists, Government, Press, Public, Victims View and Use the Media* (London: Sage), pp. 6–28.

Paletz, D. L. and A. P. Schmid (eds) (1992) *Terrorism and the Media: How Researchers, Terrorists, Government, Press, Public, Victims View and Use the Media* (London: Sage).

Paletz, D. and L. L. Tawney (1992) "Broadcasting Organizations' Perspectives," in D. L. Paletz and A. P. Schmid (eds) *Terrorism and the Media: How Researchers, Terrorists, Government, Press, Public, Victims View and Use the Media* (London: Sage), pp. 105–110.

Pantucci, R. (2011) *A Typology of Lone Wolves: Preliminary Analysis of Lone Islamist Terrorists* (London: ICSR).

Perdue, W. D. (1989) *Terrorism and the State: A Critique of Domination through Fear* (Westport, CT: Praeger).

Perl, R. (2007) "Combating Terrorism: The Challenge of Measuring Effectiveness," CRS Report for Congress, 12 March, http://www.fas.org/sgp/crs/terror/RL33160.pdf

Picard, R. G. (1991) "News Coverage as the Contagion of Terrorism: Dangerous Charges Backed by Dubious Science," in A. O. Alali and K. K. Eke (eds) *Media Coverage of Terrorism: Methods of Diffusion* (London: Sage), pp. 49–62.

Polkinghorne, D. (1988) "Explorations of Narrative Identity," *Psychological Inquiry* 7 (4): 363–367.

Post, J. (2007) *The Mind of the Terrorist: The Psychology of Terrorism from the IRA to Al-Qaeda* (New York: Palgrave).

Potter, E. H. (ed.) (2002) *Cyber-Diplomacy: Managing Foreign Policy in the Twenty-First Century* (London: McGill-Queen's University Press).

Presidential Task Force (2009) *Rewriting the Narrative: An Integrated Strategy for Counterradicalization* (Washington, DC: The Washington Institute for Near East Policy).

Quiggin, T. (2009) "Understanding Al-Qaeda's Ideology for Counter-Narrative Work," *Perspectives on Terrorism* 3 (2): 18–24.

Ragin, C. C. (1987) *The Comparative Method: Moving beyond Qualitative and Quantitative Strategies* (Berkeley: University of California Press).

Ragin, C. C. and H. S. Becker (eds) (1992) *What is a Case? Exploring the Foundations of Social Inquiry* (New York: Cambridge University Press).

Ranstorp, M. (2007a) "Introduction: Mapping Terrorism Research," in M. Ranstorp (ed.) *Mapping Terrorism Research: State of the Art, Gaps and Future Direction* (London: Routledge), pp. 1–28.

Ranstorp, M. (2007b) *Mapping Terrorism Research: State of the Art, Gaps and Future Direction* (London: Routledge).

Ranstorp, M. (ed.) (2010) *Understanding Violent Radicalisation: Terrorist and Jihadist Movements in Europe* (Oxon: Routledge).

Rapoport, D. C. (1984) "Fear and Trembling: Terrorism in Three Religious Traditions," *The American Political Science Review* 78 (3): 658–677.

Rapoport, D. C. (ed.) (1988a) *Inside Terrorist Organizations* (New York: Columbia University Press).

Rapoport, D. C. (1988b) "The International World As Some Terrorists Have Seen It: A Look at a Century of Memoirs," in D. C. Rapoport (ed.) *Inside Terrorist Organizations* (New York: Columbia University Press), pp. 32–58.

Reid, E. O. F. (1993) "Terrorism Research and the Diffusion of Ideas," *Knowledge and Policy* 6 (1): 17–37.

Reid, E. O. F. (1997) "Evolution of a Body of Knowledge: An Analysis of Terrorism Research," *Information Processing & Management* 33 (1): 91–106.

Reid, E. O. F. and H. Chen (2007) "Mapping the Contemporary Terrorism Research Domain," *International Journal of Human-Computer Studies* 65 (1): 42–56.

Reiner, R. (2007) "Media-Made Criminality: The Representation of Crime in the Mass Media," in M. Maguire, R. Morgan, and R. Reiner (eds) *The Oxford Handbook of Criminology*, 4th edn (Oxford: Oxford University Press), pp. 302–337.

Riley, N-M (1995) "The Teachers' Unions and Their Image: A Case for Branding in an Industrial Relations Context?" *Research Papers in Management Studies*, No. 11 (Cambridge: Judge Institute of Management Studies).

Rogan, H. (2009) " Al-Qaida in the Islamic Maghreb: Ideological Dissent in the Algerian Jihad," paper presented at the International Studies Association annual convention, 15–18 February.

Rogers, E. M. (2003) *Diffusion of Innovations*, 5th edn (London: Free Press).

Roselle, L. (2010) "Strategic Narratives of War: Fear of Entrapment and Abandonment during Protracted Conflict," paper presented at the American Political Science Association annual convention, Washington, DC, 2–5 September.

Rosenau, J. N. (1990) *Turbulence in World Politics: A Theory of Change and Continuity* (Hemel Hempstead: Princeton University Press).

Ross, J. I. (2007) "Deconstructing the Terrorism News Media Relationship," *Crime, Media, Culture* 3 (2): 215–225.

Roy, O. (2004) "Al Qaeda: Brand Name Ready for Franchise," *Le Monde Diplomatique*, 1 September, Global Policy Forum, http://www.globalpolicy. org/empire/terrorwar/analysis/2004/0901terrorbiz.htm

Roy, O. (2008a) *Al-Qaeda in the West as a Youth Movement: The Power of a Narrative*, MICROCON Policy Working Paper 2 (Brighton: MICROCON).

Roy, O. (2008b) "Radicalisation and De-Radicalisation," in ICSR (ed.) *Perspectives on Radicalisation and Political Violence* (London: ICSR), pp. 8–14.

Royal Canadian Mounted Police (2011) *Youth Online and at Risk: Radicalization Facilitated by the Internet* (Ottawa: RCMP).

Rumsfeld, D. (2003) "Rumsfeld's War-On-Terror Memo," *USA Today*, 20 May 2005, http://www.usatoday.com/news/washington/executive/rumsfeld-memo. htm

Rumsfeld, D. (2006) "Media's Role in the 'War on Terror'," *Taipei Times*, 28 February, http://www.taipeitimes.com/News/editorials/archives/2006/02/28/ 2003295064

Sacco, V. F. (1995) "Media Constructions of Crime," *Annals of the American Academy of Political and Social Science* 539: 141–154.

Sageman, M. (2004) *Understanding Terror Networks* (Bristol: University of Pennsylvania Press).

Sageman, M. (2008) *Leaderless Jihad: Terror Networks in the Twenty-First Century* (Philadelphia: University of Pennsylvania Press).

Sarbin, T. (ed.) (1986) *Narrative Psychology: The Storied Nature of Human Conduct* (New York: Praeger).

Schlesinger, P. (1990) "Rethinking the Sociology of Journalism: Source Strategies and the Limits of Media Centrism," in M. Ferguson (ed.) *Public Communication: The New imperatives: Future Directions for Media Research* (London: Sage), pp. 61–83.

Schlesinger, P. (1991) *Media, State, and Nation: Political Violence and Collective Identities* (London: Sage Publications).

Schmid, A. P. (1984) *Political Terrorism: A Research Guide to Concepts, Theories, Data Bases and Literature* (New Brunswick, NJ: Transaction Books).

Schmid, A. P. (1989) "Terrorism and the Media: The Ethics of Publicity," *Terrorism and Political Violence* 1 (4): 539–556.

Schmid, A. P. (2004) "Frameworks for Conceptualising Terrorism," *Terrorism and Political Violence* 16 (2): 197–221.

Schmid, A. P. (2005) "Terrorism as Psychological Warfare," *Democracy and Security* 1 (2): 137–146.

Schmid, A. P. (2010) "The Importance of Countering Al Qa'ida's Single Narrative," in National Coordinator for Counterterrorism (ed.) *Countering Violent Extremist Narratives* (The Hague: National Coordinator for Counterterrorism), pp. 46–57.

Schmid, A. P. and J. de Graaf (1982) *Violence as Communication: Insurgent Terrorism and the Western News Media* (London: Sage).

Schmid, A. P. and A. J. Jongman (2005) *Political Terrorism: A New Guide to Actors, Authors, Concepts, Data Bases, Theories, and Literature* (London: Transaction Books).

Schultz, M., Y. M. Antorini, and F. F. Csaba (eds) (2005) *Corporate Branding: Purpose/People/Process* (Copenhagen: Copenhagen Business School Press).

Schulze, F. (2004) "Breaking the Cycle: Empirical Research and Postgraduate Studies on Terrorism," in A. Silke (ed.) *Research on Terrorism: Trends, Achievements and Failures* (London: Frank Cass), pp. 161–185.

Sciolino, E. and E. Schmitt (2008) "A Not Very Private Feud over Terrorism," *The New York Times*, 8 June, http://www.nytimes.com/2008/06/08/weekinreview/08sciolino.html

Scott, J. (2000) *Social Network Analysis: A Handbook* (London: Sage Publications).

Seib, P. (2012) *Real Time Diplomacy: Politics and Power in the Social Media Era* (New York: Palgrave).

Seib, P. and D. M. Janbek (2011) *Global Terrorism and New Media: The Post-al Qaeda Generation* (Milton Park: Routledge).

Shanahan, J. (2011) "Foreword," in Fenstermacher, Laurie and Todd Leventhal (eds) *Countering Violent Extremism: Scientific Methods and Strategies*, pp. 1–2.

Shane, S. (2011) "Killings in Norway Spotlight Anti-Muslim Thought in U.S.," *The New York Times*, 24 July, http://www.nytimes.com/2011/07/25/us/25debate.html?pagewanted=all

Shpiro, S. (2002) "Conflict Media Strategies and the Politics of Counter-Terrorism," *Politics* 22 (2): 76–85.

Silber, M. D. and A. Bhatt (2007) *Radicalization in the West: The Homegrown Threat* (New York: City of New York Police Department).

Silke, A. (2004a) "An Introduction to Terrorism Research," in A. Silke (ed.) *Research on Terrorism: Trends, Achievements and Failures* (London: Frank Cass), pp. 1–29.

Silke, A. (ed.) (2004b) *Research on Terrorism: Trends, Achievements and Failures* (London: Frank Cass).

Silke, A. (2004c) "The Devil You Know: Continuing Problems with Research on Terrorism," in A. Silke (ed.) *Research on Terrorism: Trends, Achievements and Failures* (London: Frank Cass), pp. 57–71.

Silke, A. (2004d) "The Road Less Travelled: Recent Trends in Terrorism Research," in A. Silke (ed.) *Research on Terrorism: Trends, Achievements and Failures* (London: Frank Cass), pp. 186–213.

Silverstone, R. (ed.) (2005) *Media, Technology and Everyday Life in Europe: From Information to Communication* (Aldershot: Ashgate).

Simmons, B. K. (1991) "U.S. Newsmagazines' Labeling of Terrorists," in A. O. Alali and K. K. Eke (eds) *Media Coverage of Terrorism: Methods of Diffusion* (London: Sage), pp. 23–39.

Smith, A. (1990) "Towards a Global Culture?" *Theory, Culture & Society* 7 (2): 171–191.

Smith, M. L. R. (2009) "William of Ockham, Where Are You When We Need You? Reviewing Modern Terrorism Studies," *Journal of Contemporary History* 44: 319–334.

Smith, B. and **A. C. Sparkes** (2008) "Contrasting Perspectives on Narrating Selves and Identitites: An Invitation to Dialogue," *Qualitative Research* 8 (5): 5–35.

Snow, N. (2005) "Truth and Information Consequences Since 9/11," *Peace Review: A Journal of Social Justice* 17 (1): 103–109.

Snow, D. A., E. B. Rochford, S. K. Worden and **R. D. Benford** (1986) "Frame Alignment Processes, Micromobilization, and Movement Participation," *American Sociological Review* 51 (4): 464–81.

Snow, D. A., and **R. D. Benford** (1992) "Master Frames and Cycles of Protest," in A. D. Morris and C. McClurg Mueller (eds) *Frontiers in Social Movement Theory* (New Haven: Yale University Press), pp. 133–155.

Somers, M. R. (1994) "The Narrative Constitution of Identity: A Relational Network Approach," *Theory and Society* 23 (5): 605–649.

Somers, M. R. and **G. D. Gibson** (1994) "Reclaiming the Epistemological 'Other': Narrative and the Social Constitution of Identity," in C. Calhoun (ed.) *Social Theory and the Politics of Identity* (Oxford: Blackwell), pp. 37–99.

Speckhard, A. (2011) "Battling the 'University of Jihad': An Evidence Based Ideological Program to Counter Militant Jihadi Groups Active on the Internet," in L. Fenstermacher and T. Leventhal (eds) *Countering Violent Extremism: Scientific Methods and Strategies* (Wright-Patterson AFB, OH: AF Research Laboratory), pp. 164–174.

Spiegel Online (2011) "A Chronology of the Twin Attacks," Spiegel Online, 25 July, http://www.spiegel.de/international/europe/0,1518,776437,00.html

Standage, T. (1998) *The Victorian Internet: The Remarkable Story of the Telegraph and Nineteenth Century's Online Pioneers* (New York: Walker Publishing).

Stenersen, A. (2008) "The Internet: A Virtual Training Camp?" *Terrorism and Political Violence* 20 (2): 215–233.

Stevens, T. (2009) "Regulating the 'Dark Web': How a Two-Fold Approach Can Tackle Peer-to-Peer Radicalization," *The RUSI Journal* 154 (2): 28–33.

Stevens, T. (2010) "The Myth of the Lone Wolf," Free Rad!cals Blog, 25 January 2010), http://www.icsr.info/blog/The-Myth-of-the-Lone-Wolf

Stevens, T. and **P. R. Neumann** (2009) *Countering Online Radicalization: Strategy for Action* (London: ICSR/Community Security Trust).

Stohl, M. (2006) "Winners and Losers in the War on Terror: The Problem of Metrics," paper presented at the International Studies Association annual convention, San Diego, CA, 22–25 March.

Straw, J. (2003) "House of Commons Hansard Debates for 11 November 2003," Column 168, http://www.publications.parliament.uk/pa/cm200203/cmhansrd/vo031111/debtext/31111–04.htm

Sun Tzu (2009 [6th century BC]) *The Art of War* (London: Penguin Books).

Tarrow, S. (1995) "Foreword," in D. della Porta (ed.) *Social Movements, Political Violence and the State* (New York: Cambridge University Press), pp. vii–viii.

Tarrow, S. (1998) *Power in Movement: Social Movements and Contentious Politics*, 2nd edn (Cambridge: Cambridge University Press).

Taylor, C. (1989) *Sources of the Self: The Making of the Modern Identity* (Cambridge, MA: Harvard University Press).

Taylor, P. (2010) *Generation Jihad* (Part 1), video documentary broadcast on BBC 2, 13 February 2010, http://www.bbc.co.uk/programmes/b00qvq09

Taylor, R. (1992) "The Branding of Services," in J.M. Murphy (ed.) *Branding: A Key Marketing Tool* (London: Macmillan), pp. 125–137.

Temple-Raston, D. (2011) "Al-Qaida's Resilience May Mean Its Survival," NPR, 2 May, http://www.npr.org/2011/05/02/135928519/resilience-key-to-terrorist-groups-survival

The Armenian National Institute (n.d.) "Frequently Asked Questions about the Armenian Genocide," http://www.armenian-genocide.org/genocidefaq.html

The Economist (no author) (2011) "Osama Bin Laden: The Evolution of Al-Qaeda," *The Economist*, 2 May, http://www.economist.com/blogs/clausewitz/2011/05/osama_bin_laden

Theohary, C. A. and **J. Rollins** (2011) *Terrorist Use of the Internet: Information Operations in Cyberspace*, Congressional Research Service Report for Congress, R41674, http://www.fas.org/sgp/crs/terror/R41674.pdf

Thomas, D. (2008) "Al-Qaeda: Winning or Losing?" *The Economist*, 17 July, http://www.economist.com/specialreports/displayStory.cfm?story_id=11701218

Thompson, R. (2011) "Radicalization and the Use of Social Media," *Journal of Strategic Security* 4 (4): 167–190.

Thornberry, W. and **J. Levy** (2011) "Al Qaeda in the Islamic Maghreb," Center for Strategic and International Studies (CSIS), 1 September, http://csis.org/publication/al-qaeda-islamic-maghreb

Tilly, C. (2002) *Stories, Identities, and Political Change* (Oxford: Rowman & Littelfield).

Tololyan, K. (1988) "Cultural Narrative and the Motivation of the Terrorist," in D. C. Rapoport (ed.) *Inside Terrorist Organizations* (New York: Columbia University Press), pp. 217–233.

Towsend, M. and **I. Traynor** (2011) "Norway Attacks: How far Right Views Created Anders Behring Breivik," *The Guardian*, 30 July, http://www.guardian.co.uk/world/2011/jul/30/norway-attacks-anders-behring-breivik

Travis, A. (2008a) "Battle against al-Qaida Brand Highlighted in Secret Paper," *The Guardian*, 26 August, http://www.guardian.co.uk/world/2008/aug/26/alqaida.terrorism

Travis, A. (2008b) "Revealed: Britain Secret Propaganda War against al-Qaida," *The Guardian*, 26 August, http://www.guardian.co.uk/world/2008/aug/26/alqaida.uksecurity

Tsfati, Y. and **G. Weimann** (2002) "www.terrorism.com: Terror on the Internet," *Studies in Conflict and Terrorism* 25 (5): 317–332.

Tucker, S. T. and **P. M. Roberts** (eds) (2008) *The Encyclopedia of the Arab-Israeli Conflict: A Political, Social, and Military History* (vol. I) (Santa Barbara: ABC-Clio).

Tumber, H. (1999) *News: A Reader* (Oxford: Oxford University Press).

Upshaw, L. B. (1995) *Building Brand Identity: A Strategy for Success in a Hostile Marketplace* (New York: Wiley and Sons).

US Army (2008) "Supplemental to the 304th Ml Bn Periodic Newsletter," http://www.fas.org/irp/eprint/mobile.pdf

US Army War College (2011) "Information Operations Primer: Fundamentals of Information Operations" (Carlisle, PA: US Army War College), http://www.au.af.mil/au/awc/awcgate/army-usawc/info_ops_primer.pdf)

US Department of Defense (2002) "International Contributions to the War against Terrorism," Fact Sheet, Office of Public Affairs, 22 May, http://www.defense.gov/news/May2002/d20020523cu.pdf

US Department of Defense (2009) "Report on Strategic Communication" (Washington DC: US Department of Defense), http://www.carlisle.army.mil/dime/documents/DoD%20report%20on%20Strategic%20Communication%20Dec%2009.pdf

US Department of Justice (n.d.) "The Al Qaeda Manual," http://www.justice.gov/ag/manualpart1_1.pdf

US Department of State (2008) *Country Reports on Terrorism 2007* (Washington, DC: Office of the Coordinator for Counterterrorism), http://www.state.gov/documents/organization/105904.pdf

Van Dongen, T. (2009) "Break It Down: An Alternative Approach to Measuring Effectiveness in Counterterrorism," Economics of Security Working Paper 23 (Berlin: Economics of Security).

Van Ham, P. (2001) "The Rise of the Brand State: The Postmodern Politics of Image and Reputation," *Foreign Affairs* 80 (5) September–October: 2–7.

Van Um, E. and **D. Pisoiu** (2011) "Effective Counterterrorism: What Have We Learned So Far?" Economic of Security Working Paper 55 (Berlin: Economic of Security).

Viera, J. D. (1991) "Terrorism at the BBC: The IRA on British Television," in A. O. Alali and K. K. Eke (eds) *Media Coverage of Terrorism: Methods of Diffusion* (London: Sage), pp. 73–85.

Virgin.com (no date) "About Us," http://www.virgin.com/AboutVirgin/WhatWeAreAbout/WhatWeAreAbout.aspx

Walker, D. H. (2005) "Developing Metrics for the Global War on Terrorism," paper submitted to the Department of Joint Military Operations, Naval War College, Newport, http://www.dtic.mil/cgi-bin/GetTRDoc?AD=ADA464335

Webster, L. and **P. Mertova** (2007) *Using Narrative Enquiry as a Research Method* (Milton Park: Routledge).

Weimann, G. (1987) "Media Events: The Case of International Terrorism," *Journal of Broadcasting & Electronic Media* 31 (1): 21–39.

Weimann, G. (1990) "'Redefinition of Image': The Impact of Mass Mediated Terrorism," *International Journal of Public Opinion Research* 2 (1): 16–29.

Weimann, G. (2006) *Terror on the Internet: The New Arena, the New Challenges* (Washington, DC: Unites States Institute of Peace).

Weimann, G. and **C. Winn** (1994) *The Theater of Terror: Mass Media and International Terrorism* (White Plains, NY: Longman).

Weinberg, L. and W. L. Eubank (1998) "Terrorism and Democracy: What Recent Events Disclose," *Terrorism and Political Violence* 10 (1): 108–118.

Weinberg, L. and L. Richardson (2004) "Conflict Theory and the Trajectory of Terrorist Campaigns in Western Europe," in A. Silke (ed.) *Research on Terrorism: Trends, Achievements and Failures* (London: Frank Cass), pp. 138–160.

White, H. C. (2008) *Identity and Control: How Social Formations Emerge* (Princeton, NJ: Princeton University Press).

White House (2011) "Empowering Local Partners to Prevent Violent Extremism in the United States" (Washington, DC: Government Printing Office), http://info.publicintelligence.net/WH-HomegrownTerror.pdf

Wieviorka, M. (1992) "Case Studies: History or Sociology?" In C.C. Ragin and H. S. Becker (eds) *What is a Case? Exploring the Foundations of Social Inquiry* (New York: Cambridge University Press), pp. 159–172.

Wiktorowicz, Q. (2004) *Islamic Activism: A Social Movment Theory Approach* (Bloomington, IN: Indiana University Press).

Wiktorowicz, Q. (2007) "Islamic Activism and Social Movement Theory: A New Direction for Research," *Mediterranean Politics* 7 (3): 187–211.

Wilkinson, P. (2006) *Terrorism Versus Democracy: The Liberal State Response*, 2nd edn (New York: Routledge).

Wilkinson, P. and A. M. Stewart (eds) (1987) *Contemporary Research on Terrorism* (Aberdeen: Aberdeen University Press).

Wright, L. (2008) "The Rebellion Within: An Al Qaeda Mastermind Questions Terrorism," *The New Yorker*, 2 June, pp. 37–53.

Yan, J. (2003) "Nation Branding: Branding and the International Community," *Brand Management* 10 (6): 447–456.

Yungher, N. I. (2008) *Terrorism: The Bottom Line* (Upper Saddle River, NJ: Pearson Education).

Zulaika, J. and W. A. Douglass (2008) "The Terrorist Subject: Terrorism Studies and the Absent Subjectivity," *Critical Studies on Terrorism* 1 (1): 27–36.

Index

Abbott, Andrew, 184
ABC News, 98, 182
Abu Muqawama, 170, 184
actor-network theory, 4, 10, 60, 70–6, 81
Adorno, Theodor, 49
Afghanistan, 3, 9, 16, 41, 51, 52, 64, 77, 98, 99, 127, 141, 147, 150, 154, 163, 165, 181, 184
Air Force Research Laboratory, 45
Al-Awlaki, Anwar, 94, 109
Al-Durrah, Mohamed, 110
Alexander, Dean, 108
Alexander, Yonah, 36, 38, 39
Al-Fajr, 41, 142
Algerian Salafi Group for Preaching and Combat, 161
Al-Jazeera, 136
Al-Jihad, 164
Al-Lami, Mina, 183
Al Qaeda, 3, 7, 8, 9, 19, 21, 23, 24, 28, 40, 41, 48, 49, 66, 93, 99, 109, 110, 115, 127, 130, 161, 167, 170, 171, 176, 177, 180
  affiliated groups, 16, 142
  brand, 7, 8, 144, 145–50, 163
  ideology, 8, 149, 162
  narrative, 8, 31, 108, 128, 136, 141, 142, 144–5, 149, 150, 153–60, 163–4, 184; *see also* narrative
  publications, 12
  weaknesses, 161–5
Al-Zawahiri, Ayman, 3, 21, 48, 147, 153, 154, 155, 157, 163, 184
Ambinder, Marc, 12
Amm Sam, 19
anarchism, 16
Anderson, Benedict, 83, 182
Anholt, Simon, 146
anthropology, 106
  see also ethnography
anti-colonial movements, 16, 25
Antoniades, Andreas, 126

'Arab Awakening', 80, 127, 171
  see also Arab Spring
'Arab Spring', 8
  see also Arab Awakening
Archetti, Cristina, 39, 98
Armenian terrorism, 10, 77
As-Sahab, 41
audio-cassette, 123, 141
Aum Shinrikyo, 28
Awan, Akil, 29, 40, 43, 44, 47, 48
Ayers, Michael, 181
Azarian, Reza, 62, 63, 65, 66, 67, 68, 181

Bahr Thompson, Anne, 146, 147
Bakker, Edwin, 16, 66, 147
Ball, James, 49
Baranek, Patricia, 54
Barnhurst, Kevin, 38
Barrett, Richard, 149, 163, 164
Bassiouni, Cherif, 36, 38
BBC (British Broadcasting Corporation), 9, 47, 50, 52, 93, 110, 136, 181
Bearman, Peter, 63, 65
Belaala, Selma, 7, 106
Bell, Bowyer, 36
Bell, Martin, 39
Benard, Cheryl, 130
Benford, Robert, 78
Benjamin, Daniel, 166
Bentley, Arthur, 71
Bennett, Dianne, 183
Benwell, Bethan, 131
Bergin, Anthony, 109, 128, 132
Bero, David, 138
Beski-Chafiq, Chahla, 91, 117, 119, 120, 183
Betz, David, 126, 127, 136, 141, 142, 149
Bhatt, Arvin, 104
Bin Laden, Osama, 3, 8, 21, 28, 48, 56, 64, 136, 147, 162
Bjørgo, Tore, 13, 26, 27, 91, 118

Björkman, Carl, 141
Black September, 98, 182
Blackberry, 49
Blackett, Tom, 146
blog, 34, 100, 176
Blumler, Jay, 45, 53
Boer, Leen, 66, 147
Boiney, John, 32, 37
Boje, David, 140
Bonanate, Luigi, 91
Boyle, Michael, 180
Braben, Donald, 172
Braiker, Brian, 8
Brandon, James, 163
Breen Smyth, Marie, 180
Bosi, Lorenzo, 117, 119, 120, 183
brand, 1, 6
    definition of, 145–50
    identity, 144, 146–8, 150, 168
    'identity prism', 144–5, 151–7
    as narrative, 145–50
    platform, 146–7, 150, 165–166, 168
    role in measuring narratives, 143,
        145, 149, 150–1, 157, 160
    see also Al Qaeda, brand; branding
branding, 10
    in counterterrorism, 145, 160–8
    country branding, 126
Breivik, Anders, 49, 94,
        123, 176–7
Brenkel, Jos, 147
British National Party, 19, 180
Brooker, Will, 52
Brown, Gordon, 154, 157
Brown, Symeon, 49
Bruner, Jerome, 126
Brymer, Chuck, 147
Burke, Anthony, 180
Burke, Jason, 3, 36
Bush, George, 152

Calhoun, Craig, 83, 84, 92
Carafano, James, 124
Casebeer, William, 7, 129, 140, 141
Castells, Manuel, 45
causal explanation, 12, 20, 21, 23, 24,
        25–8, 33, 34, 38, 51, 54, 55, 62,
        72, 74, 103, 104, 116, 175, 180,
        181, 184

causal inference, 23, 180–1
CD, 3, 141
Cento Bull, Anna, 87, 88
Chan, Janet, 54
Change Institute, 43, 112, 121
Chen, Hsinchun, 5, 29
Chermak, Steven, 54
Chibnall, Steve, 54
Choudhury, Roshanara, 94
Choudhury, Tufyal, 64
Chrichton, Torcuil, 155, 167
Cilluffo, Frank, 173
Clan na Gael, 16
Clandinin, Jean, 140
Clark, Wesley, 179
Clifton, Rita, 146
Cohen Almagor, Raphael, 39
Cold War, 2, 29
Coleman, Stephen, 45
Coll, Steve, 40
Commission of the European
    Communities, 42
Committee in Homeland Security, 41,
    42, 92, 142
communication
    definition of, 33–4
    networks, 1, 7
    'revolution', 45
    as sharing/transmission of
        information, 1, 2, 12, 33, 49, 51,
        55, 58, 59, 60, 66, 67, 68, 75, 76,
        80, 81, 82, 84, 85, 92, 93, 100, 101,
        112, 115, 116, 118, 122, 124, 127,
        131, 133, 134, 139, 148, 174, 176
    in social interaction, 3, 4, 33
    technology, 1, 2, 4, 5, 6, 7, 8, 24,
        32, 34, 40, 41, 44, 45, 46, 49,
        50, 51, 53, 55, 58, 59, 60, 70, 71,
        72, **73–4**, 79, 80, 82, 83, 84, 93,
        95, 96, 99, 108, 109, 111, 122,
        126, 141, 164, 171, 181; *see also*
        technological determinism
    in terrorism research, 2–3
    as a weapon, 3
Communication Studies, 7, 10, 33, 54
comparative research, *see* research,
    comparative
Constructivism, 57
'contagion hypothesis', 32, 38, 52

Contest, 2, 153, 161
Conway, Maura, 40, 41, 109
Cornish, Paul, 64, 130
counterinsurgency, 3
counter-narrative, 6, 8, 55, 128–31,
    137, 142, 161
    see also narrative
counterterrorism, 1, 2, 3, 6, 10, 11,
    100, 102, 125, 127, 128, 129, 138,
    139, 144–5, 149, 150, 151, 153,
    155, 169, 175, 177, 178, 183
    measurement of success in, 145,
    160–8; *see also* branding, in
    counterterrorism
Corman, Steven, 7, 129, 138, 139
Cortazzi, Martin, 140
COT (Instituut voor Veiligheids- en
    Crisismanagement), 94, 109
Council of the European Union, 41
Crelinsten, Ronald, 2, 35
Crenshaw, Martha, 13, 25, 26, 38,
    90, 180
Critical Incident Analysis Group
    (CIAG), 41, 48, 128, 130, 131,
    136, 181, 183
'Critical Terrorism Studies', *see*
    Terrorism Studies
Cronin, Audrey, 13, 19, 22, 27, 29, 41,
    88, 180
Crotty, Robert, 172
Csaba, Fabian, 146, 161
culture, 48, 79, 112, 119, 140, 149,
    152, 153, 154, 156, 183
Curtis, Adam, 39
Czarniawska, Barbara, 131

Daily News, 178
Dalgaard-Nielsen, Anja, 112
Dall'Olmo Riley, Francesca, 146, 150
Davidson, Hugh, 146, 147
Dayan, Daniel, 84
de Chernatony, Leslie, 146, 150
de Graaf, Beatrice, 165
de Graaf, Janny, 2, 34
della Porta, Donatella, 47, 110, 111,
    112, 117, 119, 120, 183
Denmark, 10, 92, 19, 121
Department of Defense, 138, 183, 184
Department of State, 45, 108, 113

de Vaus, David, 20, 21, 22, 23, 24, 28
Deven, Josh, 162
de Waal, Martijn, 139
Dewey, John, 71
digitilisation, 3
Dodd, Vikram, 94, 109
Dolnik, Adam, 22, 181
Douglas, Frank, 127
Douglass, William, 18, 56
Dowling, Ralph, 34
Dr. Fadl, 164
Durodié, Bill, 167
Duyvestein, Isabelle, 22
DVD, 40

Eatwell, Roger, 14, 17, 30
The Economist, 8, 145
el Sadat, Anwar, 84
email, 2, 34, 83, 94
Emirbayer, Mustafa, 57, 65, 71, 75,
    85, 182
English, Richard, 21
English Defence League, 94
equifinality, 23
Ericson, Richard, 54
Esser, Frank, 52
ethnography, 7, 106, 114–15, 117–19,
    140
    see also anthropology
Eubank, William, 91
European Commission, 103
Euskadi Ta Askatasuna (ETA), 16
Evans, Jonathan, 145
Ewing, Michael, 146
extremism, 3, 6, 9, 14, 17, 30, 31,
    49, 51, 55, 88, 91, 92, 103, 104,
    107–16, 121, 122, 125, 128,
    132, 137
    countering of, 8, 45, 138, 139, 169,
    175–8
    Islamic, 30, 163
    political, 9, 12
    violent, 1, 11, 15, 19, 30, 45, 57, 58,
    65, 73, 81, 103, 107, 123, 125,
    128, 130, 173, 175–8, 179
Eyerman, Joseph, 91

Facebook, 49, 50, 127
Fascism, 16, 87–8, 89, 111

fedayeen, 96, 97
Feiser, Jonathan, 165
Fenians, 16
Fenstermacher, Laurie, 117
fight against terrorism, *see* war on
    terrorism
Fink, Naureen Chowdhury, 8
foreign policy, 2, 45, 98, 99, 103,
    159, 166
frames, 78, 78–9, 111–12, 114, 132, 182
France, 10, 97, 98, 106, 117, 119, 121,
    183
Frankfurt School, 49
Franks, Jason, 15, 56
Fromm, Erich, 49
Front de Libération du Québec, 16

Gartenstein-Ross, Daveed, 91, 103
Geltzer, Joshua, 142
Gendron, Angela, 181
George, Alexander, 23, 180
Germany, 10, 17, 26, 46, 52, 80, 111,
    112, 121
Gerrits, Robin, 36, 37
Gertner, David, 146
Gibson, Gloria, 90, 92, 131, 181
Gilmore, Fiona, 146
Githens-Mazer, Jonathan, 30, 117,
    173, 175
Glasgow airport car bombing, 39
Glasser, Susan, 40
globalisation, 1, 12, 145
Global Islamic Media Front, 41
Global Terrorism Database, 21, 180
Godin, Seth, 146
Goodall, Lloyd, 129
Goodman, Marc, 40
Goodwin, Matthew, 14, 17, 30
Gordon, Avishag, 5, 29, 154, 173
Graebner, William, 183
Gramsci, Antonio, 49
Granovetter, Mark, 174
Gray, John, 39
Greenpeace, 146
grievance, 7, 25, 26, 27, 31, 36, 66,
    79, 108, 113, 114, 117, 128, 129,
    163, 176
  narrative of, 1, 108, 145
Grossman, Laura, 91, 103

guerrilla warfare, 14, 15, 16, 40, 98
Gupta, Dipak, 46, 137
Gunning, Jeroen, 5, 30, 180

Haig, Matt, 161
Hall, Stuart, 53, 54
Hallin, Daniel, 23
Halverson, Jeffry, 129
Hankinson, Graham, 146
Hankinson, Philippa, 146
Harrison, Gilmore, 146
Hart, Janet, 126
Hasan, Nidal Malik, 109
Hashim, Yahia, 154, 156
Hay, Colin, 55
Hearst, Patricia, 38
"hearts and minds", 1, 3, 10, 138
Hegghammer, Thomas, 5, 21, 169
Hick, Steven, 181
Hizballah, 43
Hobbes, Thomas, 91
Hoffman, Bruce, 15, 16, 95, 96, 97, 98,
    162, 180
Homeland Security Institute,
    108, 183
Homeland Security Policy Institute
    (HSPI), 41, 48, 128, 130, 131, 136,
    181, 183
Home Office, 6, 7, 15, 28, 31, 44, 55,
    102, 103, 108, 121, 124, 128, 129,
    145, 153, 154, 155, 157, 161, 167
Horgan, John, 20, 22, 30, 107, 114,
    115, 117, 118, 180
Hoskins, Andrew, 29, 43, 44, 47, 48,
    49
Howard, Michael, 20
Hughes, Mark, 94
Husein, Ed, 12
'hypodermic needle theory', 52
  see also silver bullet theory

identity, 4, 8, 18, 44, 60, 61, 62, **63–4**,
    66–8, 71, 73, 75, 76, 88, 91, 94,
    100, 101–2, 104, 106, 110, 114,
    115–16, 117–18, 120, 131, 140,
    142, 143, 168, 177
  collective, 31, 62, 68, 79, 83, 84, 86,
    92, 107, 112, 114, 115
  of a group, 18, 89, 97, 100, 141, 150

individual, 58, 59, 62, 81, 82, 85,
  86, 89, 92, 93, 114, 121, 122, 132
  see also brand, identity; brand,
  identity prism
ideology, 149, 152
  of Al Qaeda, 7, 8, 147, 149, 162, 163, 164
  extremist, 1, 3, 9, 14, 15, 26, 33, 41,
  43, 48, 57, 58, 69, 88, 101, 104,
  109, 114, 118, 128, 130, 145, 162
imagined communities, 65–6, 82–3,
  94, 100, 120, 122, 182
  see also social relationships,
  imagined
imagined relationships, *see* social
  relationships, imagined
innocence, of terrorist attacks'
  victims, 17, 18
innovation, 172–4
Inspire, 12
insurgency, 14, 15, 16
  see also counterinsurgency
International Centre for the Study
  of Radicalisation and Political
  Violence, 19, 43, 103
International Communications, 7, 10
International Crisis Group, 141, 160
Internet, 1, 5, 6, 7, 8, 9
  characteristics of, 40, 109
  demonization of, 40–5
  role in supporting terrorist
  organisations, 41, 42–3, 45
  role in terrorist recruitment, 41, 42,
  44, 45, 110
  see also terrorism, recruitment into
Irish Republican Army (IRA), 21
Iraq, 3, 16, 42, 77, 94, 110, 127, 142,
  147, 160, 163
Israel, 17, 95, 96, 97, 110, 129
Italy, 10, 26, 89, 98, 111, 112, 119,
  120, 141

Jackson, Richard, 180
Jacobson, Michael, 127
Jamieson, Alison, 89
Janbek, Dana, 29, 40, 164
Japan, 26, 28
Jemaah Islamiyah, 66, 162
Jenkins, Brian, 36, 38, 136
Jennings, Peter, 98

Jermyn, Deborah, 52
jihad, 44, 47, 104, 105, 108, 109,
  110, 114, 141, 147, 154, 155,
  156, 164
jihadi groups, 5, 41, 42, 45, 108, 127,
  130, 136, 142, 162, 166, 170
'jihadisation', 104, 105, 107
Jihadism, 16, 48, 104, 170
Jihadi Studies, 169, 170
jihadi videos, 24, 48, 92, 98, 122, 141;
  see also videos, role in radicalisation
jihadi websites, 43, 44, 48, 109,
  146, 164
Joas, Hans, 90, 182
Johnson, Thomas, 9, 141, 150
Jongman, Albert, 14, 20, 171
Joscelyn, Thomas, 12
Journalism Studies, 10, 174
Justus, Z. S., 167

Kamen, Al, 161
Kapferer, Jean-Noël, 144, 146, 150,
  151, 152, 153, 154, 155, 157, 159
Kassimeris, George, 180
Katz, Elihu, 53, 84
Katz, Rita, 41, 42, 92, 142, 162
Keohane, Robert, 21, 126, 171
Kepel, Gilles, 21, 64, 149
Khosrokhavar, Farhad, 110
Kimmage, Daniel, 48, 145, 164
King, Gary, 21
Knight, Kathleen, 184
Knöbl, Wolfgang, 90, 182
Kohler Riessman, Catherine, 140, 158
Kohlmann, Evan, 47, 110, 181
Kotler, Philip, 146
Kühle, Lene, 92, 103, 104, 117,
  118–19, 183
Kuhn, Thomas, 33, 58, 172
Kull, Steven, 159, 160

Lambert, Robert, 124
laptop, 40
Laqueur, Walter, 38
Lashkar-e-Taibe, 66, 162
Latour, Bruno, 4, 60, 70, 71, 72, 74,
  75, 182
Lave, Charles, 181
Law, John, 71, 73

Lawler, Stephanie, 131, 134
Lazarsfeld, Paul, 53, 61
Lemieux, Anthony, 92, 137
Leonard, Mark, 167
Levi, Jaclyn, 163
Levitt, Mathew, 128
Lewis, Paul, 49
Lewis Mernit, Judith, 177
Lia, Brynjar, 146, 147, 158
Linde, Charlotte, 131, 132
Lindekilde, Lasse, 92, 103, 104, 117, 118–19, 183
Lindley-French, Julian, 64, 130
'lone wolf', 92, 94, 109–10, 122
    see also radicalisation, self-radicalisation
Luhmann, Niklas, 59
Lukacs, Georg, 49
Lybia, 8

Mackenzie, Iain, 49
Mahoney, James, 27
Mancini, Paolo, 23
Mansfield, Laura, 21, 153, 154, 155
March, James, 181
Marcuse, Herbert, 49
Marketing, 10
Martin, John, 35, 38
Marxism, 31, 49
Maslikowski, Monika, 167
McAdam, Doug, 27
McCants, Will, 162
McCaughey, Martha, 181
McInerney, Lisa, 40, 109
McNutt, John, 181
media, 1, 3, 5, 6, 8, 9, 10
    definition of, 50–2
    effects on audiences, 6, 52–3
    mass, 2, 32, 34, 35, 36, 38, 46, 52, 84, 97, 137, 146
    new, 40, 52; *see also* media, social
    organisations, 4, 5, 32, 50, 52, 55, 58, 59, 60, 82
    role in terrorism phenomenon, 5, 37–40
    social, 32, 40, 127, 133, 182; *see also* media, new
    sources, 10, 53–4, 98–9, 100, 133

media coverage, 1, 32, 36, 37, 38, 39, 50–4, 58, 59, 79, 82, 84, 97–9, 110, 122, 142, 158, 170
    see also news stories
'media events', 84
Media Studies, 7, 10, 52, 174
Meinhof, Ulrike, 17
Melissen, Jan, 126
Melucci, Alberto, 87
Mertova, Patricie, 139
metanarrative, 90, 181
Milelli, Jean-Pierre, 21, 64, 149
Miliband, David, 161
Miller, David, 54
Miller, Toby, 53
Mische, Ann, 62, 85, 182
Miskimmon, Alistair, 126
mobile phone, 49, 74, 123, 127, 133, 139
    see also telephone
mobilisation, *see* political mobilisation
Morgan, Nigel, 146
Moro, Aldo, 89–90
Morocco, 48, 159, 184
Mueller, John, 42, 99, 171
Muir, Jim, 8
mujahideen, 64, 153, 154, 155, 157
multidisciplinarity, 7, 11, 173, 174
Mumby, Dennis, 132
Munich Olympics, 37, 96, 97, 98
Municipality of Amsterdam, 104
Musharbash, Yassin, 8

Nacos, Brigitte, 2, 35, 36, 38
Napoli, Julie, 146
narrative, 1, 6, 61, 91, 101–2, 116, 122
    as a brand, 149
    collective, 86–8, 100, 122, 183
    compatibility among narratives, 86–7, 118, 133
    conceptual problems with, 136–40
    definition of, 7, 69–70
    dissonance among narratives, 87, 118
    individual, 81, 85–7, 93, 100, 122, 123, 182, 183

measuring of, 150–60, 176
origin of concept, 126–7, 183
'our narrative', 55, 70, 142, 150,
    153, 156, 179
'rewriting' of, 129
'single narrative', 121, 150
strategic, 126–7, 136, 140, 142, 143,
    144, 149, 150, 153, 157
of terrorist groups, 8, 61, 64, 87,
    122, 125
see also Al Qaeda, narrative;
    counter-narrative; metanarrative;
    grievance, narrative of
Nasjonalt Folkeparti, 115
National Commission on Terrorist
    Attacks upon the United States, 3
National Counterterrorism Centre
    (NCTC), 104, 107
nationalism, 25, 65, 83, 182
Nazism, 14, 16, 111
network analysis, 62, 63, 75, 108, 174
networks, 3, 6, 7, 61, 62, 116, 184
    among terrorists, 3, 4, 90, 97, 108,
    110, 162
    social, 9, 29, 63, 64–6, 67, 69, 70–4,
    75, 77, 78, 79, 80, 82, 85, 93, 94, 97,
    100, 110, 112, 113, 115, 116, 123,
    124, 134, 136, 170, 173, 174, 177
Neumann, Peter, 40, 43, 103, 109,
    128, 132
news stories, 34, 38, 52, 178
    see also media coverage
New York Police Department (NYPD),
    104, 107
non-governmental organisations
    (NGOs), 70, 113, 121, 126, 146
Nill, Robert, 92, 137
Northern League, 120
Nosske, Hillel, 99
Nye, Joseph, 126

Office for Security and Counter-
    Terrrorism (OSCT), 102, 124
Ohnesorg, Benno, 111
Olins, Wally, 146
O'Loughlin, Ben, 29, 44, 47, 49, 126
ontology, *see* social ontology
opportunity structure, 77, 79–80, 88,
    112, 113, 120

'Orthodox Terrorism Studies', *see*
    Terrorism Studies
Oslo, 10, 49, 94

Pakistan, 98, 99, 127, 159, 160, 162,
    163, 181
Pakistani Institute for Peace Studies,
    127
Paletz, David, 29, 32, 37, 51
Pantucci, Raffaello, 92, 109
paradigm, 9, 90, 169, 172, 174, 179
    definition, 58
    see also terrorism, paradigm
perceptions, 4, 8, 30, 61, 65, 76, 79,
    80, 88, 103, 107, 110, 111, 127,
    132, 148, 158, 160, 161, 165, 167,
    168, 176, 178, 179
Perl, Raphael, 165
Pfetsch, Barbara, 52
Picard, Robert, 32
Piggott, Rachel, 146
Pisoiu, Daniela, 165
Palestinian Liberation Organisation
    (PLO), 37, 95, 96
Polkingorne, Donald, 126
'political', definition of, 17
Political Communication, 7, 10, 33,
    35, 45, 52, 174
political mobilisation, 3, 4, 6, 8, 12,
    30, 31, 33, 46, 49, 56, 59, 60, 62,
    68, 75, 76, 77–8, 79, 82, 85, 99,
    101, 104, 105, 107, 111–16, 120,
    121, 127, 132, 135, 139, 140, 142,
    149, 150, 167
political violence, 17, 26, 27, 111, 112
positivism, 30, 90
Post, Jerrold, 17, 114
Potter, Evan, 45
Presidential Task Force, 45, 47, 70, 91,
    128, 129, 130, 137, 164
Prevent, 6, 7, 15, 28, 31, 44, 102, 103,
    128, 161
Pritchard, Annette, 146
process-tracing, 180–1
propaganda, 16, 21, 24, 37, 160
    centre, 41; *see also* Al-Fajr, As-Sahab
    'of the deed', 35
    material, of terrorist groups, 41, 43,
    45, 47, 92, 123, 136, 145

propaganda – *continued*
  studies, 139
  in World War I, 52
public, 2, 35, 36, 38, 39, 47, 52, 53, 55,
    89, 94, 109, 122, 144, 154, 155,
    156, 157, 158, 159, 161, 173, 179
public diplomacy, 126, 138, 184
publicity, 36, 37, 38, 46, 54, 95, 128
  as 'oxygen of terrorism', 2, 97–9
public opinion, 151, 159

Quaddafi, Muammar, 8
qualitative methods, 170
  see also anthropology; ethnography
quantitative methods, 7, 30, 63, 170
Quilliam Foundation, 162

radicalisation, 6, 7, 8, 10, 15, 21, 24,
    25, 28, 31, 36, 41, 44, 48, 51, 54,
    55, 64, 91, 92, **101–24**, 128, 132,
    133, 136, 173, 175
  causes of, 102–7
  definition of, 102–7, 183
  self-radicalisation, 44, 45, 109, 122,
    158, 162; *see also* 'lone wolf'
radio, 46, 52, 53, 133, 139
Ragin, Charles, 22
Ranstorp, Magnus, 5, 171
Rapoport, David, 2, 6, 97
rational choice theory, 57
Rayner, Gordon, 94
recruitment, *see* terrorism,
  recruitment into
Red Army Faction (RAF), 10, 17–18, 88
Red Brigades, 10, 89
Reich, Wilhelm, 49
Reid, Edna, 5, 29, 170, 172, 184
Reiner, Robert, 54
relationalism, 57–8
Relational Sociology, 4, 10, 57, 60,
    61–70, 74, 75, 81, 182
relationships, *see* social relationships
research
  comparative, 20, 22–5, 29, 74, 90,
    98, 106, 174
  empirical, 5, 11, 20–2, 23, 40, 49,
    100, 125, 139, 144, 158, 175
  descriptive, 20–2
  explanatory, 20–2

Resource Mobilisation Theory (RMT),
    112–14
  see also social movement theory
Research, Information and
    Communication Unit (RICU),
    129, 145, 161
Revolutionary Brotherhood, 16
Richardson, Louise, 13, 30
Riley, Nicola-Maria, 148, 153, 155,
    159, 184
Rogan, Hanna, 158, 163
Rogers, Brooke, 132
Rogers, Everett, 137, 184
Rosenau, James, 126
Ross, Jeffrey, 32
Roy, Olivier, 128, 145
Royal Canadian Mounted Police, 108
Rumsfeld, Donald, 3, 165, 178
Russell, James, 7, 129, 140, 141

Sacco, Vincent, 54
Sageman, Marc, 7, 30, 46, 91, 94, 107,
    108, 109, 110, 162, 176–7, 181
Salafism, 104, 108, 141
Sarbin, Theodore, 126
satellite, 133
Schlesinger, Philip, 54, 86, 87
Schmid, Alex, 2, 13, 14, 20, 29, 34, 38,
    39, 99, 121, 160, 171, 181
Schulze, Frederick, 20
Sciolla, Loredana, 86
security, 2, 20, 29, 42, 43, 44, 51,
    126, 139, 140, 143, 154, 156,
    169, 170, 175
Seib, Philip, 29, 40, 127, 164, 171, 182
September 11, 3, 12, 18, 36, 37, 39,
    84, 98, 99, 109, 120, 124, 127,
    147, 151, 152, 163, 165, 167, 170,
    171, 180
shabnamah (night letters), 9
Shahzad, Faisal, 43
Shane, Scott, 95, 177
sharia, 19, 83, 119, 146, 154, 156,
    159, 163
Sheehan, Michael, 42
Shpiro, Shlomo, 37
Silber, Mitchell, 104
Silke, Andrew, 5, 13, 19, 20, 29, 31,
    90, 171

'silver bullet theory', 52
  see also hypodermic needle theory
Silverstone, Roger, 181
Simmons, Brian, 32
Smith, Anthony, 79
Smith, Brett, 126
Smith, Howard, 98
Smith, Jacqui, 155, 167
Smith, Michael, 13, 19, 20, 27, 29, 177
Snow, David, 78, 79, 182
Snow, Nancy, 39
social movement
  definition of, 182
  repertoire of, 78, 178, 182
social movement theory, 4, 10, 76–80,
  112, 114, 132
  see also Resource Mobilisation Theory
Sociology, 7, 10, 20, 71, 72, 90, 116,
  174, 181
social ontology, 33, 55, 60, 91
social relationships, 4, 24, 44, 57,
  61–8, 70, 72, 73, 74, 75, 76, 81–3,
  85, 87, 88–9, 91–2, 93–4, 97, 100,
  103, 106, 107, 108, 112, 116–18,
  120, 121, 122, 123, 124, 126,
  132–3, 134, 135, 142, 147, 148,
  152, 153, 154, 155, 156, 157, 167,
  173, 176–7
  imagined, 65, 70, 76, 79, 83, 88, 91,
  94, 176, 183; *see also* imagined
  communities
  see also social ties
social ties, 4, 55, 62, 64–8, 75, 76, 82,
  123, 133
  see also social relationships
Somalia, 66, 167
Somers, Margaret, 90, 92, 116, 117,
  118, 131, 181, 183
Spain, 10, 16, 106
Sparkes, Andrew, 126
Speckhard, Anne, 45, 47, 110, 130, 137
Stenersen, Anne, 42
Stohl, Michael, 165
Stokoe, Elizabeth, 131
stories, 4, 6–7, 8, 12, 18, 62, 64–6, 67,
  68, 69, 76–7, 81–2, 98, 116–18,
  121, 125, 126, 128–9, 131, 132,
  134, 136, 138, 140, 141, 144, 151,
  157, 158, 159, 160

  see also narrative
Stovel, Katherine, 63, 65
strategic communication, 1, 10, 64,
  133, 138, 139, 184
  see also narrative, strategic
Straw, Jack, 39
structure of opportunity, *see*
  opportunity structure
Substantialism, 57–8
surveillance, 2, 83, 100, 183
Symbionese Liberation Army, 38
Swanson, Guy, 22
Swidler, Ann, 149

Taliban, 9, 98
Tarrow, Sidney, 4, 13, 27, 31, 46, 61,
  77, 78, 79
Taylor, Charles, 126
Taylor, Peter, 47, 110
Taylor, Philip, 39
Taylor, Russell, 146
technological determinism, 45–9; *see
  also* communication, technology
Tehran embassy crisis, 39
telegraph, 46, 50
telephone, 33, 34, 40, 49, 50, 70, 73,
  83, 87, 94, 138
  see also mobile phone
Temple-Raston, Dina, 8
terror, 14, 18
terrorism
  causes of, 12, 13, 25–8
  as communication, 2, 34–7
  definition of, **13–19**
  as mass-mediated phenomenon, 35–6
  by non-state actors, 2, 29
  paradigm, 33, 54, 55–9; *see also*
  paradigm
  as political communication, 35–6
  recruitment into, 7, 37; *see also*
  Internet, role in terrorist
  recruitment
  right wing, 9–10, 30, 87–8, 94–5, 115
  by states, 14, 15
Terrorism Studies, 5, 6, 7, 10, 11, 12,
  13, 15, 19, 20, 28, 30, 31, 49, 54,
  55, 56, 57, 58, 60, 75, 90, 114,
  169–74, 177, 180
  'Critical', 5, 15, 56, 180

Terrorism Studies – *continued*
  'Orthodox', 15, 30, 56, 180
  shortcomings of, 5–6, 13, 169–73
Thatcher, Margaret, 2
  see also Thatcherism
Thatcherism, 17
theory, 20, 21, 24, 28–31, 33, 54, 55,
  56, 75, 103, 175
  building, 21, 28, 30
  testing, 20, 23, 28, 180
Thomas, Dylan, 145
Thompson, Robin, 108
Thornberry, William, 163
Tiananmen Square, 92
Tilly, Charles, 4, 8, 27, 46, 61, 76, 77,
  78, 80, 81, 82, 182
Timms, Steven, 94
Tololyan, Chachig, 77, 90, 93
Towsend, Mark, 95
Trabelsi, Nizar, 93
Transition Network, 19, 180
Travis, Alan, 145
Traynor, Ian, 95
Tsfati, Yariv, 36, 40
Tsoulis, Younis, 109
Tumber, Howard, 52
TV, 34, 37, 40, 46, 50, 52, 83, 84, 95,
  97, 110, 115, 133, 139
Twitter, 40, 49, 50, 52, 127
'two-step-flow' model, 52
Tzu, Sun, 3

ummah, 42, 94, 122
United Kingdom, 8, 10
United States, 8
Upshaw, Lynn, 148
US Army, 40, 138, 142
Utøya (island of), 10, 49, 94

values, 3, 18, 68–70, 79, 104, 106, 112,
  113, 114, 118, 119, 120, 127, 132,
  138, 142, 146, 147, 148, 150, 152,
  153, 154, 155, 156, 159, 161, 165,
  166, 167, 168, 184

Van Dongen, Teun, 165
van Ham, Peter, 146
van Um, Eric, 165
variables, 21, 23–5, 27, 28, 33, 175,
  181, 184
Verba, Sidney, 21
video camera, 3
videos, 3, 22, 24, 40, 41, 42, 43, 47,
  48, 92, 93, 109, 110, 122, 123,
  129, 133, 137, 141, 142, 146, 157,
  164, 165, 179
  role in radicalisation, 47–8
  see also jihadi videos
Viera, John, 36
Vietnam war, 39
violence, *see* political violence
violent extremism, *see* extremism,
  violent
Virgin, 146

Walker, Douglas, 165
war on terrorism, 1, 99, 130,
  169, 183
Webster, Leonard, 139
Weimann, Gabriel, 36, 37, 40
Weinberg, Leonard, 13, 30, 91
White, Harrison, 4, 60–9, 73, 74, 75,
  76, 181
White, Hayden, 131
White House, 128, 142
Wieviorka, Michel, 89
Wiktorowicz, Quintan, 112–14
Wilkinson, Paul, 38
Winn, Conrad, 36
Woolgar, Steve, 70
Wright, Lawrence, 164

Yan, Jack, 166, 184
Yemen, 24
Yorke, Claire, 64, 130
YouTube, 40

Zuckerman, Jessica, 124
Zulaika, Joseba, 18, 56

Printed and bound in the United States of America